The Magical Guide to Bliss

DAILY KEYS TO UNLOCK YOUR DREAMS, SPIRIT AND INNER BLISS

Blessin + Bliss . God Bless xo Meg

by
Meg Nocero

ISBN: 1506183689
ISBN 13: 9781506183688
Library of Congress Control Number: 2015909713
CreateSpace Independent Publishing Platform
North Charleston, South Carolina

PRAISE FOR *THE MAGICAL GUIDE TO BLISS*

"One of the coolest things about my job is I get to see other authors' books before everybody else does. And since magic and bliss are two of my favorite things, this was the perfect book to pop into my inbox. Thanks, Meg, for including me (at least in spirit) in your power posse."
~Pam Grout, best-selling author of seventeen books, including *E-Squared* (2013) and *E-Cubed (2014)*

"It's no accident you picked up this powerful book full of love! You'll receive countless blessings as you take part in this heart journey guided by Meg, whose light, wisdom, and love will show you the way."
~Amy Butler, international artist, designer and creator of *Blossom Magazine*

"Meg is a refreshing, authentic burst of positive energy. She combines her wisdom, intellect, and unrelenting passion for life in such a brilliant fashion. You can feel the energy of her words rise from the pages as you read this gem. This is a must read for anyone out there striving to live their life with compassion and purpose…and so it is from the angels."
~Janet Woods, *Mystical Woods Healing & Learning Center*, Boston, MA

"As a pragmatist and skeptic, I am genuinely touched by Meg's *Magical Guide to Bliss*. In the face of painful personal loss, Meg has chosen to fill her world with goodwill and warmth. The magic in this book is the author's unrelenting pursuit of gratitude and inspiration and her disciplined practice of daily bigheartedness. This book is a beautiful formula for kindness."
~Michele Drucker, Coral Gables, FL

"Meg! I am such a fan! Thanks for your inspiration. You are a constant in such a crazy, unstable world. Look forward to the e-mails every day. God bless you! Big hug."
~Dr. Heather Williams, Miami, FL

"*The Magical Guide to Bliss* insight is what I look forward to every morning. Sometimes I feel the messages were written just for me...I have faced many personal challenges, and I have had many dark days. I often wondered how God could let me go through the things I went through and why they were happening to me. These challenges and dark days left me scarred and very pessimistic about life. At least, this is what I thought until the day my path crossed Meg's path. I started receiving the insights, and from that day on, my outlook on life gradually began to change. Speaking to Meg and reading the insights have made a huge impact in my life. The insights increase my spiritual energy, give me hope, and teach me to look at life in more positive ways. The insights have touched my life because they have helped me build more confidence and encouraged me to focus on the positive aspects of my life. Since reading the insight passages, I have become a more positive person, happy and spiritually energetic. I often try to apply the insight message to my daily life. I am grateful for meeting Meg. Her positive energy and outlook in life have impacted my life in the short time I've known her."
~Marlene Meyers-Owen, Dallas, TX

"Your thoughts of the day have always been so inspirational to me. It's the lovely surprise in my inbox that I cannot wait to open. It's the message I need to hear to get me moving, to inspire me to be happy, to dream, to be positive, to be grateful, and to ultimately live a blissful life on this earth. Love you, my dear friend!"
~Michelle Alberty, Miami, FL

"My mom passed away in October 2009, and I've been through the most difficult and challenging five years since. Each day, though, is brightened when I start off with your Bliss Insight e-mail—Thought of the Day—helping to shift the focus of the day onto all positive thoughts,

inspirations, and things! Many of your Insights remind me of my mom, especially the constant words of encouragement. Thanks!"
~Kelly Allocco, Miami, FL

"What an amazing journey this has been for you, and how blessed I feel to have shared part of it through your inspirational messages. It is a true testament that sometimes the most difficult of times can turn into our greatest joy and blessing. Your mom must also be very proud of you and thankful for this tremendous tribute you are honoring her with. This speaks volumes of the impact she had in your life and the woman she was. May the launch of your book be a great success, and more importantly, may your words continue to touch countless lives. Peace, blessings, and all my love."
~Patty Bustamante, Coral Gables, FL

"Your daily messages through e-mail have blessed me in more ways than you know. My mother/best friend passed in 2013, my twins started college, my oldest son entered his senior year of college, and I'm about to enter the DROP program after teaching for almost thirty years. After being the caretaker of my mom, children, and husband, I thought my world was over after mom passed and my kids left for school, so your messages have uplifted me on so many levels. I've started living for me by starting a business as a Mary Kay independent beauty consultant so that when I retire from the school system, I'm in a position to continue making money, traveling, having a sisterhood, and changing women's lives. Therefore, through your messages, I have realized that my world isn't over because Mom passed and my kids went to school. It's sort of just beginning."
~Darlene Durant, Key Biscayne, FL

DEDICATION

In Gratitude for My Mom

I contracted—you told me to expand;
I got scared—you promised to hold my hand.
I dreamed—you told me to think bigger again;
I made mistakes—you told me I was forgiven.
I faced life's challenges—you gave me hope for another day;
I always leaned on you—you told me I needed to find my own way.
I miss you so much, and it gets dark;
You assured me your light would always shine in my heart.
I will never forget you—you taught me so much;
Your legacy lives on through each life you touched.
I love you, Mom—my guide, my counselor, and my friend;
Your light will guide my journey until the end.
May your example live on through me as I do my best;
Thank you in loving gratitude for all the rest!

~ Your Meggie

CONTENTS

FIGURES

PROLOGUE

Congratulations! If you have bought or been given a copy of *The Magical Guide to Bliss:*
Daily Keys to Unlock Your Dreams, Spirit, and Inner Bliss, you had better get ready to embark on the adventure of your life. What sets *The Magical Guide to Bliss* apart from all the other books of its ilk on the market today is that the featured star of this book is *you*—a unique creation of God. Just think, no one else in the entire cosmos is like you—you are a completely distinctive individual, right down to your feelings, intellect, body, and soul. Yes, soul…because therein resides the Holy Spirit, at the core of your very existence, just waiting to accompany you on your journey to achieve not simply mediocre or even good things but *great* things.

Because God created each of us in His/Her own image, we consist not only of "star stuff" but also of "God stuff." And in His/Her great love for you—God's unique creation—God wants everything good in this existence to happen *for you*. Have faith; it is just about to happen. If you don't have faith, do not fear: Meg Nocero and *The Magical Guide to Bliss* empower you to explore your uniqueness and ultimately find faith—in yourself, in every fellow human being, and in your Creator.

Because Meg shared such an uplifting relationship with her mom—my late wife, Mary Jo—you will have the benefit of not one but two perspectives from two unique human beings who interacted in dialogue all their lives in the exploration of what it means to be human. The greatest human activity occurs in regard to your relationships with not only loved ones but also the very cosmos and, ultimately, God.

So get ready for the great ride of your life with Meg as your guide to discover the magical bliss of becoming one with your own sacred nature, the foundation on which your unique identity as a human being will unfold like the petals of a beautiful rose coming into bloom. From the day that you were born, you were meant to travel in that world, and there you will find your true self—not your false self—and your bliss will be complete. In this newfound bliss, you will transcend the old and find a new, magical place in relationship to the ones you love the most in all of their individual uniqueness.

You will be back home where you were meant to be from the start—far from the stresses of the world that do not allow you to understand your specialness as a human being. This true discovery of your humanity, guided by what you will read in *The Magical Guide to Bliss*, makes full circle in you that which you will share with your Creator—a circle with no beginning and no end—whose center is everywhere and whose periphery is nowhere.

So as you come full circle, get ready to experience the true bliss of becoming. Enjoy!

Dr. Michael Nocero Jr., MD
FACC, MACC
Cardiologist and Former Chairman of the Board of the American College of Cardiology
November 2014

INTRODUCTION

Figure 1. *Butterflies & Bliss*, illustration by Meg Nocero, 2014

The title, *The Magical Guide to Bliss: Daily Keys to Unlock Your Dreams, Spirit, and Inner Bliss*, is self-explanatory. This book is exactly what the title says it is: a guide to bliss. All guidebooks share common goals: to demonstrate the best way to reach a specific destination by outlining the journey, to describe the terrain, and to warn of pitfalls commonly encountered along the way. However, this destination—bliss—is an abstract and elusive one. Bliss is not a place but a state of mind, and to get there, you must undergo a transformation on every level. This metamorphosis is signified through the butterfly illustrations featured throughout this book.

The Format of The Magical Guide to Bliss

To guide you to this elusive destination, bliss, I describe the journey in 366 steps, one for each day of the year. I chose a specific concept for each month and illustrated its various aspects in the day's featured issue and my reflections on it. The format for each daily meditation is consistent: a title summing up the issue to tackle, a relevant quote from an inspirational author, my reflection on the subject, and suggestions for addressing the issue. Each day's meditation culminates by presenting a magical key that will help unlock the doors you may encounter on the road to bliss. There is room below the entries on each page of this book. There I invite you to journal, draw, and reflect on each meditation as you allow bliss and your creative side to take flight.

How to Use *The Magical Guide to Bliss*

*T*he *Magical Guide to Bliss* is written in a modular format, with a chapter for each month of the year and an entry for each day of the month. You choose how you would like to read *The Magical Guide to Bliss*. If you prefer, you can read it straight through from beginning to end, perhaps even according to the calendar format, reading each meditation on its particular day of the year. However, you can read the entries in any order. I chose this modular, daily presentation to provide a condensed, easily accessible format for even the busiest person. Although each entry stands on its own, there is a progression of the concepts from January to December, so reading *The Magical Guide to Bliss* straight through will deepen your understanding of how the various elements fit together.

The Content pages present a summary of the various concepts introduced in each chapter's month and the specific issues considered for each day of the year. Select sources for the quotations that precede each meditation can be found in the bibliography section, which also serves as a suggested reading list. Finally, the index at the very end of the book provides an alphabetical listing of the authors quoted throughout the book.

So let's begin our journey to the bliss of enlightenment, taking it one day at a time!

# Chapter One: January

CARPE DIEM: SEIZE THE DAY!

January, the first month of the Julian calendar, is known in Western culture as the time of year to begin anew. Characteristic of January's association with fresh starts is the time-honored tradition of the New Year's resolution. The Pulitzer Prize–winning journalist Ellen Goodman aptly stated that "we spend January 1 walking through our lives, room by room, drawing up a list of work to be done, cracks to be patched. Maybe this year...we ought to walk through the rooms of our lives... not looking for flaws but for potential." This sentiment is exactly what is meant by the title of chapter 1: "Carpe Diem." Seize the day, indeed, but also seize the possibilities for the future. One cannot seize something that does not exist, so this month, take hold of what you have. Resolve to realize your potential rather than focusing on negatives or lack.

Now is the time to close the door on the past and begin a new chapter in your life. But sometimes that is easier said than done. Remember, the caterpillar struggles on its long journey from a nymph. You must take all necessary steps on the path to complete the transformation from a grounded caterpillar into a soaring butterfly.

There is no time like the present. Are you ready? In January, seize the day!

January 1: Pursue simplicity, clarity, and authenticity today and every day.

Whether we want them or not, the New Year will bring new challenges; whether we seize them or not, the New Year will bring new opportunities.

~Michael Josephson, American ethicist and founder of the Josephson Institute of Ethics

To move forward in the New Year, repeat the following mantra: simplicity, clarity, authenticity. Eliminating the clutter and clarifying what is important in your life are crucial tasks to successfully making a new start. Review the past year and be completely honest with yourself. Ask yourself, "What has worked for me? What behavior do I need to change? How can I make informed choices that elevate rather than depress my spirit?" Instead of playing an actor's role in which you are subject to the dictates of an all-powerful director (otherwise known as fate or God), this year, resolve to become the screenwriter and tell your story the way you choose to tell it! Become the change you want to see in your world.

Challenges will inevitably arise, but as you pursue simplicity, clarity, and authenticity, so will opportunities. Once you release old resentments, learn from past mistakes, and embrace future success, you will be ready to enter a new phase. Stand in gratitude for the blessings you have already received and for those still on the way. In a state of appreciation, you are open to receive the grace, the strength, and the favor that empower you to realize your dreams and fulfill your life's purpose. Each New Year, as the picture becomes clearer, simpler, and more authentic, you will begin to seize every opportunity that enriches your life's purpose. May *The Magical Guide to Bliss* light the road on your journey to fulfillment and shower you with blessings along the way!

Magical Key to Bliss: Get ready to seize the day—today and every day!

3

January 2: Make your masterpiece glorious!

We can be tired, weary, and emotionally distraught, but after spending time alone with God, we find that He injects into our bodies energy, power, and strength.

~Charles F. Stanley, American author and pastor

You are an artist at work, and the world is your canvas. You pay attention to and experience a beautiful life precisely because *that* is your focus. Seek happy places and commit their details to memory to use in your masterpiece. When you are tired, weary, and emotionally distraught, rely on these details for the sustenance and optimism you need to continue your journey. Look to teachers and guides for help in making crucial choices as you refocus your life's direction. Seek a mentor. Seek love. Seek energy, power, and strength. Once you stop running from your fears, everything you are looking for will magically appear. Take a mini soul retreat in nature with God to remind yourself that angels guide you and dreams come true. Your life is a living prayer for which you must be grateful. You are the blessed body through which magic and miracles occur. Bright, joyful colors infuse your spirit, and you are once again renewed as you acknowledge that you are an artist at work on your greatest masterpiece, YOU!

Magical Key to Bliss: Take a mini soul retreat into glorious meditation.

January 3: **The future is completely open.**

The future is completely open, and we are writing it moment to moment. There is always potential to create an environment of blame—or one that is conducive to loving kindness.

~Pema Chodron, author and Buddhist teacher

Today and every day, you are the one who sets the tone for your life. Everything that has happened in the past is done, over, kaput, finished. A time machine is not available, at least not yet, to take you back in time for a do-over. So let it all go! Instead of dwelling on past losses, seize what you have gained: the wisdom of the lessons learned through experience. Gather all the confidence you can muster and move forward. The future is completely open. That fact alone is beyond exciting! As long as you live and breathe, you have time to write the best chapters of your life. You decide whether those chapters are filled with anger and blame or with love and kindness. Today is a new day in your journey; unwritten chapters await you. Decide now to inscribe wonder into what has not yet been written. Redirect the present moment with all that is good, trusting that the future will unfold accordingly. Declare, at this moment, that you will become a force of love, hope, and joy, and know that the associated rewards for doing so are already yours. Are you ready to experience what awaits you with an attitude of optimism, love, and kindness? Away you go!

Magical Key to Bliss: Get a pen and paper and write out your vision statement.

January 4: If you don't make time for your dreams, then who will?

Most people are so busy knocking themselves out trying to do everything they think they should, they never get around to doing what they want to do.

~Kathleen Winsor, American author

We all live very busy, stressful, and overly packed lives. Take time out of yours to ask yourself, "Am I taking the time to do the things that make me feel alive?" Never let others' mundane expectations take precedence over the activities that are important to you. In your desire to perfectly fulfill others' expectations, you could be missing out on opportunities that would bring you satisfaction and joy. You may assume that you have all the time in the world to accomplish your dreams. But in reality, you may be putting off pursuing exactly what you need to do to set yourself in a positive direction. And for what? To drive yourself crazy as you prioritize others' values over your own? Today is the day. Start thinking about what sparks your curiosity. Spontaneously brainstorm a list of activities that stimulate your creative spirit. Don't wait for the nod from another. For if you don't make time for your dreams, who will? In those sacred moments, envision yourself as a happy, innovative, fulfilled person living a truly amazing life on earth. Place your energy where it needs to be, and make your mark. Can't wait to see where it takes you!

Magical Key to Bliss: Take one small step toward furthering your dreams.

January 5: **Remember—life is an adventure!**

Because of our routines, we forget that life is an ongoing adventure.

~Maya Angelou, American author, poet, dancer, actress, and singer

W e have all been blessed with the gift of life. Sometimes, caught up in our daily routine, we forget what a precious and rare blessing this actually is. There is magic in the synchronistic timing that brought our souls into this physical existence. There is magic in the moment we took in our first breath and then cried out to the world that we are here. There is magic as we realize that we have gained knowledge from our great journey, becoming everything we are meant to be! From this positive perspective, when we look around and behold those accompanying us on our way, we can be grateful for what is in store. From this positive vantage point, when we connect with those placed on our path to bring us comfort, wisdom, or perhaps some small act of kindness, we acknowledge the blessings of the shared experience. We are here for just a short time; we must remember to seize each and every opportunity. The present moment offers so much more than we can imagine as we simply open our eyes and welcome what is right before us—breaking out of routines, taking chances, and becoming conscious of life's magic and miracles. When we start to think outside the box, we become open to the beauty that changes us for the better. And then we can come alive and participate in new adventures, grabbing others to join us on our way!

Magical Key to Bliss: Take a magical ride; rent a movie that inspires you.

January 6: Forgiveness promises new beginnings.

Forgiveness is the answer to the child's dream of a miracle by which what is broken is made whole again, what is soiled is made clean again.

~Dag Hammarskjold, Swedish author, diplomat, and economist

As you leave one year and enter another, look forward to a new start by setting forth resolutions that will catapult your hopes, dreams, and desires into reality. During the last days of the year, perhaps you prepared to start fresh with a clean slate, doing your best to put resentments in the past—even those difficult to release. In anticipation, you may have decided to clear a path that will allow your dreams to take priority in your life. Many start the New Year with high hopes, only to burn out after a couple of days. You are only six days into your journey now. Make a conscious decision each day not to quit. Accept that you will falter on your path; forgive yourself and move forward into this amazing new year of your life. Inform your resolutions with an enthusiastic belief in your potential and with compassion for yourself. Be gentle with your life; you are a child of the universal one, no matter what age. By continually seeking or granting forgiveness, you start fresh each day with a spirit of perseverance. You can and will, as you renew your spirit, move toward being whole again. Look forward to all the success awaiting you.

Magical Key to Bliss: Forgive yourself first.

January 7: Until you breathe your last breath, it is always too early to quit!

It's always too early to quit.

~Norman Vincent Peale, American author of *The Power of Positive Thinking*

Ever wonder what you are meant to do with your life? What will allow you to make a difference, leaving this world better for having known the beauty that is you? Each person has a specific mission on this journey. When each person makes it his or her goal to live out that mission, we are all blessed. As each of you delves into your own magical mystery, always be true to yourself, no matter what. Each of you must honor the music of your soul to discover what you really are all about. You must honor your intuition and not be distracted by others' expectations and demands. Keep your focus on the dream in your heart; only you can make the best decisions for your future. As you continue to learn who you are by virtue of life's unique lessons, you become perfectly in tune with the beat of your heart. As you approach goals that clarify your purpose, synchronicity abounds, and the gifts you need on the journey will magically appear. Appreciate these gifts when they appear. See each stage of the journey as an opportunity to learn; make a conscious choice to stay the course. Until you breathe your last breath—even in the face of adversity—it is too early to quit pursuing the discovery of who you are and what you can become. Remember, the very moment you decide to quit could be the moment you realize the greatest success. Are you prepared to face such an enormous risk?

Magical Key to Bliss: Visualize the amazing things you will do in your life.

January 8: **Time to shine!**

Create a definite plan for carrying out your desire and begin at once, whether you're ready or not, to put this plan into action.

~Napoleon Hill, American author of *Think and Grow Rich*

The best way to make your dreams a reality is to look within and outline a clear, detailed plan. Many people go through life putting the dreams of others before their own, and ultimately their own dreams become last on the list. Living like this serves no one. When you constantly prioritize others at your expense, you become burned out, frustrated, and tired. There is a reason that the stewards on a plane instruct you to put on your oxygen mask *before* helping others with theirs. You must breathe life into your own before you can give to others. When you energize your talents and gifts with positive purpose, your energy multiplies, and you are able to help more people than you ever imagined possible. You might think to yourself, "I don't have enough time to accomplish that now; I'll do it later" and put off your dreams; then that one inevitable day arrives, and you realize it's too late. Realize that you are actually putting off the magic that makes life worth living. Each day is a gift. If you want to see your desires come to fruition, you must take action and pursue them without delay, whether you are ready or not.

Magical Key to Bliss: Set out that guide map that will allow you to shine!

January 9: **Reinvent yourself.**

We possess such immense resources of power that pessimism is a laughable absurdity.

~Colin Wilson, British novelist and philosopher

You really can reinvent yourself. You did so many times as a child, without even realizing it, and you can do so again now. You do not have a fixed, frozen personality. You have the power to be, to choose, and to create a life that aligns with your soul. Nothing prevents you from doing this except your beliefs about your own inferiority. So banish them; you can break out of habitual pessimistic thinking that keeps you stuck. You can do whatever and be whomever you want; just follow your heart and do all that you do with passion. There is so much more to you than meets the eye; set out to discover it. You are pure potential, so let no one suggest to you otherwise. Don't give your power away by relying on others' opinions. No one knows you better than you do. No one knows what you are truly capable of better than you do. One thing is true: when you believe in yourself, clarify your direction, take action, and infuse your dreams with joy, passion, and love, there are truly no limits to how high you can soar in life! It is absurd to think any other way; surprise the world by taking hold of your life as the owner of your journey. Then fly!

Magical Key to Bliss: Say, "I believe in myself" ten times, three times per day.

January 10: Pay attention; your soul is calling!

Sometimes you hear a voice through the door calling you…
This turning toward what you deeply love saves you.

~Rumi, thirteenth-century Persian poet and Sufi mystic

Like a bolt of lightning, an event wakes you up, and something in you comes alive. You are immediately overwhelmed with a zest and enthusiasm for life that feels like a rebirth. Your senses start to respond anew, and a newfound energy is born the moment you believe in things that you never before thought possible. Electricity permeates the air you breathe as potential infuses each cell within. Start to pay attention to the magnitude of this moment as a sign that you are that much closer to your calling. You acknowledge for the first time a journey filled with new possibility. Your soul no longer can be ignored as it triggers your mind and body into action. More opportunities to grow are introduced to you, more people show up to advise you, and more good feelings infuse your growing spirit. When you honor this calling, your life just feels so right. Your sense of awareness is focused on no longer being afraid to surrender to life as it unfolds. It is that moment when your soul calls to you to connect in love, when you recognize what is important, and when life takes on a meaning that saves you. This is so magical and exciting all at once. When the bolt of lightning hits, answer the call and turn toward what you love, and it will save you.

Magical Key to Bliss: Figure out what you love most in this world.

January 11: **Be bold!**

Whatever you can do, or dream you can, begin it. Boldness has genius, power, and magic in it.

~Johann Wolfgang von Goethe, German writer and statesman

You live in a world of connections. Whether you like it or not, your life is intertwined with that of others. And thank goodness because you need other people to help you to move forward in life and realize your dreams. Technology has allowed you to reach out for miles and miles; you can meet people all over the world with the click of a button. Information and resources lie at your fingertips to help you tap into your source. The following question remains: are you bold enough to commit to your dreams, to start the process by doing the work necessary, and to engage in the important conversations to begin? When the spark of genius awakes you from a dormant life, you are inspired and start to act. When you release your ideas into the universe, there is no telling where your own brand of innovation will take you. When you allow the magic of possibility to take hold in your life, the path opens up, and you can see the way. You may be able to almost see the fruits of your labor; who would give up now? Courage is what you need to succeed. Boldness is an attitude that will aid you as you take the risks necessary to be magical. All it takes is a commitment to a new reality. Then get ready to see how the universe will provide the connections to make all your dreams come true.

Magical Key to Bliss: Set out to make one new connection today!

January 12: Enchanted by your light!

No matter how you are feeling, get up every morning and prepare to let your light shine forth. Those with eyes to see will see and be enchanted by it.

~Paulo Coelho, Brazilian author of *Manuscript Found in Acra*

Each of you has a light within. There is no reason to chase fireflies for something that is already inside you. Just acknowledge when you wake up every morning that now is the time to let it shine. Each morning when you rise to live a new day, make a conscious choice to flip the switch and tap in. No matter how you feel, decide that today you will be a light in this world, and choose to surround yourself with people whose acts of love will illuminate you as well. Today, decide to make a conscious choice to let your light show; smile from ear to ear, and just start to glow. If you beam in this way, rest assured that you will positively impact the lives of others throughout your day. Just as a child is mesmerized with the discovery of a firefly lighting up the night, those who have eyes to see you will also be elated as you share your brightness in an otherwise dark place. Just as nature enchants as flowers come alive when the sun's light shines on them, if you so choose, the spark that lights you from within can become a shared energetic force of beauty that will surely enchant those you meet. When you start your day with this magical mind-set, life really can be something to behold as it bursts forth vibrantly and in a most beautiful way.

Magical Key to Bliss: Imagine that you are a beam of light energy that shines each time you smile.

January 13: Commit positively to the "I am."

Remember, the thoughts that you think and the statements you make regarding yourself determine your mental attitude. If you have a worthwhile objective, find the one reason why you can achieve it rather than hundreds of reasons why you can't.

~Napoleon Hill, author of *Think and Grow Rich*

To take charge of your mind, simply set out "I am" statements that empower you. If you feel overwhelmed, state, "I am strong," and move through any challenging time with conviction. If you feel insecure, state, "I am a success," and start to believe those words to be true as you become the best possible you. If you feel sad, state, "I am hopeful," and seek positive support to help you break through to a better place. Take charge of whatever you want to manifest in your life by changing your own mental chatter. Do your best to set aside the negativity that can get you stuck, and start programming your mind with visions of what is possible. The world can deliver some difficult blows at times. But with your "I am" resolve, you can kick-start your potential into reality. Do your best to know that there is good and that it is in process; then plant the seeds that strengthen your positive mental attitude, and give yourself a chance to grow. This is your journey, and you will take it where you want to take it. Make your choices rather than allowing your choices to be made for you! Fear not; if you dare to dream with an "I am" state of mind, the tools you need to accomplish what you set out to do will come to you. With determination, perseverance, and uplifting statements about your potential, nothing can stand in your way!

Magical Key to Bliss: Write out one strong "I am" statement and repeat it throughout the day.

January 14: Claim what is yours!

*The internal state of your mind is the biggest single factor in
determining whether or not you succeed as a _____
(fill in the blank).*

~Lawrence Block, American author of *Write for Your Life*

Each new day, you are filled with incredible possibility and potential.
As the light breaks free from the horizon, you can also break free
from your own self-imposed obstacles laden with past doubt and fear.
The sun rises effortlessly. When it claims its rightful place in the sky as a
matter of course, you get to share in its remarkable beauty as it lights up
the day. You can also claim the light that is yours, the joy that is yours,
and the love that is yours. When the sun rises brilliantly and effortlessly, you will arise with the intention that today your mind and body
will work together to shine. For today is a new day, a new moment, and
a new chance to become all you are meant to be. When you are aware,
you can travel down your road with an empowered state of mind. With
today's sunrise, put your doubts aside and succeed in manifesting your
greatest desires. With your loving thoughts shining from within, your
life will already beam success. And as you travel through your day, the
outside events will be ready to confirm what is already on the inside as
you claim what is yours.

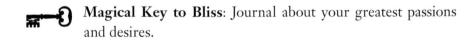 **Magical Key to Bliss**: Journal about your greatest passions
and desires.

January 15: **Trust your choices.**

Since every choice is a fork in the road, each decision brings with it new hope and promise.

~Richard Carlson, PhD, American author of *Don't Sweat the Small Stuff...and It's all Small Stuff*

In every moment of life, you get to make choices. Look at this as a very good thing. With each decision, you are empowered to take in whatever information is available and wisely set a course in the direction of your dreams. While some choices may appear big and others small, each is significant in that it could alter the trajectory of your path and bring new hope and promise. Using your sixth sense as a guide, you can be confident that when you choose what you will create, everything little thing will ultimately be all right. When you decide to live consciously, you become focused, aware, and ready for any challenge. So when you come to that fork in the road, you can be sure that as you choose what you want most in life, whatever you elect will bring beauty to your world. When you look at your life as if you are the director in your own play, you can greet whatever scene follows with enthusiasm and grace. So as you start each new act on your journey, keep in mind that you are able to choose to align your spirit with the purpose that drives your soul. This state of mind is a great way to embolden a beautiful life! Happy decision making!

Magical Key to Bliss: Decide that you will proceed today with great enthusiasm for life.

January 16: The best is yet to come.

Optimism is a muscle that gets stronger with use...it takes
courage to believe that the best is yet to come.

~Robin Roberts, American television broadcaster

Do what you love! If you have not quite figured out what that is yet, like a fastidious soul searcher, do your research and never let anything or anyone get in the way. Weed through all the possibilities that are out there, and before you know it, you will want to jump out of bed each morning welcoming the life designed just for you. Keep searching until you happen across the very thing that gives your heart wings to take flight! It will happen—even faster if you carry optimism with you. If something does not feel right or you feel stuck, look around for something else that aligns with your purpose. Don't ignore that blessed intuition; it will carry you toward opportunities that match your passion. Keep moving forward, and get creative about the theme of your dreams. Persistence pays off as long as you carry the highest virtues with you. Rest assured you will never have to give up on your dream. As long as you are steadfast, you will never have to give your soul away. Yes, it is that serious of an endeavor. Stay true to who you are, and do not buy into the false security that the world tries to present to you as the only way. It takes strength to not play it safe. It takes a strong belief that your own abilities will be your true guide. It takes courage to believe that the best is yet to come. Do what you love, and you are well on your way! Believe it!

Magical Key to Bliss: Plan a date by yourself to go somewhere that you have never been.

January 17: **Something great awaits you.**

Life is a process. We are a process. The universe is a process.

~Ann Wilson Schaef, PhD, American author

L ife is a process that unfolds before you. It is how you approach the process that dictates the experience, and that is why trust is so important. While trust itself is defined as an assured reliance on the character, ability, strength, or truth of someone or something, it can be an incredibly dualistic concept. On the one hand, to trust in life can seem challenging when you are struggling to surrender control. Yet on the other hand, to trust in life can feel like a breath of fresh air as you ultimately release into a freedom that brings great peace. When you become aware that you are a part of something greater than yourself, both the struggle and the release have a purpose in the grand scheme of things. If you become aware and trust that the reason for the unfolding of your life events will contribute to your life process, then you can stop fighting what happens and truly begin to enjoy the ride. You then won't miss out on all that is good because your focus shifts. Remember, there is always the possibility that greater magic and miracles are awaiting you right around the corner. Really, the magic is still there just waiting for you to discover it, and it can help you grow to greater heights. So just trust the process; then you hold the key to that something greater that will set your spirit free!

Magical Key to Bliss: Go for a walk in nature today, and pay attention to the effortlessness of your surroundings.

January 18: **Color your world magnificent!**

When you walk up to opportunity's door, don't knock on it...
kick that b*tch in, smile, and introduce yourself.

~Dwayne Johnson, "The Rock," American actor, producer, and professional wrestler

It's time to go out and make your own opportunities. It's time to be the designer of your own life. Take that canvas and paintbrush and splatter it with your imagination. Color it with magnificent purple to awaken insight. Color it with robust red to enliven the passion in your soul. Color it with peaceful blue to calm your spirit. Or color it with anything that speaks to you. It doesn't matter which color you choose, as long as you do choose. Life is happening all around you. Stop wasting precious time complaining, and start creating something amazing. Go for it! Get outside and connect with nature, discover new adventures, or take your everyday routine and throw in the element of surprise. Start to think differently if you want to see change happen. One day at a time, go out with your adventurous eyes and challenge yourself to see the world a little differently. Don't forget to take your daring self with you, and craft the kind of destiny you wish to see. It's time to wake up to the wonder that awaits you. Rise up and state confidently to the world that you are here—ready for whatever it throws your way! Get ready to break down barriers and to receive all the abundance that is meant for you! Each and every day brings with it new opportunities. Forget about knocking; just make an entrance, smile, and introduce yourself. Remember that when you take inspired action, something wonderful is always waiting on the other side. Get off your couch, and do something amazing with your canvas by coloring your world magnificent.

Magical Key to Bliss: Say yes to all opportunities as they present themselves.

January 19: Hold on to your dreams.

When a person really desires something, all the universe conspires to help that person to realize his dream.

~Paulo Coelho, Brazilian author of *The Alchemist*

If you are a dreamer, there is something that you have wanted very much to do, be, or have. However, there are times in life when you feel like you are just floating along without direction, wondering why your hopes and desires are at a standstill. Perhaps you are weighed down by past patterns, just wishing to be released from their very determined grip. Or your fears are taking a mental toll on your internal view of possibilities. When you are holding on to the stuff that does not serve you well, you need to stop and make a choice to consciously exchange your negative thoughts for those that will allow for all the wonderful things that life has in store. You will feel the shift when you do. You need to have faith that when you receive love in your heart for the ability to dream, this energy will greatly increase as you make your request to the universe. When you are stuck in an illusion that does not serve your highest good, allow yourself to let go one moment at a time, knowing that everything is giving you clues that will help you solve the mysteries in life and move on to greater things. When you trust this, hold on to your dreams and take inspired action to see them through, knowing for sure that the universe will conspire in your favor. And as you navigate your way through life's journey, you will rejoice as signs appear as a testament to your belief that you are moving in the right direction.

Magical Key to Bliss: Start mapping out your hero's journey on the road to realize your dreams.

January 20: Fly, butterflies, fly!

If nothing ever changed, there'd be no butterflies.

~Unknown

Don't let anyone label you! Everything that holds you down is only an illusion anyway. You are a magnificent, creative soul just waiting to shine in so many different ways. Let your eyes gaze at the beauty that surrounds you, and allow it to nourish your spirit with love. It is then you will realize that what you perceive as judgment from others is only a reflection of how you are treating yourself. With this in mind, pour love over your mirror of life and be kind to yourself; then you will receive kindness in return. For if you want to be free and released from whatever cage you have imagined for yourself, it is all about love. It is a love so simple, so pure, and so completely effortless. When you allow that transformation to happen in your heart, you will experience more love everywhere you turn. Then humbly let it come through you and set you free. Even if you are not ready to let go of your past story today, love will wait patiently for you, always, until you can handle its embrace once again. And as you accept it, little by little, back into your life and gain strength, you will burst out of the cocoon of darkness into the light. With courage, you will spread your beautiful wings, ready to take flight. And when you open your eyes again, what a majestic sight to see. The sky will be so colorful and bright as you set out to seize the new day, a new day of life to discover all the glory that is waiting for you. For when things change, you can tell yourself again—fly, butterfly, fly!

Magical Key to Bliss: Look for butterflies, real or artificial. Write down how many you see.

January 21: Follow the cheerful ones.

The cheerful live longest in years, and afterward in our regard. Cheerfulness is the offshoot of goodness.

~Christian Nestell Bovee, epigrammatic New York writer

Looking for a little cheer today? Seek out those people who will bring a little more sunshine into your life. You will be amazed at how being surrounded with positive people can make your life even more worth living. Ever notice how you feel when you are with a person who embodies a glass-half-full kind of attitude? When you are with them, you get an energy boost that can lift you up to believe in all kinds of possibilities. Your enthusiasm for life increases. And your ability to embrace a world full of magic and miracles multiplies. When you are around people of good cheer, life just feels better. And after you leave their company, you may be more inclined to share a simple smile with a stranger. You may be more inclined to take in the beauty of your surroundings. You may be more inclined to stand up confidently, chest out, heart ready to experience love. Life certainly can be challenging at times, so if you can't share a smile of your own, seek out those who can share one with you. Before long, the cheerfulness and optimism that is shared with you will encourage you to follow your own bliss and to pass on the love. And in the end, you will always remember with gratitude the goodness that was shared and will certainly be empowered to continue with this sentiment. For, if the cheerful live longest, then cheerfulness is something that you can hope will be contagious for as long as you live!

Magical Key to Bliss: Seek out the ones who make you smile.

January 22: **Take a leap of faith.**

"Come to the edge," he said.
"We can't, we're afraid!" they responded.
"Come to the edge," he said.
"We can't, We will fall!" they responded.
"Come to the edge," he said.
And so they came.
And he pushed them
And they flew.

~Guillaume Apollinaire, French poet

Do not be limited by your fear; fear is all just an illusion anyway. When you are entrenched in fear, you can feel paralyzed with no idea how to move out of it. Sometimes it is less painful to take the risk than to stay in the painful place of what we know. Sometimes tolerable risk coupled with your wise intuition can be just the thing to set you free from your imaginary cage. Life beckons to you on a daily basis to participate, to engage, and to be involved in your journey. Life urges you to come to the edge. Life invites you every day to experience all that you can while here. Life knows that if you do take some risks, what lies on the other side can and probably is more than you ever could imagine. Your world opens up to all the possibilities that are already there for you to take hold of. If you know in your heart that fear is the only thing that can hold you back from taking risks, set it aside and imagine what you need to believe: that you are a fearless being. Perhaps come to the edge, spread your wings, take the leap of faith, and fly! You won't regret it if you do.

Magical Key to Bliss: Write down your fears and what holds you back, and then burn the paper.

January 23: **Make your ideas a reality.**

Reduce your plan to writing. The moment you complete this, you will have definitely given concrete form to the intangible desire.

~Napoleon Hill, author of *Think and Grow Rich*

Creative inspiration surrounds you on a daily basis. It comes to you through nature, through your interactions with others, or through studying those who have gone before. To take advantage of the inspiration and allow your creative genius to unfold, you need to set out a plan. When you put pen to paper and capture the creative thought process as it is conceived, the path to discovery becomes crystal clear. When you take the time to set out your heart's greatest desires in a concrete way, you outline the steps needed to get you where you want to go. Carry around a notebook to capture the ideas that come at you from out of the blue. Write down on your hand inspirational concepts that get you excited to be alive. Sketch ideas anywhere you can to take a snapshot from a scene of your imagination. In doing so, you have given form to something that was previously just a part of your dreams. Thus, you have taken the steps needed to go to the next level. Get ready. These ideas will come to you when you are relaxed on a routine drive to work, are refreshed as you let the water wash over you in the shower, or are enlightened during a guided meditation. With something close by to jot down your inspirations, you will remember to memorialize these ideas for further review at a later time. Giving concrete form to what was once intangible, you become a vital part of making these ideas transform into a beautiful new reality that will give you a lifetime of fulfillment and joy.

Magical Key to Bliss: Set out a guide to fulfilling one of your greatest dreams.

January 24: You are exactly where you are meant to be.

There are no mistakes, no coincidences. All events are blessings given to us to learn from.

~Elisabeth Kubler-Ross, Swiss-American psychiatrist and pioneer in near-death studies

Everything in your life is a blessing. There are no mistakes. Accept this mantra, and you are free to see the world through grateful eyes. Accept this mantra, and you are ready to accept life's experiences with a loving heart. Accept this mantra, and allow amazing grace to encapsulate you as your soul's journey continues. There are no coincidences. Every experience is presented to you as an opportunity to bring something wonderful to your world. Each person who crosses your path delivers a message that will help you to understand the universe more fully. Each place you visit will help you to discover something that you desperately seek. The joyful moments will teach you gratitude as you celebrate life. Even the challenging moments will teach you perseverance as you value the wisdom gained through hardship. Without judgment, in both the good and bad times, you will embrace the gifts each situation offers as perfect synchronicities present to guide you along your path. Any way you look at it, as long as you adopt the perspective that you are exactly where you are meant to be, you can find peace in knowing that it is all part of some grand design as the universe is unfolding exactly as it should for your highest good.

Magical Key to Bliss: List the challenges you have had and the blessings received.

January 25: **If you chase your dreams, you will catch them.**

Chase your dreams until you catch them...and then dream, catch, and dream again!

~Dee Marie, American novelist and author of *Sons of Avalon: Merlin's Prophecy*

If you want to see life through new eyes, watch little children at play. So simply, the little ones chase their bliss as they discover the world around them. Dreaming is a fundamental part of their existence. Joy is infused in everything that they do. Connecting to others is a necessary way of life. With the task to wander into a world of fantasy, amusement, and possibility, they grab the hands of those around them and boldly engage. Although they may stumble or fall, it is just for a moment until they get up again; judgment has no place in their world. There remains only incredible wonder as they seek the gifts each new day will bring. You, too, can embrace your inner child. You, too, can chase your dreams as if they were butterflies on a sunny day. You can entertain those fanciful notions born in the imagination. You can awake into a conscious state of magical enlightenment with intention. It has always been the journey that holds the beauty of life. From the birth of an innovative idea until its ultimate conclusion, when you embrace the path with an exuberant spirit, magic is sure to unfold. So perhaps today you will choose to remain a child at heart and seek out others to frolic with. You will certainly rejoice in the fact that others are there to hold onto and help you catch your dreams, too. So chase all your dreams, sweet ones; catch them, smile widely, and then dream all over again.

Magical Key to Bliss: Start your day with a magical tone, and find ways to embrace the spirit of play.

January 26: Be not afraid...you were born for this!

I'm not afraid...I was born for this!

~Joan of Arc, Roman Catholic saint nicknamed the "Maid of Orleans"

Yes, you were born for this, this life that you are now living. Everything about it was custom made just for you. You don't have to think in terms of justifying your existence. You were born for a reason, and you have purpose. You don't need to prove that fact to anyone. Just believe it, know it, and most of all, live it! As William Shakespeare begins the monologue spoken by Jaques in act 2 scene 7 of his (1599) play *As You Like It*, "All the world's a stage." You are the principal actor in your own personal theatrical performance. You can make choices to live out your production with flair. You can choose to dance, sing, and laugh as much or as little as you like. You can choose to inspire others by being true to yourself in all that you do. You can live your life moving to the beat of your own drum and in doing so live a charmed life. Learn as much as you can as you travel your path. Take in the wisdom that is offered to you, and absorb the love that is gifted to you. Be humble when necessary, and be bold as well. And do not forget to smile when the awareness washes over you that you are exactly where you are meant to be at any given time. You are an empowered soul who is not afraid of declaring to the world that *yes* you were born for this, whatever "this" looks like to you. For "this" intricately well-imagined life has been specifically prepared just for you. There is no greater feeling than to truly believe that in whatever you do, you can boldly say, "I was born for this!"

 Magical Key to Bliss: Believe that you are here to accomplish great things. Write down what that looks like to you.

January 27: **The magic and power of dreaming.**

It is precisely the possibility of realizing a dream that makes life interesting.

~Paulo Coelho, Brazilian Author of *The Alchemist*

Life's possibilities are endless. If there comes a time when you can't see any hope on the horizon, stop and take a moment to dream. There is power in dreaming. When you spend time allowing your imagination to run wild, innovative ideas will come to you like bursts of sunshine on a cloudy day. Making it a habit to take the time to dream will catapult you to live your life with a renewed enthusiasm and hope for wonderful things to happen. When you set out to make your dreams come true, the excitement that accompanies your inspired action becomes more and more contagious. With a new, incredible goal foremost in your mind, each morning when you wake up, you will be eager to take the steps to bring it closer and closer into your reality. Each day, you will be excited to seek out opportunities to further your aspirations. Each day you will be enthusiastic about opening your gifts that allow you to discover your purpose. So if you find yourself stuck in a rut, make it a point today to connect with your personal dreams, take action to realize them, believe in your own potential, and then open your mind to visualizing whatever you deeply desire as if it already existed. It is the possibility of something wonderful happening that will shift you. So start off dreaming big, then go bigger, all the way to the biggest, most impossible dream you can imagine! Your life will be not only more interesting but also magical and powerful!

Magical Key to Bliss: Decide what your magical power will be, and apply it to your dreams.

January 28: **Stop playing it safe.**

Far better it is to dare mighty things, to win glorious triumphs, even though checkered by failure…than to rank with those poor spirits who neither enjoy nor suffer much, because they live in the gray twilight that know neither victory nor defeat.

~Theodore Roosevelt, twenty-sixth president of the United States of America

At times the world can seem very overwhelming and the unknown very bewildering. When these challenges present themselves, you need to make a commitment to dare mighty things and forge ahead. Even if you make some mistakes along the way, embrace and learn from them so that you can use the wisdom to progress in a conscious manner. You need to understand that you are looking for progress, not perfection. So when you shift perspective to accept and surrender to change, you will receive the gifts of strength and perseverance, too. If you want to live your greatest life possible, then playing it safe can never be an option. You want to have no regrets when you take your last breath, so pay attention to the messages that you receive daily. Follow your intuition so you know when it is time to act and when it is time to be still. Learn to bend like a palm tree, or you will end up breaking like an oak in a heavy storm. As a palm, you will stand strong, persevere, and never run the risk of living in the gray twilight, slowly fading away.

Magical Key to Bliss: Step out of your comfort zone and decide to do one thing that scares you.

January 29: Look forward; therein lies a brilliant destiny!

Don't look back. Something might be gaining on you.

~Satchel Paige, American Major League Baseball All-Star

If you want to move forward in life, it is futile to dwell on the past. It does you no good to judge yourself over and over again for your past mistakes. The past is done. It is the present that is bursting with potential. Give love to your present dreams, give love to yourself, and go forth. Figure out what makes you special and do that. If you make people laugh, do that. If you like to share wisdom and insight, do that. If you can heal others with your words or your hands, then do that too. Just keep looking forward and don't look back. Life is filled with many stages, each one offering you an opportunity to play a different role to further develop the amazing human being that you are. Every present and future positive action will assist you in discovering your own beauty within. Just don't look back, or you might lose your direction; choose to spend your quality time on something wonderful today. When a baseball player rounds the bases toward home plate to score a home run, he cannot turn around without losing his forward momentum. Likewise, looking forward will help ensure that you arrive at your intended destination. And the sun will rise again over your present as you no longer focus on the sunset going down over your past. Keep shining, and imitate the same light that bursts with the hope that accompanies the brilliance of a beautiful future. And know that therein lies your destiny to come!

Magical Key to Bliss: Decide on a present action that will propel you forward in life.

January 30: **Build joyful connections.**

If your guard is up, let it down. If you've constructed a defensive wall to protect yourself and keep all the bad guys out, don't forget who that wall also prevents from getting in—the good guys.

~Brendon Burchard, author of *The Charge: Activating the 10 Human Drives That Make You Feel Alive*

Instead of building a fortress to protect your heart and soul, let your guard down and open up to joy. When there are times of great loss, hurt, or disappointment, perhaps your gut instinct is to contract and push away further vulnerability. Although you may think that constructing a wall is a good option in the short term, doing so can prevent great things from coming your way in the long run. Take the risk of seeking out positive connections, and you will be well on your way to a beautiful life. If you are too walled in already, it's not too late to find ways to demolish that wall or climb over it and enjoy the colorful world on the other side. When you start letting go of your fear, you can focus on and recognize the possibilities that await you. When you turn toward love and away from fear, the good guys will come to assist you. Each time a generous soul arrives, your faith will increase. Revel in the freedom of movement that these self-imposed structures once prevented. The choice is yours.

 Magical Key to Bliss: Build a bridge of joy, and take the necessary steps to create a life from which you will never want to take a vacation!

January 31: A greater world than we could ever imagine!

There's no greater thing that you can do with your life than to follow your passions in a way that serves you and the world.

~Sir Richard Branson, British businessman and investor

Two heads are better than one. In fact, if it is on the shoulders of giants that you are able to recognize new breakthroughs and explore further innovative design, then there will always be a vital need for many thinkers to enhance the process. One person alone can never take all the credit for good works or deeds. It has often been the hero guided by the mythical mentor who gives way to informed choices as the journey continues. It has been and will always be a communal effort that leads to great discoveries that enhance the collective good. The successful performance only goes on seamlessly because each person joins together to follow his or her passions in a way that sets out to serve themselves and the world. And when you are part of that collective effort, you walk away experiencing the great thrill of being alive, connected to others for the greater good. Yes, two heads are better than one. Look around and share your ideas with others to gain perspective that will break through any illusory barrier that gets in the way. When two heads collide in a wonderful way, something amazing can be created by virtue of the talents that are put forth. You will then reap the rewards through the realization of a world that is more beautiful, kinder, greater, and more peaceful through joint effort than any of us could ever imagine alone.

Magical Key to Bliss: Discover what you are passionate about today.

# Chapter Two: February

IT'S ALL ABOUT LOVE

By the time February arrives, our journey into bliss is in full force. We have set out a road map, identified our dreams, and planted the seeds of our desires in fertile soil. By now, we have made a commitment to ourselves and will accept no excuses, only results. Even in times of doubt, we know that our efforts will pay off. This month is the perfect opportunity to infuse the foundation we have established with the only thing that can truly move us in the right direction: love. And in February, love certainly is in the air; romantic love, familial love, and love among friends. Most importantly, self-love also remains our focus during this time of year. When we set out on our journey with *The Magical Guide to Bliss*, we were hopeful of experiencing a great and wonderful change. Positive change can happen only if we bring love to its rightful place of importance—directly at the center of who we are as we become who we want to be. Love invites us to embrace the buzz that takes over as plans are made to celebrate the time-honored tradition of showering the ones we care for most with incredible warmth and affection.

The word February comes from the Latin term *februum*, which means purification. In true spirit, the second month of the Julian calendar allows us to cleanse our hearts and purify our souls by focusing on love and allowing it to wash over us in every aspect of our lives. We grow as a result of giving and receiving love; there is no other way to flourish as we trust and open our hearts to experience life this way.

Let Cupid's arrow pierce your heart during this month; truly allow the beautiful feelings of love to wash over you. Are you ready to be a part of it? In February, it's all about love!

February 1: Be beautiful on the inside and shine on the outside.

Since love grows within you, so beauty grows. For love is the beauty of the soul.

~Saint Augustine, Roman Catholic saint

In today's world, we are often too consumed with worry over how others perceive us. Unfortunately, our focus is often misplaced. Although we can decorate our faces and our bodies with clothes, makeup, and material things, we will never fully step into our true beauty until we make a proactive intention to love who we are as we are. When we shift our focus from the external to the internal, we will start to truly understand our purpose here. It is the beauty within that emanates for all to see. It is the beauty within that needs to be nurtured. It is the beauty within that we must take care to cultivate. It is the beauty within that makes us the special and unique people we were created to be. When we shift our focus to our inner gorgeousness, the world starts to make more sense, and our experiences become more and more like blessings rather than hardships. The beauty within grows when we focus on feelings of love. We are all here in this life to make connections with others coming from a place of complete love. If we shift to the internal and focus on the love and appreciation for who we are, we will see our lives through kinder eyes, with a renewed sense of zeal and enthusiasm for living. When we come from the perspective of self-love on the inside, we will get the best makeover on the outside and not even have to pay the big bucks for it. For love is truly the beauty of the soul!

 Magical Key to Bliss: Name one thing that allows your beauty within to shine through.

February 2: Love yourself first.

Love yourself first and everything else falls into line. You really have to love yourself to get anything done in this world.

~Lucille Ball, American actress and comedian

Strive for a life in which there are more joyful days than sad ones, more exciting times than dull ones, and more abundance than lack. Although the journey at times takes you through storms, you must hold on to the fact that when the rain passes, and it will, there will always be a rainbow to treasure. So when you are going through the rainy days, make a conscious decision to love yourself first, and the transition to more amazing moments will be easier. When you take care of yourself and love yourself first, you get the much-needed oxygen for your body and soul that will allow you to breathe easier as you move forward. So when you hit the bumps in the road, take the time to listen to what your heart is telling you: Do you need quiet time alone? Do you need to get a massage? Do you need to stop berating yourself and acknowledge the amazing person you are? Remember, when you are kind and gentle with yourself, you gain much-needed clarity to deal with the task at hand rather than adding more stress and prolonging the agony. So if you want to get anything done in this world, today give yourself some love, and you are well on your way to seeing more joyful days, more exciting times, and more abundance for you and everyone you meet along the way!

Magical Key to Bliss: Write a love letter to yourself today.

February 3: **Love is not logical.**

A love that defies all logic is sometimes the most logical thing in the world.

~Unknown

Perhaps it is not logical to do so, especially during the challenges, but falling in love with life is a decision that you can make on a daily basis if you so choose. Once you make a committed decision to love whomever or whatever comes your way, stand back and welcome what the universe brings. Where love is concerned, open yourself up to the highest highs and even the lowest lows. There is no logic regarding whom or what you love; matters of the heart are best encountered when you open your soul to the potential that lies there without an expectation for what should come back to you. To protect yourself from being hurt by hiding from life may seem logical at times; however, to take the risk of opening your heart to experience a love that defies all logic is more rewarding. When you love, you get to experience life, and that is why you are here. So love like there is no tomorrow; the treasures of loving may not be readily apparent or logical, but in the end they are great! Love will give you wings!

Magical Key to Bliss: Send love to someone with whom you have had disagreements, and see what happens.

February 4: You are love!

Your love of life can carry you through any circumstance.

~Chinese fortune cookie

When you wake in the morning with the desire to experience love, know that love exists right at your center, pulsating in your heart, coursing throughout your entire body. The one necessary ingredient for the miraculous discovery of love is the intention to acknowledge this fact right here and right now. It is attainable when you realize that it is you. You are love. With all your gifts and all your flaws, you first and foremost are love. And, when you reali.ze this, the love in your heart shall set you free. Free from all the illusions of the world that try to keep each of us separate and apart. Free to open your wings and let your heart fly. When you embrace the fact that you are love, stand back and watch the amazing connections unfold and a love of life take over. Let this thought take you through the challenges and catapult you forward toward an incredible future no matter what happens. May you remember that you are love and are loved, and be sure to pass on this good news! Accept where you are, embrace the love in you and that surrounds you, and keep moving forward, knowing that this love will carry you through any life circumstance.

Magical Key to Bliss: Do something special to celebrate love today!

February 5: **Plant the seeds of love in your consciousness today.**

Keep love in your heart. A life without it is like a sunless garden when the flowers are dead. The consciousness of loving and being loved brings a warmth and richness to life that nothing else can bring.

~Oscar Wilde, Irish author, playwright, and poet

Perhaps today is a day that you focus on love. With love, you can let the sunshine in even on a gloomy day. Your heart will begin to bloom again as you take in the warmth of love that reenergizes you. Perhaps today is a good day to focus on how you want to share the love that resides in your heart. When you get into a conscious state of loving others, you begin to plant the seeds to manifest a more beautiful world for yourself. With love that is shared, there is a renewed hope. When you become conscious of your intentional choices to love, things around you will change because you, at your core, change. You know intuitively that without love, your life can become dreary like an unending winter or a sunless garden. When you allow the energy of love to emanate from within, then your life is nourished once again and blooms with the vibrant beauty of renewal. With love, you recognize your greatest potential and encourage others to reach theirs too. When you plant the seeds of love in your consciousness, you will revitalize a world that desperately needs it. Perhaps today is that kind of day where you focus on love and bring warmth and richness to the world—that can make all the difference! With love lies an amazing feeling that nothing else can bring!

Magical Key to Bliss: Surprise someone with a gesture of love today!

February 6: Love is a decision.

As long as you refuse to see your inner potential for happiness now, you will not see it in the world. You will only see in the world what you're prepared to see in yourself—nothing more and nothing less.

~Robert Holden, PhD, British psychologist, author, and expert on happiness

When you decide to see your inner beauty and to love who you are, you are making the greatest and most important decision in your life. Your view of the world is a direct reflection of your thoughts about your potential. When you are convinced that you are happiness, you will start to experience a joy in your life that unleashes your soul. When you start to believe that you are love, then the world will mirror that magic that comes from inside you. When you start to feel beautiful from within, then the heaviness of the world will fall away as you prepare to see the miraculous all around you. First, clear the mental and emotional clutter that may be preventing you from seeing your own inner light. Second, make the choice to value yourself by accepting your own inner worth. Third, embrace the talents that are so uniquely yours, and replace the negative chatter that can hinder you with the love that you know resides within. You will see in your world what you believe already exists within yourself. When you make the decision to acknowledge the good that is you, get prepared to experience the good everywhere else. Loving yourself is a decision. When you make that decision, then happiness and success have a chance to come to fruition. See your inner beauty and love yourself first, and the rest will follow. Believe it!

 Magical Key to Bliss: Focus on love and happiness inside, and watch it unfold outside.

February 7: **Be a magnet of love.**

Everybody is like a magnet. You attract to yourself reflections of what you are. If you're friendly, then everybody else seems to be friendly too.

~Dr. David Hawkins, American philosopher

Are you ready? Today is going to be an amazing day. Why? Today you are challenged to partake in the love magnet experiment. Your journey begins when you awaken to focus on that wonderful, positive experience that you wish to happen. You take a moment to establish a conscious intention to dream bigger than you ever imagined. You then accept only loving thoughts into your existence, and do it confidently with a huge smile. Working with the knowledge that you attract to yourself what you are putting out into the world, you become intensely aware of how you conduct yourself. You turn on your love magnet to invite magical people, places, and things into your life. When you begin your day in a space filled with love, watch how you remain, undeterred, in that amazing place in your heart and mind. Then see and feel the magic that God intends for you as you attract that incredible energy back into your life. Start believing in and attracting love in your life. Make this a habit and visualize it, and it will permeate your soul! Then all you will see and experience is love, love, love everywhere you go! Are you ready for the challenge?

 Magical Key to Bliss: Pretend that you are a giant magnet of love, and document what you attract.

February 8: Love the skin you are in.

Try to be like the turtle—at ease in your own shell.

~Bill Copeland, American poet

Accept the body you are in as the best gift that you have ever been given—more precious than china, more valuable than diamonds, and more perfect for you than anything that you can ever imagine. Through acceptance of this invaluable gift, you recognize how lucky you are to experience your life as seen through your particular eyes— whether brown, green, or blue. How lucky you are to experience others through a rich culture; how fortunate to experience the world through your senses processed by your amazing mind. Once you get to acceptance and are at ease in your shell, the judgmental noise and criticism melt away so that you can experience the events in your life with love, joy, and peace. Remember that you are unique; there is no one else like you in the world! Bask in the beauty of that knowledge, wrapping your arms around the notion that you are perfect just as you are. With that kind of ease, your own skin becomes the best place to be! Don't you just love that?

 Magical Key to Bliss: Spread your arms out wide, and then wrap them around your body, saying, "Thank you; I love you!"

February 9: Rededicate yourself to a sense of wonder and awe!

Dwell on the beauty of life. Watch the stars, and see yourself running with them.

~Marcus Aurelius, Roman emperor (161–180) and Stoic philosopher

Be part of the beautiful fabric of this life. Each and every moment is an opportunity for you to realize that your reality is but a colorful dream—a dream you have always yearned for and desired. A dream that has given you the chance to explore the magic that lies at your fingertips. A dream you needed to rededicate yourself to discover the great wonders of this world. There are so many wonders; they are almost too plentiful to count. Start your day watching the dance of the leaves on the trees. Cherish the connections with friends as you travel down a particular path. Embrace the love that is offered to you, from the wind on your face to the caress of another's gentle hug. Become wonder filled as you navigate your quest to new heights of magnificence. Revisit a day with that childlike part of you that remains untainted by the habitual thinking that can keep you in a box too small, now, for your spirit. Choose to take risks, and break out striving for the marvelous things that call to you. Seek a new apogee as you pop the lid open on a box that no longer suits your grandeur, and see that there is so much more bliss for you in this world. Be courageous as you garner the strength to not only gaze on the mystery of the stars but also decide to run with them. For with a renewed sense of awe and wonder, you will not be the only person you inspire to run.

Magical Key to Bliss: Sit for a moment with nature, and take in the beauty of the world.

February 10: Looking for a lifelong romance?

To love oneself is the beginning of a lifelong romance!

~Oscar Wilde, Irish author, playwright, and poet

Once you start to accept yourself and love yourself exactly as you are, you will know a freedom and empowerment that you have never experienced before. It is time to fall in love with you. It is time to enjoy your own company. It is time to be kind and gentle to yourself right where you are. Don't look to change the beauty of who you are so that others will accept you. Change how you think about yourself so that *you* will accept you. Don't think that you need to live life a certain way to please others. Live your life so that you follow your own purposeful journey, a journey that calls out to your soul each and every moment you breathe. Enter into a fantastic love affair with your life, one that has you waking each day excited to be alive. Start a romance that has you dancing in your *own* shoes. Make it a love story filled with a passion and enthusiasm for new discovery, one that allows for intrigue and fascination as you encounter the beauty in the world that is just waiting to be discovered! If you are looking for a lifelong romance, start with the one who stares back at you in the mirror. Get to know yourself in a way that inspires a great masterpiece of art, beautiful poetry of the soul, and a harmonious composition of sounds that forms a magnificent symphony of life. This way we all benefit.

Magical Key to Bliss: Start a romance and buy yourself beautiful flowers!

February 11: Radiate love.

Let your light shine.
Be a source of strength.
Share your wisdom.
Radiate Love.

~Wilfred Peterson, American author

The universe is talking to you. The universe is begging for you to shine because there is no light identical to yours. The universe needs your particular brand of determination and strength, for there is no spirit that mirrors yours. The universe asks that you share your hard-earned wisdom to advance the cause of all that is good, for there is no perspective equals to yours. But most importantly, the universe prays that you choose to radiate love to others because no love can nourish this desperate land the way the love that comes from within you can. The universe is calling you, reminding you that you need to shine in order to guide your way through any challenge. For if you can see clearly, you will discover that it is in the challenge of life that you will see your strength. When you have walked through the challenge, you will have gained precious wisdom. And with that newfound wisdom, you will be able to radiate love even stronger than before. Each morning as you start your day, arm yourself with your positive intentions, write them down, and set out to act in a way that ensures they come to light. As your soul seeks, your vision will motivate you to become more alive in this world. Surrender to the process, radiate love throughout, and trust that from one moment to the next, you will rise to a place more aligned with your purpose in life!

Magical Key to Bliss: Set out a positive intention on a Post-it Note, and put it where you can see it!

February 12: Love.

Blessed is the influence of one true, loving human soul on another.

~George Elliot, born Mary Ann Evans, British novelist of the Victorian era

Souls love. That's what souls do. Egos don't, but souls do. Align with your soul, look around, and you'll be amazed. All beings that surround you are incredible souls. Be one, see one...And don't leave out the animals, trees, and clouds—for you are one with nature. It is that simple. Love resides as a part of one field of energy. The act of loving may be expressed in many different ways, but it is all the same—a beautiful reflection of self. Take a moment today to feel the love that is all around you. The creation that you see comes from your creativity within that started because of love and passion to begin with. Intend to attract the incredible bliss that comes from feeling one with the universe, and truly experience this purest form of love. You play an important role in this world. Your heart beats in tune with the universe. You are in sync if you just allow yourself to go with the flow. Go to your heart today, and feel the love that emanates from each beat. Then make a decision to be the change, and share that love with other souls through beautifully inspired acts. With your testimony, love will grow. To love one another in your own special way is why you are here. You are love, and you are loved—it's that simple. Now go!

Magical Key to Bliss: Write a letter to someone and tell them how much he or she is loved!

February 13: **Never outgrow your need for love.**

A baby is born with the need to be loved—and never outgrows it.

~Frank Howard Clark, American screenwriter

If you remember on a daily basis that you were at one time a precious little baby who needed the love and attention of another to survive and thrive, it will put perspective into each and every one of your connections throughout the day. When love and caring attention are withheld from an infant, that new life fails to thrive, and numerous complications ensue. The same goes for every human being. If love is withheld from your life, your will to live diminishes. Love, affection, and touch are so important in the general dance of life. You need the connections. You need to connect. You will never outgrow the need to be loved. You are a fragile, beautiful soul, and your mission in this world was never meant to be discovered alone. You need to reach out to others, grab their hands, and boldly embark on your adventure. If you see other people as little children needing to be shown the way, then you will easily express love and compassion. You never outgrow the need to be loved. When you realize this, you know how important it is to express kindness to others on a daily basis. Doing so literally changes you. With this in mind, ask how you can be of service today. In essence, set the intention to give *love* in all you do, and make this world a better place to live because we never outgrow that need for love.

Magical Key to Bliss: Choose small acts of love and kindness for others, and thrive!

February 14: Unlock the beauty within through love.

The present moment holds infinite riches beyond your wildest dreams, but you will only enjoy them to the extent of your faith and love. The more a soul loves, the more it longs, the more it hopes, the more it finds.

~Jean Pierre de Caussade, S. J. (Society of Jesus), French Jesuit priest and writer

Today is a wondrous day that holds infinite riches. Are you ready to experience all it has to offer? If so, be present to the people with whom you come into contact; they may offer you wisdom to catapult your dreams. Be present to the story of inspiration that offers hope, love, joy, and forgiveness. Be present to your own soul; it is calling out to you to act wondrously. Set aside your worries for now, and allow. Allow your faith to blossom as you surrender to the hope that positive change can begin with amazing intentions. Allow the seeds of love to be planted because the more you love, the more love you will attract. Allow your light within to glow, for more shiny people will surround you. Allow your mind to stay open without judgments, for you will learn. Remember that God is in everything. Once you realize that, you will experience less fear, know more enlightenment, and be more fulfilled. And it is there with faith and hope that your soul will find the riches that life offers. Unlock the beauty within through love, and get ready to experience the magical beyond your wildest dreams. Happy Valentine's Day!

Magical Key to Bliss: Send love to others today with a kind act, a loving gesture, or an open heart!

February 15: **It's all about love.**

Too often we underestimate the power of a touch, a smile, a kind word, a listening ear, an honest compliment, or the smallest act of caring, all of which have the potential to turn a life around.

~Leo Buscaglia, American author and motivational speaker

This is a beautiful way to live your life. When you really care about others, extend yourself by giving love, and are present through kindness, you can make a difference in both another's life and your own. You attract to yourself what you give away. By truly being a channel of peace rather than adversity, you bring more peace to your life. By being a ray of sunshine when you walk into a room, you attract others who will bring light to you. By striving to be a better person today than you were the day before, you will find other seekers who are on the same journey. Saint Therese said it is the small things you do in life that will make the world a wonderful place. It is the small acts of love that contribute to the beauty that already is there. So with small acts of kindness, a gentle embrace, a beautifully shared smile, uplifting words, a listening ear, or just a simple expression of love, you are transforming the fabric of your own little corner of the world. You not only *will* impact the life of another, but you have the potential to turn your own life around. It's something to think about as you start a new day. Amen and Alleluia! Remember, it is all about *love!*

Magical Key to Bliss: Share an honest compliment based in love with five people today!

February 16: Live, Laugh, Love.

Live passionately, laugh out loud, love unconditionally. Or in Italian, Viva bene, di risalto molto, spesso l'amore.

~Italian Proverb

Figure out what you are passionate about and what makes you excited to get out of bed in the morning. Surround yourself with people who find humor in life so they don't take themselves too seriously. Tune in to the most powerful force of energy in the universe, the energy that allows you to move mountains and brings miracles. When you marry a life of passion with healing laughter and then add in the purest form of love, your life changes before you. When you see your life as a series of chances where you can learn to live, laugh, and love through deepened experiences with friends, family, and even strangers, then you begin to know that each day is a gift to be discovered and cherished. You are not alone but with those who have been placed on your path. Each day with awareness, you contact your teachers who will help you further proceed on your path to live your purpose and who will laugh and experience love with you. It is in these daily contacts that you discover truth. Just sit in that awareness of this mantra for living, and don't mistake these words as too simplistic. It is in their simplicity that they are most power-ful. Just take one day at a time, one word at a time, and just for today, seek to be with your people and remember to live passionately, laugh out loud, and love unconditionally. It is there that you will find all the joy that life has to offer.

Magical Key to Bliss: Repeat the mantra: live, laugh, love!

February 17: Change now, love now, live now!

There's no need to wait for the bad things and bullsh*t to be over. Change now. Love now. Live now. Don't wait for people to give you permission to live, because they won't.

~Kris Carr, American author and wellness activist

*T*oday is the day! In this moment, at this time, you have the choice to shift your thoughts and change your mind-set. No need to wait. No need to get permission to do so. No need to pause for that perfect moment of clarity. Now is the time to begin to make the changes in your life that will set the course for a better experience. Your thoughts clearly affect your feelings about your life. If you believe you are a miracle, then your world will show you examples that match this belief. If you think you are special and are here on purpose, then watch how your life circumstances align with your belief and show you the way. Change now, love now, live now. You can make those choices. *Today is the day!* There is no better time than the present moment, and no better person equipped to live the life you want than you. Be responsible to think the thoughts that empower you, do the things that launch you forward, love this adventure now, and go for it.

Magical Key to Bliss: Today is the day; replace a negative thought pattern with a positive one—I AM____!

February 18: People remember how you made them feel.

I've learned that people will forget what you said, people will forget what you did, but people will never forget how you made them feel.

~Maya Angelou, American author, poet, dancer, actress, and singer

You want to live your life in such a way that the world will be a better place for having known you. Think about the people in your life who have made a difference. Think about those people who make you feel special as they radiate love, share kindness, and bring laughter to your world. Think about those people and imitate them. It is the lasting effect of a hug or a kind gesture that changes your world. Although day-to-day tasks take up your time, you should never be too busy to give loving attention to another. Although some of your memories can fade, the emotions tied to those loving moments will carry you. You will always remember that person who made you feel valued. You will always smile when you recall an encounter that made you feel loved, special, or accepted. Life gives you many opportunities to get it right. Opportunities to be kind and caring are constantly interwoven in your life. The question remains: will you stop and take the time to respond to that call to action? It is not the awards or promotions but rather the connections based in love that will ultimately get you through the day. Take the opportunity today to reevaluate your priorities and purpose in this context—make this journey worthwhile because it is your once around. So set out with the distinct purpose to give love to all, and you will build an amazing legacy.

Magical Key to Bliss: Think about how you are going to make people feel today!

February 19: Created by love, to love!

While I know myself as a creation of God, I am also obligated to realize and remember that everyone else and everything else are also God's creation.

~Maya Angelou, American author, poet, dancer, actress, and singer

We are all wholly created from the divine to become divine. From our beginnings, we learn what love is from our family. We continue to see how to love in different ways from our friends who have opened our eyes to so much. And, as we falter and grow, we gain the gifts of love and enlightenment that carry us further along the path. Throughout the journey, we have a sense that God, the higher power, or divine energy, has a hand in creating the story that unfolds before our eyes, a mystical and magical plot that not only amazes but excites us as well. The magical elements surround us and lift our spirits. For God is in everyone and everything. Questions may arise regarding finding clarity and love in the chaos, but as Einstein acknowledged, "When the solution is simple, God is answering." When we see one another as creations of God created to love, knowing that God is good, it follows that there is good in all. We are all here to learn and to serve. In meditation, when our minds get silent, we hear the answer to how this good source will use us today. We stand together connected to the beauty of creation, admiring the amazing works that surround us. Gratitude becomes the cornerstone of this tremendous masterpiece—one in which we are all united, created by love to love! Each of us is so different yet intrinsically the same.

 Magical Key to Bliss: Find connection where there is perceived separation.

February 20: **Share the love—no strings attached.**

Anyone who loves in the expectation of receiving some kind of reward is wasting his or her time.

~Paulo Coelho, Brazilian author of *The Devil and Miss Prym*

The greatest gift that we can give to one another is unconditional love. Love based on conditions is often misguided and manipulative. To love purely and freely is the greatest gift one person can give to another. It is an act of the greatest acceptance that is liberating to both the giver and the receiver. When your love is given for the pure sake of sharing from the depth of your heart and soul and not as a means to an end, how wonderful it can be. When you love another by recognizing or validating that person from a place that does not rely on what will be given in return, how incredibly healing. When you are embraced for who you are and not for what you have done, how this love changes you and makes you a better person. Love given without any expectations is incredibly freeing, while love given with expectation always has the potential of leaving you very disappointed. If you are going to share the love, release the strings, detach from the outcome, and just set out to enjoy the act itself. If you seek something in return, you are just wasting your time. As you use it well, your heart's capacity to love will grow greater despite how your intentions are received. So when you love, do your best to not bring conditions of receiving in return, and open your heart to the experience. The result will be better than you ever expected.

Magical Key to Bliss: Do a good deed for another today without any expectations.

February 21: **Educate yourself through love.**

The most important thing in any relationship is not what you get but what you give…In any case, the giving of love is an education in itself.

~Eleanor Roosevelt, American activist and former first lady of the United States of America

If you want a good education, you study hard and practice. If you want good relationships, the same applies. Strong friendships don't just happen by osmosis. It takes work to build a solid foundation of love, trust, and communication where your connection to others is concerned. You truly get what you give. If you are a solid support in times of adversity, then you will likely be held in your time of need. If you show up for others when they need you most, then rest assured that you, too, will not be abandoned. If you take the risk to be open to love as you journey through life with those beautiful souls, love will show up in your life again and again. Life's greatest lessons are there for the taking. Great opportunities to gain a tremendous education in love are there for the waking. If ever your efforts could make the greatest difference in the world, practice giving love, and you shall see the great fruits of your worthy labor. When you give love with great enthusiasm, the bonds that you form will sustain you for a lifetime and beyond.

Magical Key to Bliss: Experiment today with giving love to those who are not so easy to love!

February 22: Detach with love.

Let us not be content to wait and see what will happen, but give us the determination to make the right things happen.

~Horace Mann, American politician and educational reformer

When you feel called to a worthy endeavor, there is no time to take an attitude of wait and see. While there is a time for rest, there is also a time to move when the spirit calls you to do so. Superhuman status is not required to make the right things happen in life. You just need to pay attention to what shows up, set clear intentions, and move forward with inspired action. Affecting many on a grander scale requires only the determination of one to keep on doing the right thing over and over again. If you are that one person who answers the call, then detach from the result with love, and go forth planting the seeds of great and wonderful change. Accomplishments, both great and small, are realized when you identify your passions, investigate ways to make your dreams a reality, and take innovative steps to see the dreams come to light. Nothing can truly hold you captive if you follow your heart, surrender, and release the outcome. You were never meant to be a bystander; you were always meant to be an active participant on the journey. You were not meant to wait for others to take charge; you were meant to be the one to take initiative and do for yourself! So what are you waiting for? Success comes from inspired action and determination. Start now, detach from the result with love, and see where your actions take you today!

Magical Key to Bliss: Ask a question, close your eyes, and receive your inspired answer.

February 23: Love is your mission.

Have you had a kindness shown?
Pass it on;
'Twas not given for thee alone,
Pass it on;
Let it travel down the years,
Let it wipe another's tears,
'Till in Heav'n the deed appears—
Pass it on.

~Henry Burton, English Puritan and theologian

Your actions can have a domino effect on the world. In a time when the events of the world can bring a lot of sadness and anxiety to the masses, you can be part of a revolution of people who counteract the negative energy by opening their hearts to emanate love and kindness. If you show kindness to another in one part of the world, that kindness can spread like wildfire around the globe. If you give love wherever you go, you will leave a magical trail behind you. Like the wave at a sports event, it will start out slowly, but surely the excitement will catch on, and the whole stadium will be part of the enthusiasm, joy, and laughter. You *are* a wave of love and kindness. If you have been blessed in life, then go share your blessings with another. If you have been touched by compassion, go be compassionate to another. If you have been saved from loneliness, then open your heart to save another. Once your wave begins, it will start to travel down the years. And yes, you can be a part of wiping away another's tears without knowing it. Ah-mazing really! Once they are shared, love and kindness never felt so good. Make them both your religion. While spreading love and kindness, you can be a part of heaven on earth as peace comes to us all. Pass it on.

Magical Key to Bliss: Ask yourself how you can make a difference by sharing your love and talents, and go do that!

February 24: A vision of a life that is alluring...

Someone who does not run toward the allure of love walks a road where nothing lives.

~Rumi, thirteenth-century poet and Sufi mystic

A re you tempted by the magic of a love for life? When you dream, do visions appear in your mind's eye that empower you to break out on an adventurous road to see those images realized? If you are enticed by the desire to feel fully alive, start to believe in a life full of love. When you do, your enthusiasm and excitement for the experiences that come will open you up to learn through lessons that will assist you on your wonderful path. When you choose love, you make the choice to turn away from languishing in negative thought processes. When you are encased in the allure of love, you start to live from your heart space, and your tremendous potential is all that you embrace. Enticed by love, you make the decision to go within and discover the powerful and mysterious attraction to life that your soul is seeking. Your own tremendous capacity to love will positively impact your curiosity to imagine bigger and better dreams. Seek love and be charmed by what you find as you experience your miraculous journey! And when you set out to discover your world, looking through the alluring eyes of love, you will find more love for life, learning, people, and divine manifestation. Walk the road where life is abundant, where loving connections fortify your spirit, and where the allure of the miraculous draws you in and never lets you go! For that's the kind of vision of life worth running to.

 Magical Key to Bliss: Visualize your journey, be open to all the beauty, and feel the experience with gratitude.

February 25: **Pass on the love.**

And now these three remain: faith, hope, and love. But the greatest of these is love.

~1 Corinthians (13:13), *Holy Bible, New International Version*

When we experience love, we exude an energy that is beautiful and healing. This amazing experience can leave a strong impression on both those who feel it directly and those who witness it from afar. God's love given to us through many people is so filled with golden splendor that the brightness makes it impossible to keep it to ourselves. Many hearts are aching for this, dreaming of this, and asking where this is in life. We are all vessels of love to another, supporting one another on the journey and seeing what love can do—and realizing the important part we all play in making this a reality for the plenty, not just the few. People serving people giving love—so beautiful! While we are all challenged in our daily lives with the feeling that we cannot make a difference, it is in the small and beautiful acts of love that we can offer such a profound change. May we hold strong when we are faced with the challenges of life, using the music of love to touch the deepest part of our souls. When we trust from a place of love, we learn so much. We are *love* and that *is* the greatest thing to understand! So remember, if we are the lucky ones who have been blessed by so much love, don't forget to *give love* and keep passing it on!

Magical Key to Bliss: Hold on to a gratitude rock or a symbol as a reminder to give love!

February 26: Are you bringing love to this world?

God doesn't look at how much we do but at how much love we do it with.

~Mother Teresa, Roman Catholic religious sister and missionary

When it seems there is nothing you can do to bring hope to a world in disarray, remind yourself that positive change comes not from how much you do but from how you do it. You can have an impact if you make the decision to bring your own kind of love to this place that is desperately in need of it. The media presents a picture of turmoil, fear, and suffering. What the media fails to show are the people who are making amazing changes through acts of charity, compassion, service, and love. There has to be a time of enlightenment in which you start to wake up to a reality of your own creating. There has to be a time when you start to break the cycle of negativity and finally learn the lessons of the past to create a greater collective consciousness in the present that is founded on principles of love. This may seem like a request to live as a Pollyanna of sorts, but then again who is to say that a world in which humanity governs itself with the highest virtues is far off. Start a revolution of love. Instead of feeling that you cannot make a difference, ask yourself whether you are bringing love to this world. If you allow love to permeate all that you do, a different world is possible. Start inspiring this great hope to come to fruition. You can build this reality, and assuredly it will be well worth it!

Magical Key to Bliss: Be guided by your intuition, and reach out to someone in need today.

February 27: Use your life as part of the great love experiment!

Whatever we accomplish belongs to our entire group. A tribute to our combined effort.

~Walt Disney, American visionary, cartoonist, and animator

If we combined our efforts to spread more joy, imagine what a happier place this world would be. If we combined our efforts to spread more peace in this world, imagine what a different vibe and energy we would experience—and the wonderful feeling as we would recognize the gifts each of us embodies. When we unite and combine efforts to bring good to this world, the possibilities for miraculous change will multiply beyond measure. What was once a splash in the ocean becomes, combined with other small splashes, a wave of love with the potential to travel for miles and miles, far and wide. The impact, when we combine our efforts to spread joy, peace, and love, will soon become a tribute to the entire group that set out to meet this worthy goal. Together, when we reach out in love, we can eradicate the illusion of loneliness. Together, when we reach out in love, we can ensure that the epidemic of depression becomes a thing of the past. Together, when we reach out in love, we can connect and accomplish so much more than we could ever imagine on our own. Send out an invitation to others to join in and take ownership of all we can accomplish together, leaving a legacy of overwhelming love for future generations to experience. That legacy of love is something we could all be proud to belong to.

 Magical Key to Bliss: Let your imagination run wild as to the magical reality that could be all of ours.

February 28: **What is your philosophy?**

Wonder is the feeling of the philosopher, and philosophy begins in wonder.

~Plato, Classical Greek philosopher

On this beautiful day, challenge yourself to define what your philosophy of life will be. When based in wonder, this quest has the potential to broaden your horizons and expand your vision of the future. It is important to define the system of values by which you want to live. Guided by a desire to know more than you see, you can go further and ask the questions that will have you see the world and the universe with aware, open, and accepting eyes. Based on a philosophy of a life that is magical, you start to see people who cross your path as being there for a reason. Based on a philosophy of life that is inquisitive, you experience difficult events as embodying vital lessons there to guide you on. Based on a philosophy of surrender, you stand effortlessly in awe as your life unfolds beautifully in unexpected, unfamiliar, or inexplicable circumstances. Based on a philosophy of love, you begin to marvel about what you discover about yourself, conscious of the miracle that occurs because you decided to live an examined life. Look to the burning questions of your soul to set a fantastic course ahead. So on this beautiful day, the invitation is there to start a journey into wonder and embrace life through the eyes of a philosopher. Like the sage ones who have gone before, are willing to accept it?

 Magical Key to Bliss: Step back and prepare to be amazed at what you get to discover in life today!

February 29: Take a giant leap.

You will travel in a land of marvels.

~Jules Verne, French novelist, poet, and playwright

Perhaps you have thought you do not have enough hours in your days to accomplish all the good that needs to be done; today you get an added twenty-four hours to travel in this land of marvels. While this fabulous opportunity comes only once every four years, it would behoove you to not waste the chance to do something really special to advance your dreams. The leap day was added to the Gregorian calendar as a corrective measure because the earth does not orbit around the sun in precisely 365 days, and today can be seen as a magical day in which your actions can lend a restorative quality to enhance your future. Take a giant leap to right the direction of your life; take advantage of this extra time to venture forth and live your dreams. From sunrise to sunset, appreciate this extra gift in this rather uncommon year, and make plans to set a course in a better direction by letting go and leaping into a marvelous new course of action.

 Magical Key to Bliss: Close your eyes, make a wish, and ceremoniously take a leap to see it come true.

Chapter Three: March

PROFOUND WISDOM

March is when daylight saving time usually begins, marking the time of year when the days begin to grow longer as the earth slowly transitions to her springtime rising and setting positions in the heavens. Light symbolizes knowledge. March is the month in which we are blessed with more and more daylight with each passing day; thus, the concept for this chapter is profound wisdom.

As the third month of the year progresses, let the light of knowledge that shines within you also grow day by day. Make it your mission in March to learn something new each and every blessed day you are lucky enough to experience the light of the sun. As the days grow warmer and longer, so too will your capacity to give and receive love. For inherent in the ability to love unconditionally is your intimate knowledge of yourself and the profound wisdom that accompanies self-understanding. As you strive to understand others, you simultaneously strive to comprehend your own inner workings. As you walk steadily and rhythmically in step with others, it is this wisdom that will guide you as you continue to seize the day, open your heart to a greater love, and continue the journey marching forward toward a greater bliss.

March 1: Set the example.

It is difficult to bring people to goodness with lessons, but it's easy to do so by example.

~Seneca, Roman Stoic philosopher

Actions have always spoken louder than words. You can choose to be either a person who talks about change or a person who lives it. You can be either a person who complains that the world should be a better place or one who sets out to do things that make it that way. Eager to live in a world where compassion and kindness rule the day, if you start to dwell in possibility, doing something to bring joy can make joyful change happen. Better yet, if you start to believe that—showing others you can make a difference through small acts of love—then you set the tone for all to see. Be a true believer in the "good finder" mentality. If you look for the examples of good in the world and seek out those who offer empowering inspiration through their life example, you will find and be infected by the good, leaving the bad in its wake. And if you want to teach others to do the same, be the change, be the difference, be the living lesson for all to see. By setting the example through your loud and proud actions, you will embolden others to act, leading all of us to a better life that can be filled with overwhelming goodness. You are the company you keep; when you set a good example, odds are in your favor that the company you keep will be amazing.

Magical Key to Bliss: Set the example; choose one good thing to do for another today.

March 2: **Greatness through cooperation.**

Great discoveries and improvements invariably involve the cooperation of many minds. I may be given credit for having blazed the trail, but when I look at the subsequent developments I feel the credit is due to others rather than to myself.

~Alexander Graham Bell, Scottish-born scientist, inventor, engineer, and innovator

It is a humble person who acknowledges that most accomplishments in life are a result of the cooperation of many minds. It is a wise person who stands in gratitude for the influences and support that have brought success. It is a great person who realizes that we are all connected and that amazing things can happen as long as we work together. And, it is a proud person who recognizes that his or her initial innovations inspire others to rise to a higher level. We have all come to this world with our special talents. It is cooperation—not competition—that will allow each of us to use our gifts to benefit society. It is cooperation—not posturing—that will advance society for the greater good. It is cooperation—not our need to be recognized—that will foster further greatness. For we are not separate islands but a collective of very talented, compassionate land masses whose efforts allow all of us to blaze new trails. We cannot do it alone; we need one another as we look to make a difference, transforming from ego to essence. For we all have seen further and benefited greatly from standing on the shoulders of giants, and that understanding of cooperation has traditionally been the only thing that has ever led to greatness for us all.

Magical Key to Bliss: Do something to foster cooperation in your work, school, or any relationship today.

March 3: Extend kindness.

Beginning today, treat everyone you meet as if they were going to be dead by midnight. Extend to them all the care, kindness, and understanding you can muster, and do it with no thought of any reward. Your life will never be the same again.

~Og Mandino, American author

One thing is certain; no one knows what the future holds. As long as you have today, you must make the decision to be present with others. There are no guarantees in life that you will have this opportunity to interact with the same individuals tomorrow; life is a courageous and exciting journey that takes you on an ever-winding path that changes day to day. If you viewed each person as a once-in-a-lifetime blessing, you would extend care for this precious gift. If you saw each soul as offering to play a wondrous role in your experience, extending love without thought of any reward would be your priority. If you knew that this would be your one opportunity to learn something essential and profound, seeking to understand would be paramount. Beginning today, if you approach each interaction as an opportunity to extend kindness without any thought of reward, your life will never be the same, and how grateful you will be.

Magical Key to Bliss: Do something that will generate kindness today!

March 4: Give compassion, not judgment.

I got a fortune cookie that said, "To remember is to understand."
I have never forgotten it. A good judge remembers what it was
like to be a lawyer. A good editor remembers being a writer. A
good parent remembers what it was like to be a child.

~Anna Quindlen, American author, journalist, and opinion columnist

Nothing in life is exactly as it seems. Your interpretation of how the journey should proceed is based on your own small worldview and experience. To bring connection rather than separation, before you judge another based on your own perspective, bring compassion to the table and leave criticism behind. You have your own mountains to climb and your own valleys to get through. You have your own blessings to cherish and your own life to live. You were born into this world to learn, grow, and discover your purpose. Do your best to understand others with compassion and love as you move forward. As you are on your path traveling through life, many are there to teach you. As you go about your days, your journey will be even more fulfilling if you purpose to seek compassionate connections built on mutual understanding. In your interactions today, attempt to stand for a moment in the shoes of another. As you allow kindness to permeate your relationships, be a light of compassion in a world that so desperately needs it. For it is by seeking to understand with a compassionate heart, rather than by judging, that you will remember your roots even as your role changes. After all, we all once started out as beautiful little children with endless possibilities.

Magical Key to Bliss: Ask compassionate questions to learn about someone else's life story.

March 5: **Romance and its magical dance!**

Romance is the glamour which turns the dust of everyday life into a golden haze.

~Carolyn Gold Heilbrun, American professor and feminist author

To believe in romance—what a gift. To experience it—how magical. You can, on your own, convert the ordinary into something extraordinary, opening up to the feeling of excitement and mystery associated with love for all things. To surrender to this amazing dance, you can reach a new plane of joy as you journey through your day. Awash with romance, time with a friend becomes a profound connection of souls. Listening to music becomes an instant boost to your positive energetic vibration. A walk outside becomes a loving conversation with the world. Opening yourself up to a romantic life allows the seemingly unimportant to take on new meaning as you welcome the beauty of each moment. Romance can mean so much more than receiving flowers or an invitation to a special dinner by that special person. Romance can be born from appreciation for the mystery that the world has to offer you daily. Touched by its glamorous effect, you feel as though the universe is presenting you with a giant bouquet of love for all things and an invitation to an amazing feast. Open yourself to this excitement, and experience the beautiful dance of a life magically transformed right before your eyes. Keep your eyes open so you can see the dust change into a golden haze.

Magical Key to Bliss: Be romanced by your day—experience a beautiful sunset.

March 6: **Never give up.**

Your biggest break can come from never quitting. Being at the right place at the right time can only happen when you keep moving toward the next opportunity.

~Arthur Pine, American author

You are a work in progress. As long as you live with intention, you move every day toward achieving your goals whether you know it or not. The universe is presenting opportunities all the time for improvement and advancement. When you have awareness and patience, each next opportunity is exactly what you need in order to realize your fabulous life. Each challenging event offers the chance to develop a skill that will help you. Each connection you make along the way provides a network of support to assist you. And each pearl of wisdom gathered is a clue that opens doors to the next mountain to climb. It is when the momentum of realizing your dream is at a standstill that you must make the decision to never give up—never ever give up! It is when you feel like nothing is going right that quitting cannot be an option. Keep the faith, hold on tight, and remind yourself that much is happening behind the scenes to carry you on. There are messages being delivered daily that will lead you to the right place and time. By making small, inspired changes and keeping your worries at bay, you can believe that your biggest break is just over the hill and that each step forward presents the next opportunity to get a better view as you climb. A breathtaking view that will leave you grateful for never giving up—never ever giving up!

Magical Key to Bliss: Make a small change today to advance your dreams.

March 7: Laughter really is the best medicine!

The human race has only one real effective weapon, and that is laughter. The moment it arises, all your irritations and resentments slip away, and the sunny spirit takes their place.

~Mark Twain, born Samuel Clemens, American author and humorist

An explosive sound that indicates amusement, laughter has us re-placing images of other harmful explosions with those that can contribute to robust living. Bringing more life to your days, laughter feels good and is incredibly contagious. Laughter creates lasting con-nections and breaks the ice when there is tension. When you laugh at yourself for making ridiculous blunders or with others to lighten up an otherwise tense situation, the simple truth is that laughter helps you to approach life with an attitude that life really is too important to be taken so seriously. When given the opportunity to laugh, surround yourself with people who introduce the sunnier side of life back into your world. Certainly laughter lends a hand to your best physical self by contrib-uting in a positive way to overall health and well-being, boosting the good-feeling hormones in your body and soul. It can fill you up with vitality and infuse your spirit with newfound energy and light. You don't have to be blessed with comedic talents to benefit from this tool; you can come to life with just a shift in perspective that will help stress and ir-ritations simply fall away. So take an instant vacation from your worries in life, and learn to laugh more with love that will have you rolling on the floor, begging for mercy!

Magical Key to Bliss: Surround yourself with laughter today!

March 8: **Wander and discover your world.**

Not all those who wander are lost.

~J. R. R. Tolkien, British writer and poet, excerpt from
All That Is Gold Does Not Glitter

You never really know a place until you lose yourself there and need to find your way home again. It can be said, then, that you never truly know yourself and the right direction to take in life until you lose your way and need to find a new path back. When you wander, you have the opportunity to discover new things about yourself and your dreams. When you wander, you get a chance to see your world in a new light. When you wander, you unearth the most amazing discoveries that give rise to great change. For when you wander, you are not really lost. You are just opening another door in your heart to take a new look at your soul. To get out of a rut, it is sometimes important to lose yourself and wander—because there you free yourself from any labels that you have become associated with over the years. You free yourself to recharge your spirit only to return home again with a beautiful, new perspective, one that has you living this new day with a renewed hope and optimism. So, today, lose yourself and wander just a little in any way that you see fit. You never know who or what amazing things you will find. For you are never really lost as long as you are a work in progress using each opportunity to create a life inspired by so many new and wonderful things.

Magical Key to Bliss: Wander into a good book, to a new place, or with good friends, and see what you discover!

March 9: **Be open to wisdom from unlikely sources.**

I'm concentrating on staying healthy, having peace, being happy, remembering what is important, taking in nature and animals, spending time reading, and trying to understand the universe, where science and the spiritual meet.

~Joan Jett, American rock guitarist, singer, and songwriter

Today is a great day to make amazing statements of resolution, setting out positive affirmations toward the goal of living an exceptional life. If you map out a successful start, you are ready to welcome inspiration from a variety of sources. Wisdom arrives in many shapes and forms. When you open your mind to life's daily invitations, even the unlikeliest people or places can offer you life-changing advice that could be the catalyst to great things. Blessings come as you set the intention to live from a place of awareness. Relationships blossom and flourish when you focus on ways to be healthier, more peaceful, and happier in both mind and body. Perspectives change when you step out of the comfortable box you have settled in, getting the benefits of looking at the universe from both a scientific and a spiritual context. Resolve to seek a bit of inspiration from a bit of information received, and do your best to not reject the message because of the messenger. Go out into the world with worthy goals, and open your mind and heart to all the angels that will help you achieve them along the way.

Magical Key to Bliss: Follow your bliss and rock on while welcoming in what you need to hear, blessed from all sources!

March 10: Triumph through faith in the unknown.

To believe in the things you can see and touch is no belief at all—but to believe in the unseen is a triumph and a blessing.

~Abraham Lincoln, sixteenth president of the United States of America

Breathe in. Know that life is a blessing for you. Breathe out. Let go of the hardships that block your vision for just one moment so you can see the light at the end of the tunnel. Breathe in. Focus on the people, places, and things that you are most grateful for. Breathe out. Release the need to control your life as you surrender to the unseen forces that are there to support and carry you. Breathe in. Smell the roses and believe that health and happiness are yours now. Breathe out. Relinquish the need to fear the unknown, understanding that in this present moment, all is well. Just breathe. Your past is over, your present is waiting, and your future holds much possibility. If you breathe in the amazing and uplifting energy of each moment and breathe out all that hinders you, you have tapped into a source that would otherwise go unnoticed. If you hold strong with faith in your life's potential, you can stand triumphant, knowing that you are protected on a daily basis by your angels both here and above. Breathe in. You are blessed. Breathe out. Have faith and give yourself room to receive those blessings of life that are on the way!

Magical Key to Bliss: Breathe in and breathe out for five minutes, and feel supported by the unseen.

March 11: Just breathe!

Focusing on the act of breathing clears the mind of all daily distractions and clears our energy, enabling us to better connect with the Spirit within.

~Unknown

As life gets too crazy and overwhelming due to endless responsibilities, take a moment and remember to breathe. By taking a deep breath, you will better refocus on what is important as you slowly clear the mind of the clutter. As you inhale and exhale with purpose, your mind will be free to release the drama that could lead you off course. By oxygenating your body and mind, you will start to be still to really feel the love and spirit of connection that surrounds you. When you stop and breathe with intention, the answers to important questions in your life will magically come to you, and the confusion, stagnation, and frustration will blow away. Despite the chaos going on around you, you will always have the ability to breathe to take you through it. Do yourself a favor; close your eyes for a moment and just breathe. When you open them up again, you may be seeing things just a little bit clearer and will be better equipped to navigate your day. To breathe fully is a gift you can freely give to yourself at any time. Why hold back? Ah...now have a great day!

 Magical Key to Bliss: Breathe in for eight seconds, hold for four, then out again for eight seconds. Repeat three times, and do this three times per day.

March 12: Glorious living is a state of mind.

Everyone can have a luxury life. It's a state of mind. It's not necessarily about having the biggest house. It's about living life to the fullest.

~Paul Miklas, developer

Material things may give you pleasure for a moment, but they can never replace the warm embrace of a loved one. The richest individuals in this world are surrounded by love, are enveloped by joy, and are connected to something that sustains them. Though you may seek things in life that satisfy your soul, until you get in touch with what feeds your spirit, you may default to a vision of luxury that others suggest will bring happiness, such as the latest fashion accessories, the most beautiful house, or the fastest car. While retail therapy may give you a moment's high, the reality is if you don't figure out what a full life looks like to you, no amount of money will ever give you peace on the journey. The mind is a powerful asset, and you are encouraged to go within and define what glorious living means to you. It can be as simple as walking your dog as the sun rises over the bay. It can be as beautiful as a shared smile between two strangers. It can be as basic as wishing someone a good morning, listening to a friend in need, having that friend listen to you, or just opening your heart to what the day brings. When you discover what moves you and follow your bliss, you will know luxury and feel like the richest person in the world! And that, my friends, is more than glorious!

Magical Key to Bliss: Spread your arms ceremonially and welcome the opportunity to really live your life gloriously.

March 13: The fine art of balance.

What I dream of is an art of balance, of purity and serenity devoid of troubling or depressing subject matter—a soothing, calming influence on the mind, rather like a good armchair which provides relaxation from physical fatigue.

~Henri Matisse, French artist

A balanced life is a worthy goal, an endeavor that perfectly sets out to blend the rational with the emotional. When you have a balanced approach to life, your logical side works together with your senses to uncover a sane way of navigating this world. In the chaos, be grateful for artistic images and music that evoke emotions with the power to soothe the mind. Alternatively, be grateful for logic that can find some salvation in reason when panic and emotion rise to a level nearly out of your control. Your body sends you signals often when your center is out of alignment. To return to a place of harmony, pay attention to the messages you receive, and use your intuition to guide you home. Be still, listen, and allow yourself to fall into the comfort of that good armchair that supports you as you hold a centered vision of balance in your mind's eye. Stay there as long as you can, and return each and every time that chaos descends. Recognizing the discord is the first step toward peaceful existence in the world as you welcome the fine art of balance again. Your mind and body work together for your highest good as you continue to create the brilliant masterpiece that is your life.

Magical Key to Bliss: Dance and practice yoga or any position that brings your soul to a place of balance.

March 14: **Master the beauty of doing nothing.**

> *Italians are the masters of* Il bel far niente. *This is a sweet expression that means "the beauty of doing nothing." Italians have traditionally always been hard workers...But even against the backdrop of hard work,* Il bel far niente *has always been a cherished Italian ideal. The beauty of doing nothing is the goal of all your work, the final accomplishment for which you are most highly congratulated. The more exquisitely and delightfully you can do nothing, the higher your life's achievement...Anyone with a talent for happiness can do this, not only the rich.*

~Elizabeth Gilbert, American author, excerpt from *Eat, Pray, Love*

When you see yourself as a human "doing" rather than as a human "being," it may seem impossible to take the time to actually sit and relax without feeling guilty. Yet there is beauty and true balance in doing nothing. There is great achievement in taking generous breaks from hard work to benefit your well-being. If you must, plan well for these moments to rejuvenate your soul. Make it a priority to set aside time from the busyness to find enjoyment, go on vacation, or reconnect with loved ones. Italians are historically great masters at this; as you imitate their example to strive to do nothing as the final goal for which you are to be congratulated, your life will change for the better. A life of balance is a beautiful thing. While hard work is to be applauded, if you fail to enjoy its rewards by taking the time to do nothing and rest, you will never recharge to be inspired in important ways. To master *Il bel far niente,* you delightfully open yourself up to a more satisfying, stress-free life. When you embrace this reward for your achievements, you truly have won life's lottery!

Magical Key to Bliss: Every three months for the next year, plan a short vacation in which you do nothing.

March 15: Too blessed to be stressed!

If you are blessed enough to grow older...there's so much wisdom to be gained from celebrating the process with vibrancy and vigor and grace.

~Oprah Winfrey, American actress, producer, and philanthropist

If you keep your eyes open as you progress along the journey, you will recognize your many blessings along the way. You are blessed to know the beauty of this world; are you ready to see it? You are blessed to experience love through interactions with the many people who cross your path; are you ready to believe it? You are blessed to have a chance to make a difference; are you ready to take the challenge? You are blessed to gain wisdom through the pain and joy of life; are you ready to accept it? You are blessed to have a mind that delves into the mystery of creation; are you ready to be open to it? And you are blessed to share your faith in the magic that exists each day; are you ready to allow it? When you make the choice to see your life as blessed, you choose to follow a path that infuses your spirit with a vibrancy like no other. You choose to share a vision of simple grace that supports you. And you choose to tell the world with vigor and glee that you are too blessed to be stressed.

Magical key to bliss: Embrace wisdom in the process of getting older.

March 16: Instructions for living a conscious life.

Instructions for living a life.
Pay attention.
Be astonished,
Tell about it.

~Mary Oliver, American poet

As a child, you were simply conscious of your own personal identity, unencumbered by others' beliefs. As you grew and were faced with the world's attitudes, beliefs, and sensitivities, the challenge remained to be aware of the call that child was born with. To remain tuned in to your soul's purpose, pay attention to the messages that arrive on a daily basis, get ready to be astonished by the amazing *aha* moments that come your way, and be sure to share your experiences with anyone who wants to listen. These simple instructions will allow you the freedom to surrender to what life has in store as you begin each new beautiful day as the hero of your journey. When you feel the anxiety or stress of the world take over, start listening and paying attention to that little child within who knew so well life's calling and just followed his or her bliss. Do what you can to visualize floating on the lazy river of life instead of navigating the fast-paced stormy waters that you are accustomed to. Get carried to a place of astonishment, opening up to all the wonderful things that await you. Pause for just a moment to take it all in at a speed that you can handle and enjoy. Slow down just a bit so that you can be present in the moment as you embark on the next exciting part of your journey armed with these little instructions that simplify a life worth living. Come join me on the river, won't you?

Magical Key to Bliss: Tell your story so that others may also experience a newfound hope for all the great possibilities.

March 17: It's your lucky day; become the best *you* possible.

Been down one time, been down two times, never going back again!

~Fleetwood Mac, lyrics from "Never Going Back Again," *Rumours* album, British-American rock band

A lifetime ago, you were the small child finding your way in this great big world. Today, you are the strong, courageous adult who is determined to forge ahead despite any obstacles along the way. Lucky you, you have been given the tailor-made invitation to make your dreams come alive. Lucky you, you have received the greatest opportunity to unveil your passion through your God-given talents. Lucky you, you may have been knocked down once or hurt twice, but you are a fighter, and you are never going back again. You know that every joy and every pain made you the fabulous person you are today. You stand on those building blocks with pride and have a better view to see and move further on. The wisdom gained is just what you need to deliver you to the next level, so don't look in the mirror yearning to see the same person from yesterday. It's your lucky day—a new day to become even better, the best possible you. Just declare it to the world and accept the rest of your journey as something wonderful. As you move forward, let your prayer be to remember the lessons learned, to grow from the compassion felt, and to continue to become the best version of yourself. The future is bright; why would you let the past rob you of your chance to shine?

 Magical Key to Bliss: On this Saint Patrick's Day, celebrate your accomplishments. Grab a lucky shamrock, and be grateful for not giving up because three times is the charm.

March 18: Be your own biggest fan.

If we want liberation, we must rewrite the Sleeping Beauty myth, No one is coming and no one else is to blame.

~Elizabeth Lesser, American author and cofounder of the Omega Institute

Stop seeking approval from others; you must be your biggest fan! You and God—or your higher power, or whatever you want to call it—are your biggest cheerleaders! Rely on that incredible energy of love and go out into the world to do your thing. For you know in your soul what you are passionate about. You know in your heart what makes you happy. You know what you are here for. So no matter what circumstance you find yourself in, just follow that bliss and rock the world with your amazing talents. You are special and unique. Tolerate no treatment from yourself or others that is less than appropriate for your superstar status. You have to believe in yourself no matter what life throws your way. Even if you are down, you are never out if you have a sense of your own potential. You are the greatest at something wonderfully creative; there is no reason to have to take a poll as to what that is. You know deep down what you are called to do. Get in touch with that creative inner state of being that you can live right now, and start to manifest the life that you deserve. You are entitled to miracles that come from being your own best fan. With that in mind, there is nothing stopping you!

Magical Key to Bliss: Repeat the following mantra: as long as I believe in myself, good things happen for me!

March 19: With confidence, welcome a big embrace from the universe.

When we are self-confident, the universe opens its arms to us.

~Concetta Bertoldi, American author and medium

Confidently affirm that the universe is ready to help you in all of your endeavors. While this earth school can sometimes feel like an unloving place, you must remember that your thoughts play a big part in how you align to the world around you. Your reality is an illusion of sorts. You project onto your world what you believe to be true based on your story thus far. As your perception changes, you have the power to transform the tone of your life. A school of thought postulates that the very act of observation changes things. Therefore, if you take on an air of positivity and confidence, your life experience will be one in which the universe opens its arms to you. That is the beauty of the law of attraction. That is the beauty of the universe. That is the beauty of your life. If you begin your day with thoughts of self-confidence, magic, and wonder, then the world around you will match your vibration as you watch out for amazing things to come. When you set out to encounter a reality filled with great opportunity, miraculous things, and amazing people, you can be positive and optimistic that those concepts will show up for you on a daily basis. For with this approach to your reality, the universe is opening up its arms to you in an overwhelmingly loving embrace. That just feels good, doesn't it?

 Magical Key to Bliss: Start affirming yourself with words that build your self-confidence. Start today with "I am love," and see what the universe opens up to you!

March 20: Make you in peace!

"So what can we do about the craziness of the world?"
"Nothing." Ketut laughed, but with a dose of kindness. "This is the nature of the world. This is destiny. Worry about your craziness only—make you in peace."

~Elizabeth Gilbert, American author, excerpt from *Eat, Pray, Love*

You cannot control the craziness of the world. However, you can make a difference in your corner of it. Instead of focusing on what you believe is impossible, shift your attention to what you know you can do. You can create your world in peace by taking care of yourself. You can begin to pay attention to the kind of energy you bring to your life. You can focus with gratitude on your blessings. You can choose to tune out the noise and chaos with dedicated moments of focused joy. It is time to stop putting off your happiness for tomorrow by starting to stretch your body and mind for the pure love of it today. In small, manageable increments of time, take the actions necessary to breathe yourself back into balance. Worrying does you no good. You cannot be a warrior if you are a worrier. Focus on what the fighter within needs to tame those out-of-control feelings. Seek out the tools, prayer, meditation, exercise, inspired conversation, or reading that will bring you back to sanity. Slowly at first, as the old habits are replaced with new ones, the peaceful transformation will be quicker and living in the pain a lot shorter. Do what you can do now. Make you in peace, and the ripple effect that you can have on the world will go beyond even your wildest imagination.

 Magical Key to Bliss: Speak words of gratitude today, accepting your peaceful journey.

March 21: Aim high.

The greatest danger for most of us is not that our aim is too high and we miss it, but that it is too low and we reach it.

~Michelangelo Buonarroti, Italian sculptor, painter, architect, poet, and engineer

Believe in your own amazing potential to achieve any goal you set. Don't set an arbitrary bar that limits what you are capable of. You are blessed with untapped abilities that have the power to change the world for the better. You are a genius in your own right, so don't allow your fear of failure to scare you into inaction. Incredible opportunities come when you dream the impossible and take the necessary steps to make it a reality. Life bursts with excitement when you set out on a course guided by your imagination matched by your skills. Settling into a comfort zone of minor achievements only prevents you from living the life you were meant to live. Stretch yourself and aim higher. Talent is a gift that must be explored. Creativity is a blessing that must be tapped at the source. Brilliance is hard earned through inspiration and perspiration. Your beautiful vision must see the light of day. Love yourself and speak amazing words to your psyche, acknowledging how special, smart, or particularly innovative you are in any area that calls to you. In the end, if you work hard, dream big, welcome divine inspiration, and guard against the dangers of mediocrity, you are sure to rest easy as you smile well on a life well done. No regrets!

Magical Key to Bliss: Set a goal, aim high, raise the bar, and be your own version of Michelangelo!

March 22: It's not in the stars but within you!

It is not in the stars to hold our destiny but in ourselves.

~William Shakespeare, English poet, playwright, and actor

Have you really looked at a rose? Have you really seen its beauty? Then again, have you really looked at yourself and really seen yours? Each part of the rose, each petal working in concert, makes up this glorious masterpiece in nature from the inside out. Every part of who you are—your mind, body, and spirit—works together from the inside out, making up a beauty to behold. Each one of you is beautiful and blessed by the hand of God. And, if you don't yet see this, perhaps the time to begin is now. In the universe, there is a great plan. An infinite wisdom permeates your life that empowers you to take hold of your destiny, your own personal legend. As you would honor the beauty of a rose, once you start to appreciate and honor your own, free from judgment from another, you will be free to become a great admirer of the artistic creation that is within you and surrounds you on a daily basis. Once you change your perspective and own the beauty that is you, then your destiny is no longer controlled by the stars but becomes a dance between you and your Creator.

 Magical Key to Bliss: Let the music play, and be inspired by what you experience each day!

March 23: **Follow the Golden Rule.**

There's one sad truth in life I've found
While journeying east and west—
The only folks we really wound
Are those we love the best.
We flatter those we scarcely know,
We please the fleeting guest,
And deal full many a thoughtless blow
To those who love us best.

~Ella Wheeler Wilcox, American author and poet

Why is it that we save our very best for the people we work with, but when we come home we are disrespectful to those we make our lives with? Why is it that we are at our best with those to whom we have no obligations but at our worst with those we have made commitments to love? Why is it that we choose words of highest praise to win over the fleeting guest but words of lowest quality to destroy the person whose heart we are supposed to protect? Today wisdom and healing come when we choose to follow the Golden Rule: do unto others as you would have them do unto you. Simply stated, be impeccable with your words and loving in your actions with those who are closest to you because therein lies the magic of the world. When we are good to the ones we love, we gain balance in the world as hypocrisy falls away. When we are kind in our own homes, we gain peace in our lives as kindness permeates our being. When we are caring for those in our own sacred backyard, we gain the vision of how our Creator cares for us, and we are liberated from the chaos. When we love one another at the core, our experience can be greater than we could ever imagine.

Magical Key to Bliss: Do your best to follow the Golden Rule, and everything will fall into place!

March 24: **Remember to breathe.**

I am not a product of my circumstances. I am a product of my decisions.

~Stephen Covey, American educator, businessman, and speaker

Today, make the conscious decision to stop and take a deep breath many times. Whenever life feels overwhelming, stop and breathe. When you are faced with a big problem that requires an innovative solution, stop and breathe. Or when you just start to feel anxious and out of sorts, the best thing that you can do is to stop what you're doing, pause, and remember to breathe. Not a short and shallow kind of breathing but the kind of breathing that fills every part of your body and soul. Take as many breaths as you need to calm yourself. This small decision will make all the difference in the way that your day proceeds. It can clear your mind so that your focus is sharper and you are more attuned to the matter at hand. Most importantly, a deep breath can bring you to a place of peace if only for a moment. Taking deep breaths throughout the day brings you a higher level of happiness and clarity. In the deep breaths you take, you fill your cup by visualizing a more vital and robust you while letting out the negative energy, or hot air. The tension that is present in any challenging circumstance can be minimized by making this wonderful choice to stop what you're doing, breathe, and let go. It seems like a silly reminder, but when you decide to take deep breaths daily and often, your circumstances change as your spirit has an even better chance to take flight. How about that for a wise choice and investment in you?

Magical Key to Bliss: Breathe in calm; breathe out chaos. Life is precious.

March 25: Find the silver lining.

Yesterday I was clever, so I wanted to change the world. Today I am wise, so I am changing myself.

~Rumi, thirteenth-century poet and Sufi mystic

If you want to make your world a better place, instead of homing in on what is wrong with your life, decide to focus on what is right. Just watch; before you know it, you will witness an amazing shift that takes place as you start to dismantle the negative conditioning that has threatened to sabotage your incredible potential. Rest assured; what you look for, you will find. Look for the good in yourself, and you will find amazing gifts and blessings there. If you want change, the focus should be on yourself, not on others. For the more you focus on ways to change yourself, the more wisdom you will gain as you discover ways to overcome obstacles and realize your dreams. When you upload to your mind positive thoughts on how to make changes, you will start to see everything in a brighter light. And when you do, you transform for the better. The positive way you approach your world will overflow into your connections, increasing a healthier, energetic vibration for the planet. And then, before you know it, you will have positively affected your world. With a habit like this, even on a rainy day, you will be sure to find the silver lining in the clouds! Now that is not just clever but incredibly wise!

 Magical Key to Bliss: Pick one thing in your life that is working and one thing that you want to work on!

March 26: **Perhaps it's wise to be a little bit foolish.**

The point of living, and of being an optimist, is to be foolish enough to believe that the best is yet to come.

~Sir Peter Ustinov, British actor, writer, and dramatist

Sometimes when you focus on the bad things that the world shows you, you lose sight of how incredible reality can actually be. When you surround yourself with negative news, you start to lose sight of the good in the world. Perhaps when you meet up with others whose energy is depleting, you feel your own energy wane when it could use a bolster of magic and miracles. In life, you choose how to look at every circumstance. If you want to live an amazing life, replace any fear-based images with ones that foster love, and you will start to experience love. Turn off the news that focuses on shock, and look for stories in your neighborhood in which people are serving one another. Step away from those people who constantly point out what is going wrong; seek out others who choose to live their lives filled with joy. When you shift your vibration to a higher plane where the optimist resides, you will discover quickly the wisdom that even if today is not so great, the best is yet to come. And when you start to see the glass half full, recognize the silver lining, and grab onto the wonderful takeaways on the journey, then a new wisdom will soon be yours. Even if others think you are a bit foolish, don't care. Keep dreaming because living a positive and exciting life that is based on looking at the bright side is why you are here, after all. Forever the wise fool!

Magical Key to Bliss: Rediscover hope in humanity by acknowledging the unsung heroes.

March 27: We are all warriors of the light!

A Warrior of Light is capable of understanding the miracle of life, of fighting to the last for something he believes in...[He] knows that he has much to be grateful for. Angels help him in his struggle; celestial forces place each thing in its place, thus allowing him to give it his best...His gratitude, however, is not limited to the spiritual world; he never forgets his friends, for their blood mingles with his on the battlefield. A Warrior does not need to be reminded of the help given him by others. He is the first to remember, and he makes sure to share with them any rewards he receives.

~Paulo Coelho, Brazilian author of *Warrior of the Light*

We are all warriors of the light. We are all champions of this incredible, beautiful beam that guides our path and brightens our day. We have felt it, we have seen it, and we are it. And we will fight with every last ounce of strength left to keep this light burning bright. We warriors understand that the world is a beautiful place. When challenged in this belief, instead of losing our way, we will take action to ensure that others see this exquisiteness as well. As warriors, to do so is our mission. While the journey is not easy, we warriors are never alone in this undertaking. We are drawn to the strength of others, armoring ourselves with love. These angels give us the fortitude to see life through, and for this we are grateful beyond words. For we, the wise warriors, know the miracle that is life, and we bask in the brilliance of its glow.

Magical Key to Bliss: Shine, warriors, shine!

March 28: Recognize the brilliance of others.

It's one thing to feel that you are on the right path, but it's another to think yours is the only path.

~Paulo Coelho, Brazilian author of *The Alchemist*

Even if the path you choose for your life is right for you right now, you must remember that your path is not the only way to truth. While the greatest part of your soul knows your earthly direction, if you keep an open mind, you will discover many different ways to follow your course. When you start out, your inner circle may be small and the information limited. As you go, you may be exposed to others whose points of view can help broaden your mind and enlighten you to new perspectives that will help you to make better choices as you move forward. That is the beauty of the universe. There are so many ways to get to wherever you are going and so many different paths that you can take. Like other seekers who surround you, you are just making the best decisions you can with the information at hand. Yours is not to judge the choices of others, only to be grateful for the possibilities each new discovery offers each day. Strive to embrace the gift that is your path while keeping an open mind to the diversity that lies before you. Instead of staying closed in, when you recognize the brilliance of others, your horizons are expanded, and your world just got a little bit bigger. For you are blessed with a world whose fabric is made up of many different paths, all eventually leading to an even more amazing journey!

Magical Key to Bliss: Keep an open mind to what the universe will show you today!

March 29: Keep it simple—smile!

Remember, happiness doesn't depend on who you are or what you have; it depends solely on what you think.

~Dale Carnegie, American writer and lecturer

A smile goes a long way to brighten one's day! It can be the much-needed spark that shifts your thoughts to a happier expression of life. A smile requires fewer muscles than does a frown. People who smile exude happiness from within. People who smile attract others to their vibrant light. People who smile contribute to the common good by infecting others with happiness. It is true: the energy of a smile can be contagious when it allows happiness to blossom in the soul of another. When you are faced with hopelessness or despair, to shift your thoughts, keep it simple, and start to look for the smiles that surround you. These are the times when you really need to be acutely aware of what you watch, what you read, and what thoughts you let into your world. You must choose well the people you allow to influence your life. Look for the bright, beautiful smiles on a daily basis and grab on, and you will be reminded that yours will pull you through any challenge. Only then will you awaken your soul and activate a spark that can shift your thoughts to a happier expression of life—one of joy, love, and laughter!

Magical Key to Bliss: Focus on thoughts that make you smile.

March 30: **Face your fears.**

Fear is the main source of superstition and one of the main sources of cruelty. To conquer fear is the beginning of wisdom.

~Bertrand Russell, British philosopher, historian, and social activist

As we wake each and every day ready to face the world, we make choices the very moment our feet hit the floor—we get to choose to be empowered by life or to be overwhelmed by our fear of the unknown. We get to decide what we believe and what we don't believe. We get to decide what we store away and what we reject.

When you make the decision to face your fears, you see that what you fear is not real. When you lift the veil of what scares you, you begin to experience letting go of what has been your greatest burden, and you start to receive the blessings of the beauty that awaits you. When you make the choice to face your fears and call out for help in doing so, many will come to your aid. You don't have to conquer fear on your own, but you do have to make the choice to conquer fear. And when you make that choice, as Eleanor Roosevelt said, "You gain strength, courage, and confidence by every experience in which you really stop to look fear in the face" (You Learn By Living, 1960, 29–30). It is really that simple. So as you move forward, make the decision to stop the cruelty and face your fears little by little; see how far your confidence in the universe will take you. How wise!

 Magical Key to Bliss: Find a mentor who has gone through the process of clearing fear from his or her mind.

March 31: As long as you are alive, you might as well...

I believe life is a series of near misses. A lot of what we ascribe to luck is not luck at all. It's seizing the day and accepting responsibility for your future. It's seeing what other people don't see and pursuing that vision.

~Howard Schultz, American businessman and CEO of Starbucks

Seize the day no matter what life presents to you! No hardship in the world can take that choice away from you. Persevering through the challenges is what defines your strong character. You have to claim responsibility for your calling to have the kind of satisfying future that is your destiny. Make a concerted effort to truly live your vision, accept the near misses, and know that you will hit your mark as long as you get up and try again. Decide well how you will live your life. If making a difference is your call, may you be blessed with integrity. May you be vulnerably authentic as you set out a road map for the path you decide to travel. May you accept the wisdom of the ages as you navigate the course for your life. And may the light of knowledge that shines within also grow day by day. As you bring goodness to a world that desperately needs it, may you see what others do not. You might as well give love whenever you can, for you are here, and you are ready!

 Magical Key to Bliss: Meditate and receive the profound wisdom that comes from the peace of knowing you are here to be amazing.

Chapter Four: April

TRANSFORMING DREAMS INTO REALITY

Finally! Spring is in the air. You can feel the world pregnant with possibility. As you start to awaken from your hibernation, you know the renewed sense of energy will give way to that something wonderful that is about to happen. April is here, and it is the month of perhaps the most drastic transformation all year long. Gradually and suddenly, winter finally gives way to unveil new life, and the stark landscape bursts again, fresh with color and reawakened vigor. Even if you happen to live close to the equator, where there is less marked seasonal contrast, you know just how dramatic this transformation can be.

The Magical Guide to Bliss designates April as the month to make change happen through the synthesis of all the lessons we've learned thus far. Use March's wisdom to channel all the love generated in February to seize the day using the techniques we discussed in January. The most radical transformation will happen as you follow your intuition. You can't program your destination—bliss—into your GPS. However, you can keep your perception wide open; the universe will send the directions in the form of synchronicity while you're on the road. As you tune in to a higher consciousness, pay attention, and get ready to witness your dreams come true; the best is yet to come. And remember, it is OK to wander along the way. As J. R. R. Tolkien said in his poem "All That Is Gold Does Not Glitter," "Not all who wander are lost." (*The Fellowship of the Ring*, volume 1 of *The Lord of The Rings*, 1954, chapter 10) In April, get ready to actually experience your inspirational and innovative ideas as you take the steps to see them become your reality.

April 1: **Beauty in the transformative process.**

We delight in the beauty of the butterfly but rarely admit the changes it has gone through to achieve that beauty.

~Maya Angelou, American author, poet, dancer, actress, and singer

We dwell in an instant society, where we live for quick results and immediate gratification. Yet the real focus should be on the joy received from the transformative process. We bravely move ourselves forward. We go through intense darkness to better see the light, lose our faith only to find it deeper again, face our own fears and discover how courageous we are, and withstand pain that changes us into stronger people. Once we do the dedicated work, take the decisive actions, and make the careful choices, we can stand proudly looking back on the groundwork that we've laid. After recognizing our accomplishments, we can look forward and ready ourselves to relish in the joy as our dreams come to light. Even if our efforts are not obvious to others, we are honored to be our own grateful witness to the miracles that have taken place throughout our transformation. Like the caterpillar's metamorphosis, there is real beauty to be found in the journey. Just as it wraps itself in its cocoon, preparing to eventually burst into the open again as a butterfly, we too might embrace our own beautiful process as we use the lessons presented to evolve to a higher stage in our own enlightenment. Only then can we both delight in our own beauty and truly appreciate the changes we have undergone to achieve it.

Magical Key to Bliss: Accept exactly where you are on your journey, and acknowledge the beautiful person you have become!

April 2: Spring is nature's reminder to party!

Spring is nature's way of saying, "Let's party!"

~Robin Williams, American actor and comedian

In January, we plant seeds of potential as we set out resolutions and goals for the New Year. In February, we start the process of investigation to find loving ways to make those dreams a reality, finding the best soil to protect them from the harsh reality of life. In March, we start to gain wisdom as we renew our hope of incredible possibilities. In April, with renewed determination, we use the showers and the sun as the essential ingredients to nurture the seeds, allowing the buds to break through. Soon we will experience amazing things as we allow all that we have learned to transform our dreams into reality; we will start to see the proverbial fruit of our labors. Today starts a new day. We can almost smell, see, taste, and hear that something wonderful that is about to burst through and into our lives. Now, in the springtime, a celebration is about to begin, marked with colorful arrangements of flowers, and we rejoice at seeing our life's efforts blossom into beautiful achievements. Looking around and appreciating all the wonder that surrounds us is the best perspective and attitude—one that we will carry into the next month. This is our month that is filled with everything our imaginations allow. Spring is in the air; let's welcome the beauty of new flowers and opportunities into our lives. Breathe in the new life, breathe in the new beginnings—and let's party!

Magical Key to Bliss: Wake to the appreciation of everything that will unfold before you today!

April 3: **Transport yourself with beautiful people by your side.**

The most beautiful people we have known are those who have known defeat, known suffering, known struggle, known loss, and have found their way out of the depths. These persons have appreciation, a sensitivity, and an understanding of life that fills them with compassion, gentleness, and a deep loving concern. Beautiful people do not just happen.

~Elisabeth Kubler-Ross, Swiss-American psychiatrist and pioneer in near-death studies

In both times of laughter and times of tears, we reserve a special place in the heart for loved ones and give them space to experience life. With these connections, we acknowledge the existence of other individuals and expand our understanding of life in relation to them. Knowing that beautiful relationships exist, we open ourselves up to the possibility that today we may meet someone who enhances our life in an amazing way. It is time to share our special gifts and talents with our connections so that we can make an even greater and more profound difference in the world. When we work together, life becomes better, challenges become easier to handle, and success from our joint accomplishments becomes more satisfying. When we travel in a car pool with amazing people by our side, the benefits gained through our concerted efforts will help quickly catapult the realization of our dreams. When we set out to take others with us as we all contribute to successful lives, everyone benefits. And then for sure we are in beautiful company as we transport ourselves faster to our desired destinations having a great time in the process! Everything is better when we are surrounded by more love and more people to play with!

 Magical Key to Bliss: Share joy with others today by extending an invitation to play!

April 4: **Surprise yourself.**

Set a goal to achieve something that is so big, so exhilarating that it excites you and scares you at the same time.

~Bob Proctor, American speaker, author, and consultant

You know that something that you have always wanted to do? Now is the time to take the steps toward making it happen! It could be anything; it has been tugging at your heart for too long, and now is the time to take action. This is too important to let another day go by without a plan of action. You can do it! It doesn't matter how impossible the dream may be—the bigger the better! Get excited! It's time to step outside your comfort zone and into the world of risk and possibility. When you are on the right path, there will be signs along the way to guide you. When you step into your greatness and fulfill your journey, you will inspire many others to do the same. People will start to believe because of you and follow suit, and that is the kind of leadership that will be your legacy. Are you ready to move forward into a bigger reality? You are made of miraculous stuff, so don't set the bar low—reach for the stars. Get in line with your spirit and soar. You owe it to yourself and to the world! Before you know it—surprise! You are there!

Magical Key to Bliss: Dream big, baby, and make it a goal to manifest something amazing today!

April 5: What feels like an end is only a new beginning.

And so rock bottom became the solid foundation on which I rebuilt my life.

~J. K. Rowling, British novelist and author of the *Harry Potter* fantasy series

You grow spiritually as a result of many different life events. While some of these life events are difficult to endure, transformation comes quickly when you find yourself at the end of your rope, hitting rock bottom with only one way to go—*up!* Many people who hit the lowest point in life make the choice to turn inward, relying on the unseen for strength and guidance to rebuild their lives, instead of giving up. And this turning inward with love has been proven to establish a solid foundation on which to build their own legacy for all to see and emulate. This hope in possibility when the world seems to be closing in gives way to an endurance that becomes a beautiful tribute to the magic of the human spirit. Each day you decide to move forward is an opportunity to continue to build on your strong foundation and your belief in the good you can bring in the here and now. As long as you continue to act on your own guidance and incorporate your actions with love, yours will be a legacy of leadership based on solid principles and a lot of inspiration. Turning something that felt like the end of your world into a new beginning, you get to share this gift of hope with others with each new sunrise of your soul's bliss.

Magical Key to Bliss: Focus on someone inspirational and name three qualities about that person that move you! Incorporate those into your life as a part of your new beginning!

April 6: **Bring passion and enthusiasm to all that you do.**

Nothing great was ever achieved without enthusiasm.

~Ralph Waldo Emerson, American essayist, lecturer, and poet

As adults, we tend to forget the enthusiasm that we experienced as young children. It was the kind of enthusiasm that made us come out of our skin with excitement and joy. The kind of enthusiasm that is infectious. And the kind of enthusiasm that is the necessary ingredient to fuel our success in life as individuals. This is our new beginning. This is where we transform our dreams into our present-day reality. We need to plug into those emotions that had us sitting on the edge of our seats as little ones. We need to become the cheerleaders of our own wondrous future—for if we are not enthusiastic about the process, who will be? We are all destined for great things—in particular, a life purposefully lived with great passion. We need to enthusiastically release the victim role and jump into the driver's seat on our journey. Amazing things unfold every day when we decide to get off of our couch to make things happen. With enthusiasm mixed with inspired action, we will find that our experiences rise to our optimistic intentions. Attitude is everything. And with an eager spirit that yearns to follow our bliss, we no longer have to imagine how great life will be. The passion that we will bring to our practice will create the kind of success that will see all of us shine through!

 Magical Key to Bliss: Enthusiastically set a course to see one of your dreams come true!

April 7: All you need is right where you are!

The next message you need is always right where you are.

~Ram Dass, American spiritual teacher and author of *Be Here Now*

Stay in the moment! When you feel confused or overwhelmed, clarity will come if you keep things simple and focus on the here and now. When you are searching for answers to certain challenging questions, get still and get ready to receive the next message you need right where you are. Don't complicate the process with worries about the future. Don't be jaded by happenings of the past. Do pose your questions as clearly and simply as you can, and get ready to receive the answers as they come to you in many different ways. Awareness comes when you stop, listen, and experience the present moment. Information arrives exactly when you need it, in the best way that you personally can hear it. Understanding comes at a quickened pace when you quiet your mind, put your fears aside, and believe that all is well. For the knowledge that you are complete and have everything you need at any given moment is a mantra that allows for new and positive beginnings to take hold. As a dreamer, you need to be open to guidance for the next step on your path. As a seeker, you don't have to go far for enlightenment because the next message is always in that moment right where you are! Are you ready to stop and take it all in?

 Magical Key to Bliss: Set out your questions to the universe, sit for as long as you need in silence, and receive what comes next—because that is your answer!

April 8: Away we go!

Start by doing what is necessary; then do what is possible; and suddenly you are doing the impossible.

~Saint Francis of Assisi, Italian Catholic friar and preacher

Away we go, pledging to start doing what is necessary to survive on a daily basis. We believe in a sacred world of possibility where peace can be ours and connections will assist us. We nourish ourselves with words of strength to flourish. We are cleaning out the clutter to thrive. We are expecting to match our reality with what we already know is truth; after all, we are part of the divine, and we are extraordinary. We start doing what is necessary to begin. We begin to see what is possible in order to continue. Then, before we know it, we are moving past the impossible, one step at a time. Away we go; we will look back one day to see how far we have come. The mountain that once looked insurmountable becomes the podium on which we now stand, seeing farther and gaining more confidence in our abilities and talents. We bring the magical to life once again by acknowledging that the necessary, the possible, and the impossible are virtually all the same. We turn any task into an adventure in which perspective is the cornerstone that guides our success, stepping into our bliss as we move our dreams out of the realm of fantasy to a state of reality.

 Magical Key to Bliss: Turn your problems into projects. Break it up into smaller goals, and set deadlines for completion. Add some magical pixie dust for good measure. Then begin!

April 9: You never need permission to play.

The one thing that you have that nobody else has is you. Your voice, your mind, your story, your vision. So write and draw and build and play and dance and live as only you can.

~Neil Gaiman, British author of the comic book series *The Sandman*

You get the opportunity to play today. Just imagine how much fun you could have engaging in activities for their pure enjoyment. Even the most tedious tasks become exciting because you never know whom you might meet. Even the most challenging experiences become an exciting adventure because you never know what you may learn. Even the most humdrum occurrences become eventful because you never know what may fascinate you. With a sense of zeal and enthusiasm, you get to bring your voice, your mind, your story, your vision to live this day like no other. Everything changes when you come to the playground of your life with this attitude. The universe will unfold new adventures as you are reintroduced to joy. Get ready to claim a golden ticket to the greatest show on earth—yours. Look around at your new playmates who are ready to take part in the pleasure as well. Now it is up to you to decide if you will actually use the ticket to build a life based on more laughter, fun, and merriment. Remember, you never need permission to play, write, draw, build, or dance because you alone get to choose how you live your day! You get to look for the magic, miracles, butterflies, and blessings in a serendipitous way.

Magical Key to Bliss: Invite someone special for a playdate today.

April 10: Congratulations for who you have become!

Personal transformation can and does have global effects. As we go, so goes the world, for the world is us. The revolution that will save the world is ultimately a personal one.

~Marianne Williamson, American spiritual teacher, author, and lecturer

First matter of business today: you are going to acknowledge your own personal growth and transformation. Yes, you have come so far. Just take a good look in the mirror and accept the beauty that is before you. It was not an easy road at times, so today you must acknowledge the strength and joy it took for you to accomplish all that you have in your development. Like the caterpillar, you do not bear witness up close of each and every step involved in creating such a magnificent butterfly. Like the caterpillar, you may not have noticed the intricate details that have occurred in your own life as you continue to surrender to the process. On this auspicious day, feel the results of the positive transformations that have entered your life. Thank your angels, whether spiritual or physical, for guiding you. Congratulate yourself for never giving up. And embrace the changes and shifts that have liberated you from the dictates of a stagnant society. Well done; you have accepted your personal responsibility as you do your part to bring positive change to the world. After you acknowledge and applaud the beautiful butterfly that you have become, you will reflect outward the beauty of your own inner personal transformation for all to see, imitate, and experience.

 Magical Key to Bliss: Look in the mirror with gratitude for who you have become!

April 11: The energy of affection.

We can live without religion and meditation, but we cannot survive without human affection.

~Dalai Lama, leader of Tibetan Buddhism

A mother's love is the first and greatest gift of human affection that we receive. This amazing bond of energy is vital to each individual's growth. As a human race, we can survive without many things, but affection is not one of them. For us to thrive, we must reach out to one another with care and empathy. When we know we are loved, we are able to accomplish so much more, emboldened to grow beyond belief, spiritually as well as intellectually. Relationships are such an important part of our lives. While we are here, we have the power to liberate another from loneliness with love. While we are here, we have the power to impact another by including him or her in a life experience colored with joy. While we are here, we have the power to mother another once again with the kind of love and support that we desired in our first days. For the beauty comes from the realization that while our mother was our first and most important introduction to love and affection, she is no longer the only source available to us. We receive this energy from so many other people on the path as we set out to build a community of kindness. If we take the gifts received from the kind and gentle affection in this world and make the commitment to share them with one another, we all flourish. Mirroring the love of whoever chose to mother us out into the universe, we set the world afire with warm embraces, supportive handshakes, kind words, and loving attention.

Magical Key to Bliss: Show affection to someone who needs it today, and share this incredible energy.

April 12: So never quit, never quit, never quit!

If you live long enough, you'll make mistakes. But if you learn from them, you'll be a better person. It's how you handle adversity, not how it affects you. The main thing is never quit, never quit, never quit.

~William J. Clinton, forty-second president of the United States of America

If you dream big, don't get discouraged on the journey. As long as you put one foot in front of the other, you are one step closer to realizing your dream than you were the day before. So never quit! If you dream big, don't let mistakes turn you away. As long as you make them a part of your learning process and take the lesson as you go, your reward will be great. Continue to make commitments that you proudly stand by. Set firm yet flexible deadlines to guide you along. Never quit! If you dream big—even if you falter along the way—as long as you keep your vision close, you will continue to guide yourself despite the enormity of the task at hand. As long as you do something each day and use your intuition as a guide, you will meet success face-to-face with the pride that comes from never having given up on that burning desire within. So never quit! With your dreams, your life journey becomes exciting. With your dreams, you will know magic. And with your dreams, you must be open to all the connections that you attract to yourself. As long as you proceed to manifest your dreams, the field of potential will react in kind and deliver those miraculous surprises if you stay the course. So never quit!

Magical Key to Bliss: Never quit, no matter what!

April 13: **Be true to yourself.**

The privilege of a lifetime is to become who you truly are.

~Carl Jung, Swiss psychiatrist and psychotherapist who founded analytic psychology

Children are often asked the age-old question, "What will you be when you grow up?" The response is generally enthusiastic as the child ponders all the possibilities that his or her future could hold. When adults are asked the same question, the reaction is generally limited by the belief that it may be too late to change the path that they have already chosen. If we shift our approach and believe that it is our privilege to daily become who we truly are, then it must follow that the best of our story is still being written. Think about it. We are born with a purpose. In that little body and mind, the seeds have been planted that, if nurtured and cared for, will allow talents and skills to be developed that will serve us well. As we are delivered opportunities along the way, we have the privilege to know ourselves more. When we accept that everything is unfolding as it should, we can truly trust that the choices we continue to make are perfect for what we need to learn. And we can continue to become as we go. We must stand proud with no judgments, only the desire to be true to our path. This is truly the privilege that we all have as we experience life. Thank each and every one along the way for being true to themselves because their doing so gives others permission to do the same!

Magical Key to Bliss: Shift your perspective and become a work in progress each and every day!

April 14: God helps those who help themselves—*Aiutati che Dio t'aiuta*!

Be careful of the environment you choose for it will shape you; be careful of the friends you choose for you will become like them.

~W. Clement Stone, American author and philanthropist

Aiutati che Dio t'aiuta is an Italian proverb that means "God helps those who help themselves." While it is a good reminder, sometimes it is hard to know exactly where that divine hand is, especially when you feel that no matter how hard you try, nothing helps. In the middle of the frustration, perhaps the key to experiencing an intervention when you need it most is to do something, anything you can, and then relax, knowing this loving presence will take care of you. You will see clearly the image of life's puzzle only if you choose to sort through the pieces before you, looking for the best ones to fit your own vision. When you get perspective, you shift to a mind-set of empowerment even at your lowest point. You will gain clarity, tenacity, patience, guts, and divine assistance as you put one foot in front of the other and trust your instincts, choosing where to go next and who shall accompany you. Each new addition to the whole picture diverts your current course toward miracles and your own masterpiece. For there are miracles in doing what you can. Your good associations in this life will dictate all the good that you will attract, your relationships will feed your soul, and the places you go will shape your world accordingly! All will lead to a vision that unfolds wonderfully before your eyes!

Magical Key to Bliss: Observe the happy ones and where they go, and look to join their fun!

April 15: From a place of worthiness, you will blossom.

Do what you did in the beginning of a relationship and there won't be an end!

~Tony Robbins, American author and motivational speaker

The people you love are blessings in your life. When you are introduced to someone special, you recognize the energy of the other as it aligns with your own. Be it a friend or a lover, there is beauty in the desire to get to know such a person on a deeper level. As a result, you are awake when you are around him. You are happy when you do things to make her smile. You are excited when you share fun and exciting times as your heart expands. Over time, if you do not protect this bond, these very special relationships can be taken for granted. If you are not careful, anger, distrust, and miscommunication can chip away at that initial strong foundation of love. Do not give up hope, for the wise person knows what to do to rekindle the embers that first sparked. When you nurture others from a place of love as you did in the beginning, you remind them how important they are to you. Even if you cannot see results at first, you set out on a path to align yourself with that energy once again. It is never too late to begin today and start to show those who are blessings that they mean the world to you. Before you know it, any remorse regarding the past will fall away, and the relationship will transform before your eyes. Not only will there be no end, but ultimately you will change because from a place of worthiness, you and your loved ones will blossom!

Magical Key to Bliss: Reach out to someone you love, telling that person how much he or she means to you!

April 16: Plant the seeds of a magnificent life.

Don't judge each day by the harvest you reap but by the seeds that you plant.

~Robert Louis Stevenson, Scottish novelist, poet, and essayist

With practice, patience, perseverance, and passion, we plant the seeds of life, hoping they will grow into something amazing. The fact that we don't see the fruits of our labors each day does not mean that something magical is not happening beyond the physical plane. Although we may get disillusioned when the results of our hard work fail to break ground immediately, we need to continually care for what has been planted. For as long as we pull out the suffocating weeds and foster an environment where we can grow, the wonders instilled in our beautiful garden will soon reveal themselves. Each friendship we make and opportunity we take, like a beautiful flower, started out as a seed. Each step that we take toward worthy goals nurtures the relationships and events that provide a foundation for a fertile life. Then with faith in the outcome, we allow the light of the sun to do its thing. As we take in the positive energy from above and below, our garden is in the process of realizing its glory. It does not serve us well to judge each day by the harvest we reap because so much is going on behind the scenes. It serves us well to come to joy based on how we care for the seeds that are the foundation of our dreams. For it is only in time—divine time—that the seeds we have planted will burst through and explode with magnificence! Know this!

Magical Key to Bliss: Nurture your dreams with inspired action, and trust that they will grow.

April 17: There is always hope for positive change.

There is no such thing as a hopeless situation. Every single circumstance of your life can change!

~Rhonda Byrne, Australian television writer, producer, and author of *The Secret*

If you are in a rut, do not despair. Keep placing one foot in front of the other as you go through it. You are brave, and you shall not hide. You will face whatever life presents to you and do whatever is necessary to catapult you forward. Keep reminding yourself that pain will transform to joy if you allow it to do so. As long as you keep your vision of a magnificent life close at hand and never lose sight of this, it will guide you even when you cannot see. Go within and gain your strength from everything that has made you the person you are right now. For you have everything that you need to get you through; change is the only constant, and this too shall pass. Everything does happen for a reason. Strongly believe in your heart of hearts that the reason you are going through any experience is one that will change and transform you for your highest good. Never lose hope because it is true that there is power in each moment. And with each moment, the opportunity exists for miracles. There is no such thing as a hopeless situation; if you think you can pull yourself up and out, you are right! So hold on to your hope that at a moment's notice, things can go from what is perceived as bad to spectacular. Never lose your hope; something wonderful is always about to happen when you wake up and breathe in the air of positive possibility.

 Magical Key to Bliss: Embrace the spirit of positive change in the air.

April 18: Dream big, baby!

Dreams are today's answers to tomorrow's questions.

~Edgar Cayce, American mystic

You are ready to transform your life. It is time to do something about what you have always wanted to do. It is time to take steps toward realizing your goal! Whether it be starting a professional degree, finding the cure for a certain illness, experiencing something that allows you to see life in a different way, asking out someone you have had a crush on for some time, inventing something beyond your wildest imagination, or just meeting someone you have admired, it's time. Nothing was ever achieved by numbing your mind day after day watching television for hours on end or blaming the world for not helping you. Take action—get excited—be proactive! It's time to step outside your comfort zone and into the world of risk and possibility. At night as you sleep, your vision comes to life. When you wake, set out the steps to bring that vision to reality. When you are on the right path, there will be signs along the way that will guide you. Pay attention to those answers, and tomorrow's questions will be more defined. When you dream big, you will inspire many to do the same. People will start to follow suit, and you will lead them on the way. Don't set the bar low; reach for the stars. Get in line with your spirit and soar. You owe it to yourself and to the world. Waste no more time. If you are going to dream, dream big.

Magical Key to Bliss: Remove limitations and allow yourself the chance to live your calling!

April 19: **Run quickly so you can fly.**

Run, my dear,
From anything
That may not strengthen
Your precious budding wings.

~Hafiz, fourteenth-century Persian poet, excerpt from
"Run My Dear"

There is so much power in the symbolism of the butterfly. There are miraculous stages that the butterfly must go through to achieve such beauty and effortless grace. There is incredible evidence of metamorphoses as we watch the butterfly accept the changes that nature brings. The butterfly is the ultimate symbol of a soul that is expanding as it undergoes growing pains. We can follow the example of the butterfly as we experience our own magnificent transformation. We can support our journey by visualizing our beautiful wings getting stronger and stronger. We can come into contact with others while protecting this growth. We can become instinctively aware of our surroundings and keep the faith that all is unfolding as it should. As we blossom, there is a magical sense of purpose through expansion. As we embody self-love and prepare to fly, using the unfurling glory of the butterfly as an example, we quickly learn to run *from* anything that does not strengthen our confidence and *toward* those things that assist the development of our budding wings. And as we learn and grow into our own beauty, soon we shall fly!

Magical Key to Bliss: Pay attention to conversations today, and lean toward those that strengthen you.

April 20: You get to choose how you are going to get there.

Everyone is going to die; how you get there is up to you!

~Paulo Coelho, Brazilian author

D on't keep your distance from love when all that you want or need in life is to be hugged and connected to others. It is so much better to travel on the path of life with enthusiastic, positive, and loving people who support and honor your dreams. Say yes to each person who crosses your path offering you an opportunity to be in the world as part of the great interactive mystery. There are only two guarantees: you are born and, when you are done here on earth, you will die. Everything in between is really up to you. So get out there, lose yourself, find your truth, and discover what feeds your soul. While you are at it, make sure that you share it with people who bring you joy, passion, fun, and love. Have the courage to live your dreams in concert with a desire to step away from fear, embracing love. The incredible energy of optimism will have you and your companions changing the world in no time! There is no doubt that the choice is yours—do not waste another day. The sun has risen, and so will you as you ascend the spiral staircase of life, ready to take in its majesty one step at a time. *Now go!*

Magical Key to Bliss: Make the decision that as master of your destiny, you will live in love with others, not in fear!

April 21: **Failure is not an option.**

Act as if it were impossible to fail.

~Dorothea Brande, American writer and editor

It is time to manifest the life of your dreams. After setting aside time to clarify what that life looks like to you, the key ingredient to making this vision a reality is to infuse confidence into your every next action. As long as you keep moving forward with a positive mind-set, this belief in yourself and conviction that all outcomes will be favorable will empower you to do what is necessary to meet success. You are the only person who can give yourself permission to embark on a journey to fully realize your potential. Don't waste a moment more of your life doubting your abilities. Don't waste a moment more of your life with self-deprecating behavior. Don't waste another moment of your life buying into someone else's limiting belief of what the universe has waiting for you. You have dreams and ability; now make the decision to act and see it through. By using creative visualization, set out a road map that will guide you wherever you need to go. If you follow your passion and your bliss, failure will never be an option. This faith in yourself and resilience will take you far. Go out and set the world on fire by manifesting your own destiny. Today is a new beginning to believe in your potential, and with an air of confidence, you are one step closer to making all your deepest desires come true!

Magical Key to Bliss: Act as if it were impossible to fail!

April 22: Enthusiasm is the spice of life.

We act as though comfort and luxury were the chief requirements of life, when all that we need to make us really happy is something to be enthusiastic about.

~Charles Kingsley, Evangelical priest of the Church of England

We can all agree that life is a journey of many transitions. Looking back, we know that we are not the same person we were yesterday. Looking forward, we are enthusiastic to welcome tomorrow as we continue to transform our dreams into reality. Enthusiasm is the key to getting the momentum to see this through. For life takes on a greater meaning when we wake up each day excited about what is to come. When we make the simple choice to seek inspiration, our hearts are set afire to look for those opportunities daily. When we wake up to a life of enthusiasm, no longer deceived into believing that material things will buy happiness, we discover what makes us feel alive, and every cell of our bodies begins to rejoice. As we assist one another along the way, passion will take over its rightful place on our journey, and a different and more magnificent conversation will start. Enthusiasm is contagious. Enthusiasm is the spice of life. With enthusiasm, we can accomplish anything. In addition, when we start doing things that we love with great enthusiasm, each day lends its hand to magic and miracles. So, let today be the day where you shake off the doldrums and enthusiastically embrace writing and living the best chapters of your amazing life journey. That is where real happiness lies anyway.

 Magical Key to Bliss: Identify something that brings great enthusiasm!

April 23: **Strengthened by your faith.**

Just as a small fire is extinguished by the storm whereas a large fire is enhanced by it—likewise a weak faith is weakened by predicament and catastrophes whereas a strong faith is strengthened by them.

~Viktor E. Frankl, Austrian neurologist, psychiatrist, and Holocaust survivor

Without question, on the journey of life, a strong determination will be the driving force to guide you to achieve a desired end. Without fail, even in the toughest circumstance, a strong faith in the unseen will carry you there. Transformation is a process that can involve both struggle and triumph. Any worthy endeavor will encourage you to adapt to get to where you are going. Although the process is enjoyable on those bright, sunny days, the proverbial storms do come and shake things up significantly. When they do, sometimes you are prepared, and sometimes you are not. When your internal flame is shining bright, you feel like you can weather any challenge. It is when you are repeatedly faced with damaging blows that the gusty winds can seriously weaken your light and your resolve to see things through. It is during these times that instead of giving up, you must grab onto a deeper trust that all is well exactly where you are. Not only will this knowledge empower you to take the necessary steps forward, but this faith in something greater than yourself will strengthen you beyond measure. And when you believe that you are protected, whatever problem you face on any given day will leave you stronger than before as your light returns and you come to know that with faith all things are possible.

 Magical Key to Bliss: Write down your problems and ceremoniously ask for divine assistance to help you with the solutions!

April 24: **A new world awaits you.**

Following the light of the sun, we left the Old World.

~Christopher Columbus, Italian explorer, navigator and colonizer

To get to where you want to go tomorrow, you need to leave behind the habits of your past that no longer serve you today. Congratulations! You have successfully separated the gems from the junk and are ready to set out to further enrich your life. As you continue to follow the light of the sun, new and wonderful things will be illuminated. It is through the process of elimination that you will be guided and enlightened. It is through the process of discernment that new, wonderful paths on the journey will be revealed. You can discover a whole new world by taking a risk, leaving the known behind. You can unleash a new key to the mystery of life when you no longer hide from the light inside and the magnificence of the world at large. As you remember to follow your own bliss and listen to your internal guide, you can get past any fear or doubt. You can leave behind that Old World that served a purpose for a time, but still hold on to its value and lessons. Ultimately, you will take what you like and leave the rest. And as you continue your voyage into the new, you will make marvelous discoveries about yourself that open a greater path of magical understanding and untold riches of the heart. Just continue following the light of the sun!

Magical Key to Bliss: Follow the light in your life, and you will discover things beyond the imagination!

April 25: Boldness, be my friend!

Boldness, be my friend.

~William Shakespeare, English poet, playwright, and actor

Boldness is magical. Boldness is adventurous. Boldness will set you free. If you make boldness your friend, you will begin to imitate that fearless and daring spirit that encourages you to stop talking about doing the things that call to you and just do them. Begin today; begin now. Don't wait for permission to go after your dreams. Make a plan, set a strategy, embrace your vision, and move into it. Things that are created by your very powerful mind need to be set into motion to become a reality. Don't let the beauty of your dreams fade away. Do not let the fear of failure stop you. Do dare to be brave. Do dare to be confident. Make boldness your friend; it is your time to act. If your intentions are good and pure, then the outcome will bring you closer to your own personal genius. With boldness, whatever you do will guide you through life with great purpose while serving the greater good. Take a deep breath, or whatever you need, to free yourself from insecurity and stand out prominently. No longer remain stuck in indecision due to insecurity. No longer permit obstacles to stop you in your tracks. With an audacious air, allow your genius to take flight. It takes guts to be bold, and rest assured that when you embrace the magic inside of you, you will know that you have what it takes! Watch out, world, here you come!

Magical Key to Bliss: Gather all the courage you can muster, and do the thing that calls to you!

April 26: **It's time for your dreams to take flight.**

If one advances confidently in the direction of his dreams and endeavors to live the life which he has imagined, he will meet with a success unexpected in common hours.

~Henry David Thoreau, American author, poet, philosopher, and transcendentalist

In this season, you are ready to graduate from one point in your life to another. You are always moving upward on the ladder, ascending gloriously as you take on the next step or stage in your evolution. As you advance confidently, truly consider with conscious awareness what your new phase will look like. Ask yourself what you have prepared for thus far. Contemplate the life that you have always imagined, and get clear as to how you will welcome it. As you prepare your own commencement speech, look back and treasure the work, the sacrifice, and the enthusiasm you have invested to get to this point. Be grateful for the opportunity to surrender your past story, and confidently embrace the present moment and all that it has to offer. This is truly the beginning of your dreams taking flight. As Thoreau points out, only when you are confident in all of your possibilities and what you have accomplished will you be able to transform the ordinary into what is your extraordinary. Only then will you meet with a success that is yours to discover. With your imaginary cap and gown, accept your diploma with grace, and get ready to believe that now is the time for rebirthing a new beginning. Get ready to fly!

Magical Key to Bliss: Get creative and make a diploma setting out your triumphs over obstacles and your accomplishments. Display it proudly, and get ready for the next act.

April 27: Watch your amazing life unfold!

Arrange whatever pieces come your way.

~Virginia Woolf, twentieth-century British modernist author

L et your prayer today be that you see everything that comes your way as a blessing. Instead of wanting what you do not have in life, know that you already have everything you need. Instead of rejecting what is, accept where you are and arrange those pieces that come your way. Instead of dwelling on and complaining about life's trials and tribulations, understand that everything on your path is exactly what you need for your journey to continue. Remember that the universe is unfolding exactly as it should. Observe well as you open your arms to receive the beauty of its splendor. The mystery is revealed as the unknown unfolds into something amazing! As your prayer is answered, the blessings acknowledged will fortify your spirit and urge you on to greater heights of consciousness. Arrange well, and watch your amazing life unfold!

Magical Key to Bliss: Be the observer of your life today, and say thanks for each piece of your amazing puzzle!

April 28: **Come alive before the world.**

I am beginning to learn that it is the sweet, simple things of life which are the real ones after all.

~Laura Ingalls Wilder, American writer and author of the *Little House on the Prairie* books

When you are present in the moment, you get to witness the simple things that make the experience of living worthwhile. Each event in life offers an opportunity to learn, heal, grow, transform, and rejoice. Each sweet, simple thing that you encounter adds to your big, beautiful, bold, awesome, and amazing life. Embrace this gift without fail. Take in those moments of wonder as you actively enroll and engage as a student of love. For the sweet, simple things of life are what it is all about. They are waiting for you in plain sight, begging for you to come alive. As simple and obvious as a hug, a smile, or an interaction that bolsters your confidence, each one drifts in and out of your life, as real as can be. Each thing is ready to teach you well that life is all about love. As you go out into the world, understand that your lesson plan becomes your everyday simple occurrences. Every opportunity is an experiment in the humanities, giving you a chance to share your joy and vulnerability. Every moment is as real as you make it. As you find the connections to your soul, wake up to your moments, and they will transform you ever so beautifully. As you become alive right before the world, rejoice; this is really just the beginning.

Magical Key to Bliss: Take a deep breath now as you allow and surrender to love in its truest and simplest form.

April 29: Take the hero's journey.

This is a tale I pray the divine Muse to unfold to us. Begin it, goddess, at whatever point you will.

~*The Odyssey of Homer,* Ancient Greek epic poem attributed to Homer

You are the hero of your own life! Declare it. Do not shy away from the power and transformation that comes with this role. Own it. The path is yours to discover, through your own eyes and distinct perspective, each and every step of the way. You have been on this journey your whole life, revisiting the cycle of learning over and over again as you go. Yes, yes, yes. Know it. You are living your own mythical adventure of wonder, magic, and intrigue. You are truly here with purpose for great things. Believe it. If your path touches only one other than you with goodness, then you are making and have made a difference. Rise with it. When you hear the call, answer it. Embrace the role of hero because only then will you truly know your own power to heal yourself and those around you. Begin it. Yes you can heal yourself and others. Knowing your purpose and honoring it has that kind of power. Do not delay. Although you are not alone, the journey is ultimately yours, and the choices you make are yours. Pray to the divine Muse that each decision you make honors your precious light within. This is your tale that is unfolding in you and around you. Love it!

Magical Key to Bliss: Go forth, fellow companions, and begin it at whatever point you will.

April 30: **Are you ready to make the shift?**

When I started counting my blessings, my whole life turned around.

~Willie Nelson, American singer, songwriter, and activist

You are doing the work and are a direct witness to your life as it unfolds in a wonderful way. You have paid attention to the opportunities and wholeheartedly opened your heart and mind to experience an incredible transformation. Now, before you move on to the next step, it is time to be sure to count each one of your blessings received. Name them aloud and be thankful for the chance to do so. Recognize the importance of shining a bright, beautiful light on all of the wondrous things that have touched your life since you began your journey to bliss. When you are thankful for the big and small treasures, the world will respond lovingly. When you acknowledge your gifts with joy and delight, you are consciously creating a positive shift in the direction that your life takes. When you are grateful for the opportunities and people who have gotten you this far, your whole life turns around. When you feel the blessings of a life guided by your divine intuition, you feel loved and supported as you move forward. When you decide to shift your attitude to one of gratitude, you will experience a burst of energy that has the power to change the world. Before you shift to awaken your creativity, start with gratitude for the transformation of your dreams into reality so far! Then move effortlessly into a whole new month in which you just flow with the magic that this intentional vibe creates.

Magical Key to Bliss: Count each blessing that you have received from January through April, name each dream that has been born, and give thanks!

Chapter Five: May

AWAKENING YOUR CREATIVITY

When you awaken to your creative self, you start to truly understand what it means to be human. When you awaken to your creative dreams, you start to believe in your ability to chart a new direction for your life. When you awaken to your creative energy, you start to feel the power of possibility pour over you. As Julia Cameron, the amazing author of *The Artist's Way* (2002), points out, "There is no such thing as a noncreative person." Each one of you *is* a creative artist perhaps just waiting for the invitation to come alive.

As you begin this new chapter on your magical journey to bliss, you are invited to do just that—to come alive. The month of May, named for the Greek goddess of springtime, Maia, is a time of greatness in which you are called to engage all your senses to open up the amazing *you*. When you arouse the sleeping beauty of your creative side, you will see for the first time a palette of color that brings vibrancy to life; you will hear music that wakes up your spirit; you will touch another as your great dance unfolds; you will experience the sweet smell of success that comes from new discovery; and you will taste the richness of this new, eye-opening experience. In May, get ready to inspire as you shake up your creative energy and release your talents onto the world. Look out, baby, here you come!

May 1: There is beautiful music in you—start dancing to it!

Most people go to their graves with their music still inside them.

~Oliver Wendell Holmes Sr., American physician, writer, and poet

It is May Day. A time of great celebration. A time of merriment as you tap into your creative spirit. A time of blossoming as you prepare for the festivities that a creative lifestyle brings. A time of choosing to make miraculous shifts as you start paying attention to what brings you joy. Get enthusiastic for your party. Reprogram your past negative chatter into uplifting affirmations. Move into a belief that you are the only one who can give yourself the permission to be anyone you want to be. You have been blessed with the music that is in you. Own it and start to proudly sing your aria, your amazing song that comes from within. Let it come through you as you act in divine service to your greater purpose, whether in the role of doctor, lawyer, Indian chief, social worker, performer—you name it. When you start to honor your talents by offering them to the world, you will feel more alive than ever before, inspiring more people than you will ever know. And what was once your own melody will conspire with the melodies of others to create an operatic masterpiece. What was once your own solo will blend with others' songs to create a symphony of delight. And what was once a party of one will turn into a rave in which the dancing will never end—all because you decided to release the beautiful music and not take it to the grave. Sing on, play on, and dance on!

 Magical Key to Bliss: Find a mentor who inspires you, and imitate what he has done to let his music be heard.

May 2: **Dance, love, sing, and live life to the fullest!**

You've gotta dance like there's nobody watching,
Love like you'll never be hurt,
Sing like there's nobody listening,
And live like it's heaven on earth.

~William W. Purkey, American author of *Becoming an Invitational Leader*

We are on this earth in this body for just a short time, no matter how you look at it. Even in the time given, we have the opportunity to dance, love, sing, and live life to the fullest for as long as we can. We have been born into this magical place to experience life. It does not matter who is watching or listening; we have a mission to unleash our soul. When we remember that we are on our own journey and in this moment exactly where we are meant to be, we can surrender to the fact that the present is perfection. On the front of Emile Zola's book *Nana* (1880), he wrote, "If you ask me what I came to do in this world, I, an artist, will answer you: I am here to live out loud." So don't hide from the world, missing this chance to live out loud, dance, sing, and—most of all—love! The beautiful music of life plays and invites us to move to its beat. There is a beautiful song in our hearts that needs to come out. Tap into the source that provides endless and abundant energy, and let go. When we do, this place can be heaven on earth. Look up and start to see, feel, hear, and live in a world connected to the life that has been wonderfully laid out. The choice is ours anyway, and there is so much to gain by saying yes!

Magical Key to Bliss: Start loving what you've got, dance, love, sing, and live life to the fullest!

May 3: **Color the world with creativity.**

The secret to a happy life is to recognize that no matter what the situation, there's a creative opportunity in it.

~Deepak Chopra, Indian-born American author, speaker, and alternative medicine advocate

With a brush in one hand and a palette of color in the other, set out to create a world that defies your limits. The canvas of life is laid out before you. Guide yourself each and every morning toward a place where you will have every possibility to let your imagination come alive. The tools in your artist's box are waiting for you to sketch the life of your dreams, to fill in the gaps with details so exquisite they take your breath away, and to paint with bursts of color that make it all come to life. Every chance you get to color your world with creativity is a blessing for the whole. Just feel the creativity of your life course through your veins, seeking to be released in a grand show for all to see. Each artist's journey is different. Each of you brings your own color to this world. Your contribution has great meaning and purpose as it brings happiness to those lucky enough to experience the beauty of your masterpiece. Be willing to share your gifts as you color the world with your own creativity. You will succeed in making the world brighter, which in turn will alleviate the heaviness of worry from your shoulders. In turn, the canvas you create with your inspired genius will carry all of us to a happier place! In essence, you are coloring the world with love.

 Magical Key to Bliss: Make it your goal to take the opportunity to open your own artist's toolbox and create with great abandon and happiness today and every day!

May 4: Inspiration comes from everywhere—are you paying attention?

Inspiration comes from everywhere. Often my art is a reenactment of my own personal feelings. I am inspired by my own experiences, emotions, and the journeys I am taking.

~Nathan Sawaya, New York–based artist best known for his work with LEGO toy bricks

Your creative self is ready to burst from inside you like the first rays of sunshine on a cloudy day. Absorb the inspiration that emanates from your life journey, and use it to create something so magical that it evokes amazing fits of passion in the observer. Fear has no place there. It is only an unwelcome visitor who attempts to distract you from the greatness that is yours to discover. You feel the stirring in your soul when you happen upon something that brings you great joy. You know how your feelings guide you and lead you to become more of the artist you were born to be. Follow that inspiration, and you will choose bliss. It is the only way to live. Choose bliss. It is the only way to honor those gifts that have been bestowed on you. Choose bliss. Anything else would lead to a life of frustration and hardship. When you are faced with choices, follow bliss, and trust that whichever choice you make will lead you in the right direction to the right connections, who will reveal themselves as guides to validate your path. Get inspired today, and engage the dormant creativity that lies in your heart waiting to be exposed. Then when you surrender to the inspiration from wherever it arrives, you will become free to not only awaken your spirit but also stir the souls of others.

Magical Key to Bliss: Pay attention to the messages you get today; inspiration comes from everywhere!

May 5: **Remember to play.**

While we try to teach our children all about life, our children teach us what life is all about.

~Angela Schwindt, American mom and coach of the One Wheel Wonders unicycle team, quoted in *The Zen Mama's Book of Quotes: A Collection of Thoughts and Wisdom throughout the Ages*

Looking through the eyes of a child, we see a deep sense of gratitude for the second chance to experience life for the first time all over again. Experiencing life as a child, you once again learn what love is; you learn how to crawl before you run, you learn the importance of creativity and dreams, and you learn to enjoy the simple pleasures. Children live in the world of their imaginations. That very special place is protected from the external society that clouds one's vision. It is a special place where you sing loudly, dance without abandon, giggle at silliness, and question with courage those things that you do not understand. If you are lucky enough to remember how to sing, dance, laugh, and be brave, do your best not to squander it. When you emulate the inquisitive nature of a child and experience things that you may have missed on the first go around, you experience a time of innocence, wonder, and magical play! While there is so much you can teach children, the world would be a much better place if you opened up to what children can teach you. There is that renewed sense of freedom when you once again surrender to the gift of life that is present when looking through the eyes of a child. They will teach you what is important in life as you recapture a playfulness that reenergizes the spirit. And then you will begin to see the world as it should be.

Magical Key to Bliss: Make sure you take time to sing, dance, laugh, and play today!

May 6: **Let your creativity inspire others.**

If your actions inspire others to dream more, learn more, do more, and become more, you are a leader.

~John Quincy Adams, sixth president of the United States of America

W herever we go and whatever we do, we are on a mission, a mission with great purpose. We are here at this time to be leaders. No matter what role we assume, we set an example by our actions, inspiring others to dream, learn, do, and become more of who they are meant to be. This is our service to the world. We can spread our creative dreams through the majesty of art by engaging our eyes, through words that wake up the soul, through music by engaging the ears, or through dance that stirs the spirit. Whatever the preferred language, we all can lead by tapping into our passion and using our gifts to bring something beautiful to this world that just might spark that creative energy in another person. Nothing stands in the way of our boundless and limitless potential that can be ignited when we are doing something that we really love. There is no greater sense of accomplishment than when we witness another stepping outside of her comfort zone to soar all because she was inspired by us to do so. The greatest leaders in the world know that to fully realize our purpose here, we need to touch the life of another and ignite his passion within by virtue of what we do. For this is the greatest connection one could ever be a part of; to lead and inspire others is truly the greatest expression of creativity and love.

 Magical Key to Bliss: Be true to your language of love to inspire another; teach the way only you know how!

May 7: **Creative surrender.**

The creative process is a process of surrender, not control.

~Julia Cameron, American author of *The Artist's Way*

Let's really get creative today by letting go of the notion that we are in control of the outcome. Yes, we are in control of our creative choices, but once we make them and release them into the universe, they take on a life of their own. Once we relinquish our need to control our artistic expression, we can also release our fears and expectations regarding what should happen next. Once we decide to stand in the beauty of our creative self, we relinquish the need to control and start to relish the freedom that comes from creative surrender. If we take on our creative journey feeling good about who we are and knowing our beauty within, then whatever comes from our process will be magical. In developing our creative muscle, we are daily given lots of material to work with. We have many opportunities to embrace the creative side of our brain and let the adventure begin. We are given many chances to continue to evolve and bring the blessings of our own special talents to the world. When we radiate with passion and enthusiasm, the creative possibilities evolve effortlessly because what we uncover comes from within. And when we are able to share with others the fruits of our creativity, the joy and happiness that we have been looking for finds us. It is as simple as that—so let's get creative and begin to surrender to our own process so that we can all benefit from the best that is yet to come.

Magical Key to Bliss: Surrender to your creative process and open up to possibility!

May 8: Be inspired by your glorious uniqueness.

While we have the gift of life, it seems to me the only tragedy is to allow part of us to die—whether it is our spirit, our creativity, or our glorious uniqueness.

~Gilda Radner, American actress and comedian

We all have a glorious uniqueness all our own. We are born with the gift of life and a defined spirit that wants to soar. Each of us is blessed with a tremendous capacity to bring our creative talents to everything that we do. For we are the lucky ones, and as such, we need to remember that with the gift of life comes great responsibility to make the most of our time here. Sometimes we do lose sight of our purpose, go through the motions, and get stuck in the rut of a routine that does not enable exploration of our creative spirit. Awareness is the first step toward breaking free of the chains of monotony. We must pay attention to the yearning of spirit pulling at our heartstrings, begging to be realized. Responding to that yearning will allow us to break out of whatever we feel is holding us back. We become whole each time we answer the call to inspired action. We become whole as we unwrap the pieces that lead to growth. For it would be a tragedy to allow any part of us to die. We are the ones who need to share our glorious uniqueness with the world. We are the lovable beings setting out to embrace the gift of life that is ours to live until the last day.

 Magical Key to Bliss: Set your spirit free, let your creative mind go, and share with all of us the beauty that is your glorious uniqueness!

May 9: The secret to a happy life.

You being you is the blessing. You being you is the miracle. You being you is enough. You being you is your soul signature.

~Panache Desai, British spiritual teacher and author

Breathe in, breathe out. Anytime during your day, take a moment to feel the air enter through your nose; fill your lungs only to release the air again. Sit with yourself and welcome the opportunity to be present. In the stillness, be the observer of your thoughts. Pay attention to the ideas as they introduce themselves. Choose the ones that bring an energy of vitality, wellness, and light. As you remain there, open to the gifts as they pass by, you—the artist of your life—are invited to find inspiration as you fine-tune your desire to authentically contribute to this world. This is a blessing, you being you, looking for what emanates from your creative soul. For it is in the energy of these moments that you can best hear your inner voice guiding you. It is there you will be able to hear the muse as she attempts to get your attention. It is there you can hear your soul approve the path that you are taking or decide to alter the course in another creative direction. Breathe in, breathe out. These are not wasted moments but important ones that will assist you with the opportunity to stamp your own signature to a life, exploring the miracle you are as you go.

Magical Key to Bliss: Get comfortable in your own skin by closing your eyes and feeling the vibrant spirit that is you!

May 10: Do not be afraid to stand out in a crowd.

> *The truth is that it doesn't matter that people will laugh at you, think you are weird, or feel your dreams seem totally unattainable—You must not listen to them. They are too entrenched in the limited herd mentality to see the greater possibilities that are available...What is different about you is what makes you special.*

~Bernard Hiller, Argentinian actor, singer, and producer

Take a moment today and remember a time when you felt invincible: when you felt like you could become whoever you wanted to be and do whatever you wanted to do, a time when you embraced the endless possibilities for your life. Now, stay in that moment, feel that reality, and experience the amazing and miraculous dreamer who you are. Let that sense of wonder and potential permeate every pore of your being. Disengage from any fear that people will laugh at you, think you are weird, or feel that your dreams seem totally unattainable. Hold onto that vision of your life, and get comfortable with standing out in a crowd as you are. You are special, and this world needs you. There is a loving energy urging you on, and your inner voice stands ready to guide you. Embrace who you are, and you will attract the most amazing, exciting, and eclectic group of fellow travelers that is perfect for you. You will attract individuals who think outside the herd mentality. And you will flourish without fear as you dance on a journey that will be all sorts of colorful instead of gray any day! When that happens, hold onto your unicorn; it is going to be an amazing ride!

Magical Key to Bliss: Expose a part of your crazy, wonderful, different creative soul to the world today.

May 11: **Mentoring creativity!**

Mentoring begins when your imagination can fall in love with the fantasy of another.

~James Hillman, American author and psychologist

So many doors lead to discovering a soul. Which one will you open today? When you open the door to your heart, you get more opportunities to love. When you open the door to your mind, you get more chances to learn. When you open the door to your imagination, you get more possibilities to meet the perfect mentor who will help you to develop creative power. You may have heard the Buddhist proverb that says when the student is ready, the teacher will appear. When you open the door to truly experience a life outside the box, you will recognize the teacher who will take you to a new level; you will grab onto the lessons that are prepared just for you. Be courageous, trusting that as you open your doors to the connections presented, the teacher will guide you and be an incredible mentor to assist you in fulfilling your purpose. Your mentor will appear as the person whose imagination falls in love with your creative dream and honors the open door of your soul. A mentor is there to believe in you, to see your talents, and to support and guide you. A mentor is there to connect with the fantasy as it begins to emerge as your reality. There are so many doors that lead to discovering a soul. To be honored by another person who helps you open up and creates a safe space for you to grow is a powerful gift. Stand in gratitude as you watch the door to your creativity open further in the process!

 Magical Key to Bliss: Take the risk and think about which door you will open today to start the process!

May 12: So you want to be a dancing star?

One must still have chaos in oneself to be able to give birth to a dancing star.

~Friedrich Nietzsche, German philosopher

Good news! All great ideas in life come from chaos. All great dreams are born out of chaos. All great enlightenment develops from a state of chaos. For it is when utter confusion and complete disorder presents itself that we are forced to think outside the box to come up with solutions that will free us. For it is when we embrace the chaos that beauty and grace can effortlessly appear before our eyes. The challenge lies in the surrender. That is it. When we are in the middle of what we perceive to be madness—children screaming, people talking over one another vying for attention, or loud noise from traffic—if we close our eyes with the intent to stay centered and let go of the need to control what surrounds us, the cacophony that could cause headaches transforms into a symphonic melody that brings peace. As we allow our mind to stop and our body to start the dance, surrendering to the chaos becomes exactly the beat that we need to put our soul back into alignment. There we capture the precise moment when we release the negativity that stalls us to embrace the positivity and release our dancing star!

 Magical Key to Bliss: Think differently today when things get chaotic—stop, take a deep breath, and listen to nature's orchestra play—then dance!

May 13: You are here on purpose; make it *fabulous*!

> *Your work is going to fill a large part of your life, and the only way to be truly satisfied is to do what you believe is great work. And the only way to do great work is to love what you do. If you haven't found it yet, keep looking. Don't settle. As with all matters of the heart, you'll know when you find it.*

~Steve Jobs, American innovator and cofounder of Apple Computer

Follow your passion. Don't give up on discovering your bliss. Don't ever stop the search for what aligns with your heart and soul. If you have not found it yet, keep searching, and you will eventually find what moves you. This is your once around, so don't give up; you are meant to be *fabulous*! When you challenge yourself to look for opportunities that give you joy each and every day, you are sure to find them. When you focus on things that you love and are passionate about, don't be surprised if opportunities to do what you love appear over and over again on your radar. Work is such a huge part of daily life; you must strive to be proud of what you create by your words and deeds so that your body and soul will align with *fabulousness*! With your gifts and talents, you want to leave your beautiful mark on this universe; to do so is your great purpose here. You won't be satisfied unless you do. As a result, there is no telling what kind of legacy you will leave behind! And for sure, if you do what you love, it will be an adventure.

Magical Key to Bliss: Write down your dream, and then focus and record how many times it is mentioned today!

May 14: **Your words have more impact than you know!**

Be impeccable with your word. Speak with integrity. Say only what you mean. Avoid using the word to speak against yourself or to gossip about others. Use the power of your word in the direction of truth and love.

~Don Miguel Angel Ruiz, Mexican author of Toltec spiritualist texts

You have the power to manifest miracles or to foster great harm simply by the words you choose. Words are charged with a very powerful energy, at times wonderful and at others times harmful. The words you use can either build a person up to believe he can do anything or completely destroy his hope. The words you choose can spark a fire, igniting a passion that was once dormant, or they can devastate dreams. Words can either inspire a revolution to bring down corrupt individuals or hold people in a state of fear. It is imperative that you be cognizant of the words you choose on a daily basis if your goal is to introduce energy that empowers truth and love rather than harm. If it is peace that you seek, your words must mirror that sentiment. If it is strong direction that you desire, your words must inspire a belief that will guide you. If it is love that you want, your words must empower with kindness. By being impeccable with your word, you can bring good to your life and the lives of others. For when you use words that uplift, you are choosing to share the beautiful energy of speech that can impact the world in an amazing way.

 Magical Key to Bliss: Feel the energy behind what you intend to say, and proceed in the direction of truth and love!

May 15: Take risks—what do you have to lose?

You have to take risks. We will only understand the miracle of life fully when we allow the unexpected to happen.

~Paulo Coelho, Brazilian author of *By the River Piedra I Sat Down and Wept*

In the first step, you identify your dream. In the second step, you believe that realizing your dream is possible. In the third step, you risk making that dream a reality. Have courage to take the risks necessary to see the life you have always wanted play out. While this is no small undertaking, it is a worthwhile endeavor. Although you may meet rejection along the way, do not worry. That door was closed to you because it was never meant for you. The lessons learned from the rejection are as important to your life path as any other. You have to continue to take creative risks, authentically living out your purpose and allowing the miracles of life to unfold. Allow the world to witness what comes from within you, and get a glimpse of your soul, whether it is well received or not. As you live your creative truth, you don't have to believe everything you hear. Choose wisely what feedback will guide you. You have nothing to lose and everything to gain. When you go out into the world, take risks and release your creativity without a censor, and the unexpected will happen. This is what life is all about—facing your fears with courage, allowing your creative spirit to shine through, and enjoying the miracle of the experience!

Magical Key to Bliss: Take a risk, and do something with your creativity outside your comfort zone.

May 16: **A shining star detached from the outcome!**

Keep on shining like a star. May you always laugh and dance and sing. May your light, light the way for another. May you stay true to the inner flame that makes your heart yours.

~Ashley Rice, American illustrator and creator of greeting cards for Blue Mountain Arts

We are shining stars. When we are in the flow of the universe, there are times our light is bright. We move forward each and every day laughing, singing, and dancing as we embrace the process of becoming. There are times our light is not as bright, and we struggle. We forget our faith as exhaustion sets in. We feel stuck yet simultaneously pulled in too many directions, out of focus, and gasping for air. While we are still shining stars, the intensity of our brightness strengthens and fades as we ride this roller coaster of life, going up then going down, thriving then surviving. As long as we stay true to the knowledge that we are shining stars, this knowledge will save us. Our light will never go out as we benefit by detaching from the outcome, opening up to receive wisdom during times of uncertainty. When we take a moment to breathe into our light, as Deepak Chopra profoundly stated in *The Seven Spiritual Laws of Success* (1994), "We surrender ourselves to the creative mind that orchestrates the dance of the universe" (The Law of Detachment). It is a universe that allows us to return to a state of balance, where our inner flame grows stronger. If we give up too soon, we will never see beyond our present to know the beauty in store. So, beautiful star, keep shining regardless of where you are on the ride, and together we will light up the sky!

 Magical Key to Bliss: Take a moment to meditate as you listen for wisdom and feel your light shining brighter.

May 17: **A life led in creative abundance!**

It's not about how to achieve your dreams; it's about how to lead your life...If you lead your life the right way, the karma will take care of itself, and the dreams will come to you.

~Randy Pausch, American professor and author of *The Last Lecture*

A h, karma, what a wonderful and beautiful thing. With the understanding and heightened awareness that our actions now can affect our lives in unexpected ways later, we set out to live the best version of ourselves. This concept of living a purposeful life, empowered by consciousness through which we act rather than be acted on, is freeing. Instead of being controlled by fear of what negative karma can bring to us, we are liberated by ideas that will allow for more love, hope, joy, and abundance. What karma we build in this life will lay the path for our divine destiny. It can be a life based on strong virtue and character in which we participate in positive creativity or not. The choice is ours to make each and every day. The way we decide to live is the most important indicator of whether we live a life filled with abundance or not. There is nothing more empowering to achieving abundance than to take on the idea of cooperation rather than competition. For it is in the connections of those kindred spirits that each of our paths is bolstered with pure joy as we each fulfill the divine promise of our heart's desire. And that feeling we get from incredible, karmic right action is a wonderful thing as our dreams come to us!

Magical Key to Bliss: Focus on ways to cooperate with others to bring creative abundance!

151

May 18: Creative, amazing you!

To be yourself in a world that is constantly trying to make you something else is the greatest accomplishment.

~Ralph Waldo Emerson, American essayist, lecturer, and poet

Be true to who you are! It is your job to be your most authentic self. The simplicity of standing confident in your skin becomes difficult only when you listen to a world that offers distorted images of worthiness. When you allow your self-esteem to be hijacked and easily swayed, you parade around in a fog of uncertainty. Yet when you stay true to you, you'll be sure to live out your truth and present the most authentic version of yourself. And when you do this, no degree of outside influence will threaten this divinely inspired knowledge that guides you to march to the beat of the music that emanates from your heart. It is in listening to that music, playing, dancing, and singing that you achieve the greatest sense of accomplishment. Regret can come only from not adhering to the promise that is your life. As stated in the title of Wayne and Serena Dyer's 2014 book, *Don't Die with Your Music Still in You.* Follow your heart as your own soul dictates, and your life will be filled with abundance and promise. Just go at your own pace, and be true to yourself! Allow your intuition to guide you! Then you will know the strength that comes from a confidence that authenticity allows! This is a promise!

Magical Key to Bliss: Figure out what kind of music you would play if you could do anything today!

May 19: With loving attention, life is destined to be glorious.

You don't know what you're going to get into when you follow your bliss.

~James Hillman, American author and psychologist

Be present to the bliss that surrounds you, delighting in the moment. Joy is celebrating each event as it unfolds, no matter how big or small. Surround yourself with a loving group that supports you and makes you feel good about yourself. Close your eyes and let the sounds of joy fill your entire being—the laughter, the giggles, the love. Breathe in each morsel of bliss. Experience delight without question, and savor the beauty of the present moment. Life is too short not to experience each and every moment, so keep your dreams alive, and know that you are living them every second of the day. Visualizing the kind of life you desire is so important to realizing it, so once you set your intentions through visualization, it is time to fall in love with whatever comes your way. You can do this! Have fun, and dance when you get the chance! Embrace the magical, marvelous, and magnificent *you*! Grab onto life and let it take you away. Enjoy your once around and smile. If there is to be happiness in your life, you just gotta go with it and follow your bliss. Grab onto the balloons and fly—no questions about it.

Magical Key to Bliss: Give loving attention to a life destined to be glorious!

May 20: **Dare to do great things.**

Nothing splendid has ever been achieved except by those who dared believe that something inside them was superior to circumstance.

~Bruce Barton, American author and politician

We were all born with the ability to nurture ourselves beyond any hurdle or challenge that life presents. Couple the nurturing with a fastidious belief in all that is possible, and we are not stopped by our experience of what is. When we make the decision that today is the day to start to nurture the vision that we have for our life, then we will be able to whittle away our insecurities only to find that confident person waiting to burst out and onto the scene. It is time to start believing that when the going gets tough, we are all superior to our circumstances! And that is the truth. If life is all an illusion anyway, then wouldn't it be fantastic to choose the illusion that we so desire! Dare to do great things, friends, and the universe will answer to the call! Think big and we shall flourish. Just don't give up, and we will never know defeat even in failure. We shall know only success because as we keep moving forward and dare to do great things, we will have accomplished more than we could ever imagine.

Magical Key to Bliss: Dare to do great, creative, amazing things today!

May 21: Live in a world of pure imagination.

The great successful men [and women] of the world have used
their imagination...they think ahead and create their mental
picture in all its details, filling in here, adding a little there,
altering this a bit and that a bit, but steadily building—
steadily building.

~Robert Collier, American self-help author

With your imagination put to the test, there is no telling how your creative spirit will blossom. Imagine a world where you construct bridges, not walls; then visualize the first brick joining your imagination to your reality. Imagine a life filled with adventure and excitement. Get a clear mental picture of where you will travel first, how you will get there, the people you will meet, and what you will learn along the way. Imagine whatever you will because you have the ability to think of new things that have never been seen before. You have the ability to form a picture in your mind of experiences that are yet to come. You have the ability to create other worlds that have not been perceived in reality just yet. You are blessed with an imagination that can take you to places, to know people, and to experience amazing things if only you let it take flight. Today is a good day to exercise your creative muscle by choosing to live in a world of pure imagination. You will feel great success as you share with the world your imagination through your artistic and intellectual creations, no matter how bizarre they may be. If you imagine with wonder, it may just be a preview of what is yet to come.

Magical Key to Bliss: Imagine a world of your own creation; then write, sing, or draw about it!

May 22: **Take time to dream!**

It's the possibility of having a dream come true that makes life interesting.

~Paulo Coelho, Brazilian author

When we don't take the time to dream, we are susceptible to getting caught up in the routine of everyday comings and goings. When we fail to dream, we are subject to losing sight of the beauty that surrounds us with all the magic it holds. When we forget to stop and schedule moments to dream, we miss out on that precious time to connect with that place inside waiting to blossom. Our dreams keep our passion alive. Our dreams make life worth living. Our dreams need to be recognized and validated so that we thrive. In the reaching for our dreams, we reach for something greater than ourselves. We push past obstacles and revitalize our purpose and path. Yes, we wake up, get dressed, and go to work or wherever else we are scheduled to be. Yes, we have responsibilities to tend to that seek to fill the hours of our days. However, we can focus, plan, and take moments to think about what gives our hearts wings. That time invested in ourselves will be key to mapping out our personal plan for finding joy through our dreams. Yes, our spirits depend on the time we take to be innovative by imagining what we are capable of. When we start out by focusing on our dreams and setting out to follow them, life gets more interesting. As we open the doors for a whole world of possibilities, we enthusiastically experience a universe where dreams really come true!

 Magical Key to Bliss: Draw a map to guide you in the direction of your dream!

May 23: **Create brilliance with kind words.**

Kind words do not cost much. Yet they accomplish much.

~Blaise Pascal, French philosopher

Whether written or spoken, the words we use form the basis of our relationships as we move through this journey. When we choose to use kind words as part of our daily rhetoric, what we foster becomes the virtue that creates brilliance in our lives. By making kindness the cornerstone of our life's work, we can affect everyone we touch with our presence in a magical way. It is hard to deny the power of generosity and genuine concern for one another. Some historical leaders have used kindness well as they inspired others with speeches that have long remained great examples for many generations. If we pause to think of the most influential, positive people in the world, we know their gift lies in the energizing, kind words they use to empower others to live the life they so desire. We are moved by their compassion that allows them to create an environment for building bridges based in understanding. We are compelled to imitate their graciousness that is the foundation for the development of a better world. As we follow their example, we know kind words are powerful. We know kind words make all the difference. We know kind words are the beginning to creating brilliance in life.

Magical Key to Bliss: Find a leader who used kindness to make a difference in this world, and pick out attributes that you would like to imitate.

May 24: When you pray, move your feet.

When you pray, move your feet.

~An old African proverb

Frustration occurs when we find ourselves stuck in difficult circumstances for quite some time. Instead of moving through this period, we feel trapped in a state of hopelessness. Although we seek positive change, even praying for it to come, each morning we wake feeling destined to repeat bad patterns. While prayer is powerful and can move mountains, begging for a miraculous shift must be coupled with action that will deliver us out of the uncomfortable situations we find ourselves in. Loosening the grip of stagnation on our lives does not require a grand gesture; all we need to do is take one baby step after another toward the light of our dreams. When we pray and then move our feet through the challenge, we will manifest the events or people who will take us even further on the journey to a place greater than we ever imagined. Dreaming without sharing those dreams with others will only keep us in a state of fantasy. Dreams coupled with action will take us to a new reality. So when we feel frustration, we need to take out a journal and start writing to get clear. As the winds of change start to blow, and the cobwebs fall away, hope returns, and each inspired move forward will boost our prayer to another level of heightened vibration. Bringing back a sense of enthusiasm and passion for our dreams, we set a new course built on creative insight that comes from a newly minted approach to life.

 Magical Key to Bliss: Get inspired to journal about a problem that you are experiencing, and come up with one step toward a solution.

May 25: Music stirs the soul.

If music be the food of love, play on.

~William Shakespeare, English poet, playwright, and actor

What brings great joy to your life? What brings great happiness to your days? What brings great passion to your endeavors? What brings great love? Music, music, music, music: magical melodies that have you tapping your feet; lovely verses that speak to you in both the good times and the bad; incredible beats followed by catchy refrains that encourage you and give you great hope that nothing is ever as desperate as it seems; an incredible energy that enters through your ears and invades your very soul—this is the medicine that heals you. Look to the music of life, and let it guide you to the exact place that you need to go. And at that place, you will meet yourself for the first time again. You will nourish yourself because music is the food of love—love that ebbs and flows with the rhythmic sound that awakens the power within and energizes your creative spirit. The weeping of the violin that begs you to unleash the passion in your soul; that gentle breath of peace that is inhaled as the beautiful aria of a soprano takes you to an otherworldly place; the vibrant musical beat that releases the dance inside, enabling you to begin the celebration of life once again. Music is food for the soul especially when you need an immediate boost. So if you desire to hear universal love, play on, play on, play on, and play on!

 Magical Key to Bliss: Put on your favorite song, turn up the radio, or even grab an instrument and just play, and let the love permeate your soul!

May 26: Master a healthy habit.

Repetition is the mother of all skill.

~Tony Robbins, American author and motivational speaker

You will master the actions you repeat over and over again. It has been proven that it takes about twenty-one days to develop a habit, regardless whether it is a good or bad one. With constant dedication, chances are good that you will become skilled at whatever task you undertake. With perseverance, when you set out to master a habit that is healthy, productive, and positive, it is highly likely that success will be yours. You can start with something big or with something small. Just start today to add one thing to your life that is bound to make a difference in how you live. When you add just one healthy habit that you practice and repeat over a period of days, then that one small, positive change will have an incredibly profound impact for years to come. As you become skilled in whatever area you focus on, your experience of the world will be better and better, and you will set in motion a positive chain of events for yourself. So start with repeating a positive mantra over the next twenty-one days; get up earlier in the morning to add exercise, or learn balance by choosing carefully when to say no and yes—just make the commitment to add something worthwhile each day, and infuse that sentiment with a can-do attitude. Keep reminding yourself that it may be difficult in the beginning, but in a short time, it shall become second nature to you—and you will embrace it even more.

 Magical Key to Bliss: Start your twenty-one days today, and develop a wonderful skill that is bound to multiply the good in your life.

May 27: It is all part of your amazing dance!

When you stumble, make it part of the dance!

~Suzy Toronto, American illustrator and creator of the label "Wonderful Wacky Women "

As you embrace your season of creativity and start to dance again, focus your attention on your accomplishments! When you focus on all of your achievements, you bring an incredibly uplifting energy to what lies ahead. That magical and miraculous strength that you have developed over time has allowed you to build a solid foundation to grow even more. The belief in yourself that arises from standing steadfast and true to who you are is a gift gained as your confidence blossoms. And instead of crumbling under what you perceive to be the weight of the world, you rejoice as you stand strong and let the weight fall from your shoulders to persevere again. There are two sides to every coin. With sadness comes much happiness from the outreach of a warm embrace when you least expect it. With financial hardship comes a sense of abundance through the love and support you receive along the way. With sickness comes a sense of appreciation for the health and harmony that you do experience and otherwise take for granted. When you stumble, adding love, laughter, fun, joy, and happiness can be a part of your dance. Moving forward is not a cause for alarm because it becomes a part of the celebration that you are alive in this moment. And as long as you make the decision not to quit, that celebration can be yours every day you open our eyes to the potential that lies ahead.

Magical Key to Bliss: Choose to experience days filled with love, light, and happiness—and celebrate!

May 28: **Allow your imagination to take you away.**

A drum and a mouth—to play music and sing. Use your
imagination to create happiness.

~A Buddhist saying

The greatest tool that you have is your imagination. There have always been great individuals whose imagination has taken them from ordinary to extraordinary. They are the ones who dreamed they could fly like birds before the first flight. They are the ones who went to the moon in their minds before the actual first journey. They are the ones who visualized a world made smaller by enhanced means of communication before the first phone appeared. They are the ones who imagined a world brought together to celebrate the beauty of differences before it actually happened. There are so many wonderful things your imagination can do, so many wonderful places your mind can go. If you just surrender to it, you will be surprised by the joy it will bring as you visualize all the possibilities, never hindered by any of the limitations. Your imagination can bring magic. Just look at children at play—dancing with the snowflakes, singing to the tunes that emerge from nature, or creating a world of joy by allowing their minds to experience it. With the capabilities to use your imagination to create your own brand of happy, if you just let go for a moment and do it without judgments, you start to bang on your own drum, sharing your music with the world. On this journey into bliss, the gift of your imagination is miraculous as you get just a preview of where life can take you! Allow it to take you away.

Magical Key to Bliss: Empower yourself to imagine the greatness within!

May 29: **Have a celebratory theme to guide your days.**

Everyone needs a theme song! It should make you feel like a million dollars.

~Zooey Deschanel, American actress and singer-songwriter

At times you may need an infusion of passion or enthusiasm to take over and enliven your spirit. If you find yourself needing some inspiration, it is time to shift your attention to a theme that can help you discover something a bit more magical. It is time to refocus and set a wonderful tone by picking a melody that has the potential to catapult you to the next level of amazing. Visualizing what you intend to experience in your life has always been key to achieving goals, and preparation is essential to seeing your goals come alive. You want to imitate a successful planning process and choose a corresponding theme because what you visualize will take you from ordinary to extraordinary. When you magically set out the arrangement for fun, joy, or love, you establish a positive foundation for the necessary building blocks of an incredible year. With a perfect theme in place, you will take actions that set the stage as the amazing story of your life plays out. Choose a song that corresponds to the desires of your soul. Choose art as the background because colors bring happiness and cheer to stir your vision. Choose creative activities that will inspire. By setting out a theme for your life, you will inspire the heart to aim higher, open the doors of your mind, and keep the journey going in the direction that best serves your purpose.

Magical Key to Bliss: Set a theme to guide your day, your year, and your life!

May 30: The magical power of creativity.

The idea flow from the human spirit is absolutely unlimited.
All you have to do is tap into that well. I don't like to use the
word efficiency. It's creativity. It's a belief that every person
counts.

~Jack Welch, American businessman

An abundance of tremendous and powerful creative energy flows through the veins of each and every one of us. Do not give your creative power away. Grab your magic wand and summon the power within you. In each of you is embedded the seed of something that starts as an idea and becomes whatever your heart desires. As long as you are alive and allow your spirit to be free, there is no telling what wonderful potential lies within you just waiting to burst out. The power of the mind is beyond fascinating. Couple it with the power of visualization, get to playing, and enjoy. If you pay attention on a daily basis to life's cues and inspiration, there is no telling what kind of beauty you can bring to this world or how much fun you can have with it. Leave your mark in a way that benefits the world and has many standing in awe. Tap into your hidden and unhidden potential, and let what is inside flow out. You matter, and you are here on purpose. Each one of you has the power to make something extraordinary from the ordinary. You just need to believe and know that creativity is your birthright.

Magical Key to Bliss: Create with the unlimited opportunities that life presents today.

May 31: Create a fairy-tale ending.

If you want your children to be intelligent, read them fairy tales. If you want them to be more intelligent, read them more fairy tales.

~Albert Einstein, American, German-born theoretical physicist

Welcome to the world of make-believe! There is a treasured art in the telling of fairy tales. When you open your mind to the mystical realm and allow your imagination to soar, possibility abounds. What role will you assume as the protagonist in your own fairy tale? What challenge will you take on and overcome as you venture further on your journey? What phenomenal ending will you visualize for this amazing chapter in your life? You have awakened the incredible, creative spirit within, and you are ready to go on flights of fancy. You are ready to live the magical tale as you discover fantasy in faraway lands. You are ready to engage in crafting the most incredible success story of all, opening a path to reawakening and rediscovering consciousness. And if you need guidance, read more fairy tales. There is nothing better for this world than all its inhabitants having the magical experiences of living life connected to its mystery beyond the veil. Your taking in all the signs, symbols, and synchronicities as they are received increases your intelligence as you experience the world all over again through the eyes of a child. Believing once again in the adventure of the fairy princesses, frog queens, and magical unicorns, you surrender and enjoy your own life as if it were the fairy tale you've always dreamed of, creating an amazing ending each time.

 Magical Key to Bliss: Believe in the magic, and welcome your creative life!

Chapter Six: June

EMBRACE YOUR JOY

In June, *The Magical Guide to Bliss* invites you to embrace joy. Joy is at the core of who you are and is the primary contributor to a peaceful state of mind. True joy is not based on anything external but rather comes from your very nature. It is at the very heart of you and all that you do. Now that you have spent time in May awakening your gifts and talents, it is time to understand fully that the foundation of your creative expression comes from tapping into its joyful source. As you peel back the layers that have threatened to hide your true essence, you will begin to embrace your joy at its source, and your spirit will freely shine through.

At the start of June, as you prepare for the end of spring and the beginning of summer, the great outdoors call to you. You can venture out both physically and spiritually. You can take advantage of the many new opportunities to change your routine, beginning to explore your world in a different way. The school year is over, summer vacations are planned, and the beach or mountains beckon you as you set your sights on slowing down a bit in the heat. You can appreciate being with others as the days are a little longer. The year is halfway over, and you have come so far. Look back and congratulate yourself on your accomplishments. Now it is time to truly surrender to the fun and excitement that rises from that inner state of joy in your heart. Are you ready to sing about how happy you are because you have embraced your bliss? If so, away you go!

June 1: You are here on purpose for a great purpose.

Do what brings you joy, and your purpose will unfold.

~Iyanla Vanzant, American inspirational speaker and author

When you feel like you have lost your way, go back to the basics at the beginning of your day. Focus on the words joy, gratitude, praise, and love. Make these words a launching point, and the energy behind them will not lead you astray! Words and intentions have power. When you refocus on what gives you joy, you will align with a feeling that gives you great delight and pleasure. When you have gratitude and embrace your blessings, that recognition of the good in your life saves you when times of despair and darkness threaten to take over. When you give warm approval and praise for the life you have been given, your ad-miration begins a ripple effect that will carry you far. Most of all, when you focus on spreading love, this beauty shared with others becomes a bright and powerful light in this world. So refocus on joy, embrace with gratitude, give praise, and spread love. This powerful word formula will start to take you from the darkness into the light just one small step at a time if—you allow it. And soon enough, you will discover the joy that is your life showing you that you are here on purpose for a great purpose. The sooner you make the shift, the better; the fun begins when you get to share your inner beautiful essence with the world!

Magical Key to Bliss: Focus on what gives you joy!

169

June 2: Count your joys.

Man is fond of counting his troubles, but he does not count his joys. If he counted them up as he ought to, he would see that every lot has enough happiness provided for it.

~Fyodor Dostoevsky, Russian novelist and philosopher

Today you will officially count your *joys*! Write them down one by one to get started. While you may think it is easier to focus on what is going wrong in your life, rest assured that when you seek out what is going right, you will feel the love. So what is it that makes you happy? Perhaps the joy you get from waking up in the morning—let's start there! Or maybe you have new opportunities to explore your talents. Even better, you have a roof over your head, clothes on your body, and food to eat, to name a few basics. You know you have so many blessings, if only you are willing to release your painful story for a moment to recognize them. Life is meant to be filled with joy. The law of attraction gives you what you are willing to give out. If you concentrate too much of your time and energy on what is wrong in your life, you may get more of the same. However, if you shift your focus to what is going right in your life, your joy will multiply! If you name your joys and talk about them, your energy will change, and your life will turn around. Start with five minutes and count your joys, taking a holiday from your woes. That may just be what the doctor ordered!

Magical Key to Bliss: Count five blessings in your life today, and be grateful for the joy!

June 3: Invite in pure joy!

I cannot believe that the inscrutable universe turns on an axis of suffering; surely the strange beauty of the world must somewhere rest on pure joy.

~Louise Bogan, American poet

Being surrounded by constant challenges makes it very difficult to see beyond the next obstacle. When we are subjected to a routine that squeezes our spirit, it is no wonder we want to pull the covers over our heads to return to our slumber once again. But going through life asleep and numb is no way to live. The universe offers all of us its beauty. For when we walk through the storms of life, we are sure to find our big beautiful rainbow. We must keep walking. We must keep looking for our rainbows. We must keep seeking pure joy. But we have to get up. We have to get dressed. We have to put on our best self, and we have to allow the beauty to come shining through the clouds. The storm will pass if we start to dance in the rain. Joy is there as the water washes us and recharges our spirits to let the difficulty and suffering go. Joy beckons to us as we take the chance to face a new day and change what we can on a daily basis. If we make joy a part of our lives as a healthy habit, one day at a time, we will spend more of our waking hours experiencing the beauty of the world. And when it is time to rest again, we will cover ourselves with the love that comes from pure joy!

Magical Key to Bliss: Seek out a rainbow after a storm; get up and put on your Sunday best—go out into the world, and invite joy in!

June 4: Practice joy today!

The world is given to you as a beautiful garden. You diminish the garden if you do not enjoy its fruits.

~Brian Weiss, MD, American psychiatrist, hypnotherapist, and author

Joy: a simple word with a powerful vibration behind it. We do not need anyone's permission to experience this joyful vibration. We just need to be aware and open our eyes to the beautiful, joyful garden that we have inherited, take care of it, and enjoy its fruits. Joy is all about appreciation and gratitude for daily life. Joy is about taking it all in and learning to be satisfied with the simple pleasures that are right in front of us. It is time to begin to practice *joy*. We must step outside and breathe in the air, feeling happy as it fills our lungs. Practice joy! Seek out those people who are the happiest, and imitate their approach to life. Practice *joy*. There we will find fulfillment in our gifts rather than diminishing ourselves by focusing on our shortcomings. Practice *joy*. Don't put off until tomorrow the joy that we can experience today. Practice *joy*. The world is given to us to protect, and by emitting vibrations of happiness and glee, we nourish our garden so we can enjoy the fruits without harming anyone. We must embrace our right to delight in this beautiful garden of life on a daily basis. Realize that today is as good as any other day to write a story armed with the rose-colored glasses that enhance life's journey. So practice *joy*, and surrender to bliss as we enjoy the fruits of life that are laid out before us. That, I can guarantee, is something that we will never regret!

Magical Key to Bliss: Practice *joy*, and your life will bear the fruits from this joyful habit.

June 5: Let your focus be joy!

Find a place inside where there's joy, and the joy will burn out the pain.

~Joseph Campbell, American mythologist, writer, and lecturer

All your life you are encouraged to focus, focus, focus. As children, your teachers taught you to focus on the lessons of the day, your parents taught you to develop skills through focus, and your friends demanded your focused attention when you hung out together. As an adult, you get to choose what you focus on. No one will dictate your focus if you do not allow it. While you have so many more responsibilities pulling you in various directions as an adult, you are the navigator of your ship. You can sail through your days placing your focus on the joys of life or on the pain. Ultimately, it is your choice. Take a moment and evaluate. Focus on how you feel about certain areas of your life, and make a concerted effort to shift to the good if there are places for a more positive energy flow. Focus on what tools are available to you, and use them to guide you on your path. Focus on teaching yourself the habit of uplifting thought processes, and they will become your default mode. You are the captain of your journey; you are the master of your destiny. When you choose to focus and travel to the places of joy in your world, you take a small vacation from the stress, anxiety, and pain. And the once-tumultuous sea will be calm once more.

 Magical Key to Bliss: Make a twenty-one-day commitment to thinking about something each day that gives you joy.

June 6: Take a joy inventory.

To find joy in work is to discover the fountain of youth.

~Pearl S. Buck, American writer, novelist, and author of
The Good Earth

Today, take a glass-half-full attitude when looking at your life. Get in a mind-set of intense gratitude, and start to name the people who make your life richer, the events that make your life meaningful, and the knowledge that opens your eyes to something bigger and better than you could ever imagine for yourself. Then take action. Call a person who has enriched your life to tell her what she means to you. Reminisce on that very meaningful event that changed the course of your life. Pick up a book that has had a great impact on the way you see the universe. Then sit in awareness of the feeling of joy, beauty, and love that you have reawakened. Remind yourself of all of your blessings, and the joyful awareness you have gained for yourself will benefit the whole. To find and acknowledge the places of joy in your life is the greatest work that you will ever do and the key to staying young at heart. So remember, when you are going through a rough patch, take a joy inventory. You will help yourself to realize that this, too, shall pass, and the sun will shine again on the beauty that is your life.

Magical Key to Bliss: Take a joy inventory today!

June 7: Happiness exists on earth!

Happiness exists on earth, and it is won through prudent exercise of reason, knowledge of the harmony of the universe, and constant practice of generosity.

~Jose Marti, Cuban poet and journalist

When you practice generosity with yourself and others, you see how even little gestures can make a huge difference. Opening a door, listening to another in need, smiling as you pass by—these are all small practices that can change the world, moment by moment. By choosing acts of kindness and selflessness, you create harmony in the universe that can contribute to a euphoric high on a global scale. This emotional boost in spirit can lead you and many others to appreciate the ideal state of happiness that is your divine right and that exists here on earth. If happiness is your goal on the journey, then get in touch with that part of you that seeks to dwell in a place of unfettered joy by reaching out with love. Exercise your reason well, and do your part to promote harmony and wellness through caring and bigheartedness. Buy some unknown person a cup of coffee, acknowledge another soul traveling this earth, or offer a kind word of gratitude; these gestures will make you feel happy right away. One by one, you can change the world with your generous spirit, and therein you will find joy.

Magical Key to Bliss: Choose one person and send love his way with a call, e-mail, or letter!

June 8: **The joyous adventure of learning is yours to share.**

The more that you read, the more things you will know. The more that you learn, the more places you'll go.

~Dr. Seuss, born Theodor Seuss Geisel, American writer and illustrator of children's books

From stories relayed over the years, our roots lie in a rich tradition of immigrants who came to this country in search of a better life through education and hard work. Members of our families became teachers, lawyers, doctors, and judges, all with the underlying expectation that they would pay back this great opportunity through knowledge, public service, and acts that make a difference in the lives of others. We are part of a valuable tradition that lends a hand not just to being in this world but to leaving it better than it was before we came—one that encourages reading to expand our conscious awareness of the universe and its actors; one that infuses meaning in the small acts of kindness as we connect with others on a daily basis. It is a tradition where our love of learning and perseverance follow us throughout our days. That love of learning will take us to new places, allow us to discover new cultures, and have us living our life outside the figurative box. We will never be stuck in life as long as we don't limit our own self-actualization. Be creative. Draw and design visions of how we wish to see the world, and then get busy making it happen. Build on a hearty tradition of education and hard work. Then the joyous adventure will always be ours to share.

Magical Key to Bliss: Keep the door open to learning, and in an act of service, invite others to join you.

June 9: Look beyond imperfections.

Being happy doesn't mean everything is perfect. It means you have decided to look beyond the imperfections.

~Gerard Way, American musician and comic book writer

On any given day, as we strive for perfection, our constant self-examination has us looking for ways to further improve our lives. While a healthy desire for enhancement is not necessarily a bad thing, when we become consumed by what we perceive to be flaws, we take on an unhealthy evaluation that risks overshadowing our beauty within. This can eventually steal from our serenity, happiness, and joy. While betterment is a worthy goal, it is the satisfaction with progress—not perfection—that will liberate us to truly enjoy life. When we choose to be happy with who we are today—the beautiful work in progress that we are—we get the chance to embrace the gift of life. When we choose to be happy, looking beyond our imperfections, we empower ourselves to increase our potential for a great life. The empowering energy that is in us and surrounds us has a different vibration, one that is illuminating and inspiring. And that energy is what we all need to move us forward, happily experiencing all that life has to offer.

 Magical Key to Bliss: Embrace the beautiful work in progress that is you, and keep moving forward!

June 10: Cheers, pass it on!

You find yourself refreshed by the presence of cheerful people. Why not make an honest effort to confer that pleasure on others? Half the battle is gained if you never allow yourself to say anything gloomy.

~Julia Child, American chef, author, and television personality

Wake up to the notion that each person you meet today will happily bring love to your life. Expect to go out in the world, where each individual you come into contact with will point out something wonderful, and do your best to leave any note of complaint and sarcasm behind. Seek to find people in good spirits who are bright, cheery, and buoyant with joy and affection. Go after the cheerful ones, and leave no stone unturned until you surround yourself with an army of sunny and upbeat spirits. Then do your part, making an honest effort to return the same sentiment to the world. Today is not a day for a pity party, in which you allow gloominess to take up residence in your surroundings. Today is a day when you become the ambassador of cheer and not only pass it on but even magnify this energy throughout the universe. Not only will you experience great joy and feel reinvigorated by this incredible feeling based in joy and love, but you will have the opportunity to revitalize others as well.

 Magical Key to Bliss: Wake up with the goal of being a cheerful one today!

June 11: **See beauty in everything.**

Everything has beauty, but not everyone sees it.

~Confucius, Chinese teacher and philosopher

Bring a little magic into your life today. Take a moment, close your eyes, and take four deep breaths. When you open your eyes, determine that everything you experience from that moment on is a gift that will be beautiful, enhance your life, and make living this day amazing. Believe that everything that comes into your world and attaches to your senses will bring you beauty and love. Know that all who come into your life today will bring you the gift of their presence, their words, their smile, and their laughter. You get the gifts of life when you embrace the beauty of life. Every gift is packaged in a different way. Remember that even the unappealing stuff is a gift if you see it that way. So bring a little magic into your life today. Take a moment, close your eyes, and take four deep breaths. Remember that everything has beauty; today is your opportunity to see it. 1, 2, 3, 4...Go!

 **Magical Key to Bliss**: Set aside time to bring magic into your world, and determine to see beauty everywhere you go!

June 12: God winks throughout the day!

When we take time to notice the things that go right—it means we're getting a lot of little rewards throughout the day.

~Martin Seligman, American psychologist, author, and avid promoter of positive psychology

From small acts of kindness to the biggest of them all, when you are on the lookout for the good in your world, you are likelier to experience more joy throughout the day. When you take the time to acknowledge the things that make you feel jubilant or even just make you smile, you are noticing your blessings. Regardless of whether you even realize it, when you are conscious of the things that go right, you are being rewarded mentally, physically, and spiritually as a result. If you seek to place your attention on only what goes wrong, you can be sure you will find that too. So set out and focus on the miraculous and magical on a daily basis, and observe how often the miraculous and magical will show up for you. The synchronicity will blow you away each time as you are rewarded for your positive awareness. When you look for the good, you will become a good finder in all that you do. And each time you experience something that positively charges your soul, look up to the heavens and nod your head in gratitude—consciously experiencing and accepting your "God winks" throughout the day is a wonderful way to live!

Magical Key to Bliss: Be sure to notice all your little rewards as you take the time to notice the things that go right!

June 13: Share the joy.

Joy is a net of love by which you can catch souls.

~Mother Teresa, Roman Catholic religious sister and missionary

Looking into the eyes of a young child at play, return to a time when worry was a foreign concept, love surrounded you, and your imagination took you on many flights of fancy. Life was an adventure. Life was mysterious. And better yet, life was moment by moment. It was in those moments of connecting with friends that you created a world that was a joyful place. There is no reason that you cannot still experience the joy of a child as an adult. Even when times are challenging and you are faced with unbearable experiences, if you take a step back from that reality, you are able to transport to a place of gratitude for those things that bring you unfettered joy. For the joy comes moment by moment. In this moment, grab onto a memory of a time when joy permeated every membrane of your body. Let this focus on the joy be the gentle push that allows you to release the stress and embrace a joyful life in the most simplistic way. No one can take joy from you if you make the conscious decision to hold on to your moments. And in each moment, create a net of love to catch more souls. Joy reawakened encourages you to make this world a better place for you and others. In each moment that you share the joy, you shall find bliss.

Magical Key to Bliss: Embody joy, and be a net that catches many souls!

June 14: **Open your eyes to the beauty in the world.**

Anyone who keeps the ability to see beauty never grows old.

~Franz Kafka, German novelist and short-story writer

When you choose to see the beauty that surrounds you, you become what you see. You start to recognize the beauty that resides in you, in all people, in animals, in nature, in all things, and in all places. When you choose to see beauty all around you, you soften to your experience of the world and in this world. By becoming a softer person, and you allow the worry, stress, and fatigue of life to just melt away while love, joy, and beauty take over. A soft person who embraces beauty never seems to harden to the experience and never seems to grow old. As your eyes take in all the beauty that life has to offer today, your body will embody a youthful glow when you choose to feel exuberant about this incredible opportunity to be alive.

Magical Key to Bliss: Open your eyes and take note of the beauty that surrounds you!

June 15: Make a conscious choice to enjoy the ride.

Take pride in how far you've come. Have faith in how far you can go. But don't forget to enjoy the journey.

~Michael Josephson, American ethicist and founder of the Josephson Institute of Ethics

No matter where you are on the journey of life, be proud of how far you have come, and of both big and small accomplishments. Look to yourself for the validation that you seek, and resist looking for approval from another. Your life is not for another to judge. Be gentle enough to not judge yourself based on what you perceive to be another's path. While you are moving forward, keep the faith that you, too, shall be protected to rise from the ashes of your pain and see the light from the sun beaming down on you anew. Keep the faith that as long as you listen to your internal guide, you will experience your reality with a gentleness that makes the path easier. Keep the faith that everything happens for a reason, and perhaps you can more fully experience *la dolce vita*, the sweet life, by living well, laughing often, and loving more fully. Live in gratitude for each day, laugh with your friends at the amusing parts of life, and love others as you want to be loved. If you have not already, you will truly begin to enjoy the journey more and more each day. It is priceless when you experience a rebirth, a renaissance, and start to love the journey for all that it has to offer.

 Magical Key to Bliss: Make the conscious decision to just embrace your own existence, and make it a priority to do your best to enjoy the ride!

June 16: Obstacles are teachers to reawaken joy.

Stand up to your obstacles and do something about them. You will find that they haven't half the strength you think they have.

~Norman Vincent Peale, American author of *The Power of Positive Thinking*

Find a new way to see obstacles. They can be our greatest ally. They can be our greatest teachers. They can be the challenge that we need to reawaken the joy in our hearts, forcing our imagination to come to life again. Many of the greatest thinkers of our time made the greatest discoveries because their obstacles required them to come up with solutions that catapulted their ideas further. We, too, can use obstacles as tools to inspire new directions in our life. When we stand up to our obstacles, we bring a revitalized enthusiasm because we have surpassed something we initially believed was unsurpassable. When we face our blocks and see them for what they are, we muster the strength to face whatever life throws our way. When we experience something stopping us in our tracks, we become very grateful for the message that the challenge will teach us. When we overcome these obstacles, we will discover a renewed will and determination. We will fully appreciate the euphoric aroma of a life well lived, a life in which our spirits run carefree, souls forever young. And we will recognize that these obstacles did not have half the strength we once believed they had. When we face our obstacles as they arise, we must ask—"Teacher, what is my lesson here?" Take the time to listen as the answers come; they are the universe speaking to us, helping us to follow the path that will best serve us.

 Magical Key to Bliss: Let your obstacles guide you toward reawakened joy!

June 17: From pain to joy through music!

One good thing about music, when it hits you, you feel no pain.

~Bob Marley, Jamaican reggae musician and singer-songwriter

We are all connected. While the connections often introduce us to a great deal of love, sometimes they can introduce us to a great deal of pain...pain from being misunderstood, pain from being treated poorly, and pain from a lack of love that leaves us feeling a tremendous loneliness even though we may not be alone. When we experience connections in life that leave us feeling overwhelming waves of pain, there comes a point when it is necessary to figure out a way to disconnect from the source and plug into joy. That is where music comes in. Music is the easiest outlet for spiritual healing. Music has the ability to soothe our souls when they have been wounded. Music has a way of giving hope for a better tomorrow. And when we connect to the kind of music that touches us at our core and hits us, the strength of our spirit is reawakened, and for that moment we no longer feel pain. In time, the shift that happens changes our energy, enabling us to walk away from the connections that harm us and toward those that build us up. And as we continue to move to the place where our spirits feel free again, we happily enter a new dance of joy.

 Magical Key to Bliss: Listen to uplifting music that speaks joy into your soul!

June 18: No one alive is you-er than you are.

Today you are you, that is truer than true. There is no one alive who is You-er than You!

~Dr. Seuss, born Theodor Seuss Geisel, American writer and illustrator of children's books

I woke up this morning, and there I was. Me! One day older, one day wiser. I woke enthusiastic, excited to meet new people and discover something about myself by stretching outside of my comfort zone. I made the decision to take advantage of the opportunities that find me…to get up, get dressed, and look for the magic out there waiting for me. And I made the decision to share my take on my own life lessons with whomever was willing to listen—mantras that have made a huge difference in my life, such as "Follow your bliss," "Ask, believe, receive," "Attitude of gratitude—what are you grateful for?" and "Give love through service." I accept myself just as I am, where I am, ready to be in the world, and proud of the person I have become, flaws and all. Today, I am. I am whatever I decide to be. I am who I am. Truer than true, I realize there is no one alive who can be me! And there is no one alive who can be you! Together, we make up the beautiful canvas of life. Just for today, I will make my choice to be in the moment as I am, letting down my walls and exposing myself and my gifts to the world. I challenge you to do the same. If we all do that, my dear friends, it just has to be good. Soaring together to great heights, seeing so much more as we rise above together!

Magical Key to Bliss: Rejoice and share *you* with the world!

June 19: **Reminder to laugh!**

*I love people who make me laugh. I honestly think it's the thing
I like most—to laugh. It cures a multitude of ills. It's probably
the most important thing in a person.*

~Audrey Hepburn, British actress and humanitarian

Everywhere you look nowadays, the media is offering pictures of doom and gloom. It seems that many in today's society are so overwhelmed by their responsibilities and obligations that they can barely get through the day. Maybe you are one of the many. Before you throw in the towel and give up, figure out a way to bring laughter back into your world. In life there are serious matters that can make you feel out of sorts, but choose to keep a sense of balance and to not lose your sense of humor. Seek out those people who are able to bring a little sunshine back to your days. You will know them when you see them. They fill a room with merriment while rejoicing in the light of laughter. They will help turn your switch from despair to delight. With their infectious guffaws and tittering, their joy will invade your very being. For when laughter returns, you have allowed hope in once again as you choose to let go of some of the heaviness and replace it with love. You will rejuvenate yourself and in return pass on the laughter to others, inviting them to embrace the lighter side of life. Pay it forward in a world that begs for less doom and gloom and more unfettered glee as you remind others how important it is to laugh!

Magical Key to Bliss: Laugh; it is clearly the best medicine!

June 20: Take a leap of kindness.

With one kind gesture you can change a life. One person at a time you can change the world.

~Dr. Steve Maraboli, American author, speaker, and behavioral scientist

You can change the world for the better, and you can do so with the simplest of acts. Knowing that people are fragile, do your best to bring light to another human soul in some way. If you live your life channeling kindness, you will be secure in the knowledge that it will find its way back to you or may even change the world. Sometimes you need to be inspired. Seek out examples of uplifting people whose actions embody the word kindness on a daily basis. You know who they are— the ones who almost always have a smile to share and choose to treat others, no matter who they are, with dignity and respect. When you are in their presence, you feel their warmth; they make you want to be a better person and inspire you. Imitate those people and take a leap of kindness. Start with one person at a time, and be part of a wave of love that you can be proud of. It is the month of joy, so start with one kind gesture, keeping your eyes and heart open to a more beautiful place to live. The magical feeling that you will get in return will be the greatest gift you will receive.

Magical Key to Bliss: Start by being kind to one person at a time, and be part of a wave of love!

June 21: **An invitation to joy.**

I respectfully decline the invitation to join your hallucination.

~Scott Adams, American cartoonist and creator of the *Dilbert* comic strip

Today and every day, decline all invitations in life that keep you in any state of mind other than joy, because joy is the only invitation worthy of your precious time. If others live in a mistaken reality that suffering is the foundation of human existence, choose to say no to this unfounded hallucination. The reality is that when you choose to accept only the invitations to live and experience life through a heart that seeks joy, joy will infuse your world! Accept such invitations, and change the trajectory of your day! When you accept an invitation to joy, you welcome all the wonder that the creative can bring through magical music, delightful dance, and amazing art. When you happily respond to an invitation of love, you alight with all the emotion brought to you through laughter, smiles, and excitement. Joy is everywhere; you are invited to experience it today. Through your connections, breathe it in. See your world as an opportunity, not a burden; as joy, not suffering. Then that kind of world will be your reality, not a figment of your imagination. Open your mind, heart, and soul to the beauty that surrounds, and see your world change. Decline anything to the contrary, and open your life to *joy*!

Magical Key to Bliss: Commit to the following mantra: "I will light up every room I walk into."

June 22: **Stop, connect, breathe, and enjoy the ride.**

I believe we're all put on this planet for a purpose, and we all have a different purpose...When you connect with that love and that compassion, that's when everything unfolds.

~Ellen DeGeneres, American comedian and television host

We are surrounded by so many different beautiful faces. Each time we meet one another, we get a chance to experience the magic and miracles of our connections. When love and compassion are introduced into these encounters, the world opens up to us in an amazing way. The journey will be kinder, the experiences will be more joyous, and the gifts we receive will be more meaningful. We are here with so many other wonderful people wandering through the hills and valleys of life. We don't have to go it alone. We have one another if we are vulnerable enough to reach out and grab the hand to the left and to the right. We need one another. When we reach out, we stand together as beacons of light in an otherwise dark world. When we connect with love and compassion, we share an incredible power that can spread blessings of grace throughout. We all have a purpose in this world. When we realize this and come together in love and compassion, what unfolds has the potential to set off a chain reaction that will be remarkable to witness. So stop, connect, and breathe love and compassion all around you, and remember to enjoy the ride!

 Magical Key to Bliss: Let your life unfold from a place of love and compassion!

June 23: **Don't postpone joy for the future— it is yours today.**

Happiness is emotional, it comes and goes. Joy, on the other hand, is a way of being. It's a choice. I can choose to live my foundation of joy—the joy of being alive.

~Robert White, American executive coach, and author of *Living an Extraordinary Life*

When you start from joy, whatever life brings you today will be lived from that place of being. As you continue on the path of life, you may get caught up in the notion that if you work hard today, you will be able to retire and enjoy life in the future. You may be walking through your days asleep, not experiencing the opportunities that present themselves. The reality is you are guaranteed only the moment that you are living right now. It serves no one when you postpone joy for another day. Simply live in joy minute by minute, not based in plans for what the future may hold. For example, when you take a shower in the morning, be in joy! When you eat your breakfast, lunch, and dinner, be in joy! When you drive home in rush hour traffic, turn on the music, or sit in silence, and be in joy! Life is going on all around you. It does not hurt to put on the rose-colored glasses and see the beauty, joy, and miracles all around. It really is your choice. Even on a rainy day, the weather is offering you an opportunity to enjoy the beauty of nature regardless of whether it may be a little difficult to get around. Make the choice to embrace the joy of being alive while you can!

Magical Key to Bliss: Enjoy being alive today!

June 24: Life is a wondrous, joyful adventure.

The big question is whether you are going to be able to say a hearty yes to your adventure.

~Joseph Campbell, American mythologist, writer, and lecturer

L ife is a big, wonderful adventure. For each one of you, the path to fulfill your destiny awaits. You allow yourself to wholeheartedly go about discovering something new each day. You allow yourself the luxury of liberating your inner happiness by following your bliss. While you may be a frustrated dreamer, when you choose to break out of your routine, life's adventure can play out just the way that it should. You cannot afford to ignore that call to adventure. You cannot afford to ignore the signals to awake. Life is too short to put off what must be done today, thinking that tomorrow is a guarantee. Answer the call. Accept the invitation to go on the greatest adventure to truly experience what is meant for your life. Follow your gut and say yes. Allow yourself the opportunity to break out of the known to connect with the greater consciousness of the unknown. Use your gifts, share your talents, and soar. Greatness arises from ordinary people who respond when called. It is that simple. Start your journey today. Look for the people or angels who will help you on your way. Step by step, the path will unfold before you. Trust. It promises to be the most incredible trip that you will ever take as one by one the blessings will come.

 Magical Key to Bliss: Follow the call and say yes to your adventure!

June 25: **Dream it, wish it, do it!**

All our dreams can come true, if we have the courage to pursue them.

~Walt Disney, American visionary, cartoonist, and animator

Dreaming is as important to the spirit as breathing is to the body. In the physical sense, we need to nurture our bodies by exercising and eating well. In the spiritual sense, we need to get in touch with the passion in our souls that makes living worthwhile. And therein lies the dream. When we are born into this world, our parents have hopes and dreams of greatness for our future. As we start to grow wings, we dream for ourselves and travel through worlds created by our own unique imaginations. We continue to build on the hopes of our parents and the fertile imaginations of our youth. We continue to foster the dreams that were born in our hearts on our first day of life, and we now have the tools to bring those dreams forth into our realities. All we need is the courage to see them through: the courage to step beyond our fears of failure, the courage to meet doubt head on, the courage to pursue the ideas we discover as we enjoy the fantastic world, ready to explore. If we ask, believe, have the courage to act, and begin to receive signs, the life we have imagined can soon be the life we are living. When we start to believe and have faith in all that is possible for us, then we align with the hopes of our parents, the child within, and the adult whose courageous acts of faith allow those dreams to become a reality.

Magical Key to Bliss: Pursue one of your dreams today!

June 26: **Remember what is important to you.**

Things which matter most must never be at the mercy of things which matter least.

~Stephen Covey, American educator, businessman, and speaker

In these times of uncertainty, the challenge is to avoid getting stuck in the fear and worry of the moment. For when fear and worry are present in our lives, the best thing we can do is shift our focus from what scares us toward what is most important. Hold on to what is most important in order to get through times of strife. Things happen all the time. Life is not perfect, and sh*t happens. But it is how we react to what is going on that will determine what kind of outcome we experience. And when we remember and focus on the things that matter most, we have a better chance of not getting lost or being at the mercy of things that matter least. People have egos, people grandstand, and people do things without thinking about the full impact of their actions on others. To a certain extent, we are powerless regarding the choices of others. But remember this: we still have power over how we choose to move forward regardless of another person's poor decisions. Our choices do not have to be at the mercy of others. So take a moment today to focus on what matters most, and continue accordingly. The universe will support all of us if we are clear with ourselves and do not get caught up in unnecessary drama while remembering what is important.

 Magical Key to Bliss: Remember what is most important in your life, and never lose sight of that!

June 27: Discover the joy of cocreating!

Unity is strength…when there is teamwork and collaboration, wonderful things can be achieved.

~Mattie Stepanek, American poet

Working together on a worthy endeavor is probably the most satisfying adventure that you can undertake in life. Where two or more people collaborate on an important task, the resulting accomplishments can be magical. Unity is strength in which many come together to share their talents. One person may be good at organization, while another may be great at innovation. One person may be great at creation, while another may be amazing at presentation. When individuals come together to cocreate, all involved get to discover the joy that comes from combining joint efforts to make something wonderful. No person is an island when it comes to creating. Great ideas evolve when individuals are willing to work together to produce something both amazing and useful. The only way you will ever discover the joy of cocreating is to take the risk of sharing yourself with a team willing to work together with clear focus and expectation in mind. Within this framework, there is no doubt that something wonderful will be achieved.

Magical Key to Bliss: Pick a good team to advance your dreams joyfully!

June 28: Bloom where you are planted.

Be content with what you have; rejoice in the way things are. When you realize there is nothing lacking, the whole world belongs to you.

~Lao Tzu, Chinese philosopher and poet

There is a reason you have been planted in the here and now, in this place and time. Stand rooted in a foundation supported by fertile soil and light, and welcome blessings into your life. Be grateful for the tremendous abundance that you get to experience on a daily basis. Life is the gift; becoming the best person you can be is the only thing expected of you in return. And with this belief that things are perfect the way they are, you experience a sense of freedom to discover the joy in each and every moment. Even with the hardship you may face, and even if you face obstacles along the way, you can still be amazed at the places you get to discover. Even if you find yourself challenged by what appears to be lack or scarcity, you will feel triumphant when you take care to nurture your soul by leading a virtuous existence. You were born with everything you need; you were surrounded by the perfect guides for you. No matter where you find yourself at any given time, believe that you are there for a reason, and embrace the moment. Stand confident in the knowledge that you will be guided to the perfect place to grow; just make the decision to bloom beautifully. And when you feel the momentum that allows you to bloom, smile knowingly because in this perfect moment, the world belongs to you.

 Magical Key to Bliss: Bloom and share with all of us the beauty of your life!

June 29: **Patiently allow the joy to come.**

Even a happy life cannot be without a measure of darkness, and the word happy would lose its meaning if it were not balanced by sadness. It is far better to take things as they come along with patience and equanimity.

~Carl Jung, Swiss psychiatrist and psychotherapist who founded analytic psychology

Thank goodness the sad times are balanced out with the happy times. You may be strong when you first face the storm, but the punishing waves can prove overwhelming if they continue for too long. When the sea of life is too much to take, look for the life raft that is waiting for you. It could be that magical, synchronistic moment when the spiritual world is communicating on the physical plane. Or it could be the loving and kind soul who comes into your life as a guide to remind you that you are loved and that this, too, shall pass. Even in your most difficult moments, don't close up to possibility. Open your soul to allow the good in life to come to you. Open your eyes and be ready; there will always be a life raft waiting for you. Have a patient heart and a persevering spirit; the universe will not abandon you, and good will come again out of the darkness. And when you rise from the ashes of your pain, the happy times will be even that much sweeter. Ah! *La vita e bella*! Ah, life is beautiful! With patience, you allow the joy to come.

Magical Key to Bliss: Be patient; this, too, shall pass into joyful times again!

June 30: Something wonderful is about to happen.

Something wonderful is about to happen!

~Matthew Kelly, Australian motivational speaker and author of *Rediscover Catholicism*

Post this saying on your bathroom mirror. Read it aloud at the beginning of every day. It just brings you into the miracle of living. These words will move you. These words will change you. These words will have you looking for the possibility in your world. There is magic and power in words that inspire enthusiasm. There is excitement in words of optimism that you declare in your life. There is beauty and grace in the idea that you are in the process of becoming the best and most wonderful version of yourself today and every day. If you believe that each day you wake the universe has something exciting and special waiting for you, then your attitude toward every person, place, and thing will change. When you accept the invitation to allow something wonderful to happen, you open your eyes in wonder and engage in what life has in store for you today. Have a beautiful day, and believe that something wonderful is about to happen! And from the joy you have gained, you will find your freedom to thrive!

Magical Key to Bliss: Make a Post-it Note to remind yourself that something wonderful is about to happen.

Chapter Seven: July

FABULOUS FREEDOM

July is the month you celebrate your freedom. This is the month that you get to liberate yourself from the prison of a negative state of mind and surrender to the pursuit of what gives you utter and complete bliss. It is time to break out of routines that no longer serve your spirit. It is time to plug into your calling and go for it. And it is time to claim what is yours and release everything you think is holding you down.

Many countries celebrate their Independence Day in July, and you, too, should consider your own personal independence each day this month. If you feel as though you are not free, instead of lamenting the ways you feel constricted or confined, assess the impediments to your independence and devise a plan for addressing and overcoming them. Perhaps it is a physical, mental, social, or financial restriction that causes you to feel constrained. Whatever it is, have faith that you can transcend it. It might take some effort, diligence, and willpower to make freedom a reality in your life, but trust in the process. As you continue on the journey and embark on the second half of the year, choose to wake up to this beautiful life and embrace the fabulous freedom of leaving the suffering of an unconscious existence behind!

July 1: What do you want to create today?

Life isn't about finding yourself. Life is about creating yourself.

~George Bernard Shaw, Irish playwright and cofounder of the London School of Economics

You are born into this world armed with everything that you need for your journey. Have you just forgotten this and need to be reminded? If that is the case, and you find yourself experiencing the "lost" sensation, perhaps you are just not looking in the right direction. Perhaps, if you focus your mind's eye within, you can finally remember all that you have forgotten. If you set your sights on your talents and your gifts, you will begin to realize that you already have the building blocks to catapult your greatest and wildest dreams into reality. Your tools are there for you to create the greatest vision of yourself possible. Don't deny what you have already been given; why would you do that to yourself, anyway? You are always where you need to be. You are exactly who you need to be! Now, what do you want to create? If life is about creating you, then start there, start now! Do you want to dance, sing, paint, inspire, heal—what is it that sparks the passion within? *You* are the foundation. Look to create more of the awesomeness that is in you just begging to be let out and freed! Simply tap into the source, and you can share it with the world. Get acquainted with the wonderful person you know yourself to be, and ask yourself what you want to create today.

Magical Key to Bliss: Align thought with your soul, and then just create today.

July 2: Be authentically *you!*

You may as well be yourself; everyone else has been taken.

~Oscar Wilde, Irish author, playwright, and poet

Although this statement is extremely humorous, the reality of it remains fundamentally true. Bombarded on a daily basis through the media with images of glamorous superstars and lifestyles, you are encouraged to dream of being anyone other than yourself. You are faced every day with the suggestion that as you are, you are not good enough. With all the external and unnecessary pressures that you place on your life to be something that you perceive the world sees as acceptable, you completely miss out on the big picture and end up totally and completely exhausted in the interim. And what is the big picture? Well, it is really very simple. Be true to yourself no matter what. Follow your heart, follow your own dreams, and just *go for it!* Don't waste your time trying to match up to someone else's expectations of you, chasing after someone else's standards. For this life, God has given you everything you needed the day you entered this world. And you shall have everything to sustain you until the last day you are on this earth. Shine bigger and better, get in touch with your internal spirit, and allow that inner flow to just burst out of you. Express yourself in alignment with all the amazing potential that is waiting to come out. You were planned according to a divine blueprint, so embrace it! You may as well; by embracing all that is you, you give others permission to do the same. Besides, everyone else has already been taken, and thank goodness for that!

Magical Key to Bliss: Choose to see the beauty in the differences.

July 3: Let your inner child see the light of day.

I'm happy to report that my inner child is still ageless.

~James Broughton, American poet

You may worry about time passing and losing your youth and vigor. You may lose hope that change is even possible for you at this late stage of life. You may even think that the door to opportunity to do something amazing has closed. With a small shift, you can return to a time in which magic and flights of fancy were commonplace. And what a delight for all the senses—what a rejuvenating experience this would be. What if you spend your entire life looking for the fountain of youth only to discover that it has been within you all along? As the American poet James Broughton reminds us, "Despite what I might hear to the contrary, the world was not a miserable prison, it was a playground for a nonstop tournament between stupidity and imagination. If I followed the game sharply enough, I could be a useful spokesman for Big Joy" (*Coming Unbuttoned* 1993). So if it is Big Joy that you seek, join the tournament and get into the game. Remember that age should never limit your potential to continue as a seeker, and follow your heart in the direction it leads. For it is true that your inner child is still ageless; sometimes you need to let that inner child out of your self-imposed prison so you can benefit from the beauty that has been there all along. Do not let age stop you from following your passion in life; start looking around with the bright eyes of a child, and see all the opportunity that is there for us all.

Magical Key to Bliss: Start to enjoy the playground of life.

July 4: Let your light shine.

As we let our own light shine, we unconsciously give other people permission to do the same. As we are liberated from our fear, our presence automatically liberates others.

~Marianne Williamson, American spiritual teacher, author, and lecturer

Each of you brings your own special light to this world. You were born with one purpose: to let it shine. The brighter you allow your light to shine in this world, the more incredible will be your influence on others daily. Can you imagine a world where you embrace your gifts and those of others? Can you imagine a world where you encourage others to push past the set point to do and achieve more than you ever believed possible? Can you imagine a world where you set your fears aside and wrap your mind around the reality that you are here for a reason? Each day you are learning from your experiences in life. Each day you are taking every challenge as an opportunity for growth. Each day you stand grateful for the gift that is you. This is your chance to shine your light so brightly that you light up the sky, almost blinding others with love! By shining, you liberate others to free themselves from their own chains that bind. And that is where you will experience a world filled with peace, joy, and love—that is where true freedom resides, that is true liberty, and that is true independence. Happy Fourth of July—shine on and enjoy the fireworks!

Magical Key to Bliss: Liberate yourself from fear, and become the person of your dreams.

July 5: **Freedom lies in choosing to follow your truth.**

God isn't about making good things happen to you, or bad things happen to you. He's all about you making choices—exercising the gift of free will. God wants you to have good things and a good life, but He won't gift wrap them for you. You have to choose the actions that lead you to that life.

~Jim Butcher, American author of *The Dresden Files*

Freedom to make your own choices in life is a beautiful thing. Free will allows you to voluntarily select which decisions to make and what direction to take on your journey. Through the process of discernment, you learn over time which philosophy for life makes sense to you. Then with great conviction you move from an adolescent stage of the process into adulthood, where you better know your own truth. If you do not take the time to study and learn what resonates with you, you will live your life as a victim, stumbling along until your wake-up call shakes you out of an unconscious stupor. And the wake-up call can be the best thing that happens in your life, giving you freedom to figure out your truth and ultimately take action to follow it. You can do this before an alarm goes off. You can turn yourself around, shift your perception, and awaken to a better experience of your reality before emergent circumstances cause you to do so. It's your choice; God wants the world for you. Make your intentions clear, and choose the actions that will lead you to the good life. Freedom lies in choosing to follow your truth! It is ultimately up to you.

Magical Key to Bliss: Free will is yours; choose the good life today.

July 6: Rejoice in the joy that lies before you.

We can complain because rose bushes have thorns or rejoice because thorn bushes have roses.

~Abraham Lincoln, sixteenth president of the United States of America

A rose is a beautiful thing. At the beginning, there is a bud waiting to freely blossom into a masterpiece of nature that is both aromatic and colorful. As it develops, the thorns have a purpose as they protect the stalk so that a glorious presentation can break open and delight all of the senses. If you focus only on the negative aspect of the thorns, you will miss out on the beauty of nature's incredible design. The same thing applies to your life. You are a beautiful person. At the beginning, you are a perfect little baby waiting to learn and freely blossom into an amazing adult who is intelligent and kind. As you develop, each part of you serves the greater purpose as you come into your own and discover your individual calling. If you focus on your flaws for too long, you will miss out on your positive traits, filled with wonderful potential. In life, choose well on what thoughts you decide to dwell. In life, choose well what kind of judgments you make. Be your greatest advocate and ally. Do your best to choose to see everything about you—even though parts are a bit prickly—as a positive. Remember, you are as beautiful as a rose. Everything about you is important to the whole. There is no point in complaining about your thorns when there is so much more to them than meets the eye.

Magical Key to Bliss: Choose to see the beautiful roses today!

July 7: **Be true to yourself.**

When we are true to ourselves, each of us becomes a light for another to follow.

~Nina Wise, American author of *A Big New Free Happy Unusual Life*

Imagine if everyone were true to his or her calling. Imagine if everyone followed the path that provided the most joy. Imagine if people took the time out of the busyness of life to check in on their callings and determine what gives them the most joy. If that happens, get ready to witness a great transformation of this world. People would start to understand what true happiness is. People would start to connect from a profound place of sharing that which is divinely inspired. People would feel the freedom from fear as they choose their own truth in order to serve using their gifts and talents. There would be a lot of bright and shiny people walking around with big smiles on their faces. Their truth would set them free, allowing magic and miracles into their lives. When one person is true to the light in her soul and shines brightly, she can light the way for those who are lucky to be close enough to follow. Your light will travel from one candle to another until eventually the entire world will shine just because you decided to be true to yourself!

Magical Key to Bliss: Light up the world with your smile that comes from knowing your truth!

207

July 8: Set yourself free.

I saw the angel in the marble and carved until I set him free.

~Michelangelo Buonarroti, Italian sculptor, painter, architect, poet, and engineer

Your greatest responsibility in life is to learn to set yourself free. As the artist/sculptor/painter of the greatest masterpiece—*you*—you are tasked each day to get in touch with your beautiful spirit. You need to figure out how to nurture its growth. And when you are ready, you must set it free into the world to make a positive contribution to the whole. Through discernment, you are given the key to opening up the many doorways that will lead you down a path of greater freedom and enlightenment. You are given the magic sculpting tools that help you carve out the greatest sculpture you can ever imagine. You are given the inspiration to think outside of the box, guiding you to wonderful experiences. Tap into your wild side and your inner self to find the will to run free, and then invite someone else to do the same. Let what is weighing you down fall from your shoulders, and nurture your inner artist to do the work that you are here for. Be the Michelangelo of your own life, and with the help of your angels, unleash whatever is worthy of your beautiful life—for you have everything you need within you! Before you know it, you will be free!

Magical Key to Bliss: Get in touch with who you really are, and set him/her free!

July 9: **Choose to keep your soul alive.**

To know what you prefer, instead of humbly saying Amen to what the world tells you that you ought to prefer, is to have kept your soul alive.

~Robert Louis Stevenson, Scottish novelist, poet, and essayist

Why would you give your choices away so willingly when you can live the life you prefer? With courage, you can take a stand. You are given a wonderful mind that can examine life as it comes. You are given feelings that allow your body to assist with the decision-making process. You are a thinker, a feeler, and an amazing spirit. When you educate yourself with an open mind, you can make a true evaluation as to what life presents and proceed accordingly in the direction of your dreams. It is only then that you will come into your own. By getting to know yourself better, you safeguard what makes you soar. Embrace what you prefer in this life and go with it. Balance the concerns of others, leaning toward the yearnings of your soul, and you will feel more alive than you ever thought possible. When there are things you do not understand in life, don't defer to those you consider authorities. Gain a deeper and more abundant understanding, holding onto your aspirations by relying on your own understanding. Listen, process, engage, and find your flow by asserting your own preferences, and you will boldly rediscover the path that is meant just for you. Choose to keep your soul alive; go forth and surely you will set the world on fire.

Magical Key to Bliss: Allow yourself to choose your bliss!

July 10: **There is no greater freedom than awareness.**

Action without vision is only passing time, vision without action is merely day dreaming, but vision with action can change the world.

~Nelson Mandela, South African anti-apartheid revolutionary and president of South Africa

We run from one place to another, sometimes with a checklist in mind—not thinking, not stopping, no vision; perhaps just passing time. Consciousness falls by the wayside. We move from one point in time to another, from one place to another, moving without direction, acting without thought. What is it that we truly need in this life? Always in a hurry, we will never know. When we slow down and enter into a state of awareness, we start to notice what our souls yearn for. There is a shift. Then life starts to change. We stop, share a smile, and acknowledge the existence of another. We acknowledge our daydreams and think about the next steps to realize them fully. If we are free, we must be able to articulate a plan that is different from the chaotic one we currently subscribe to. For without the chaos, we invite a new paradigm that will give our lives a peaceful tone, a compelling meaning, and enlightened action. Without the chaos, we can really experience life. Action with vision can change our own world—perhaps the whole world. We will no longer be passing time, scurrying along. We will have greater awareness as to which direction to take, and there is no greater chance at freedom than that.

Magical Key to Bliss: Reflect on your vision of life, and choose well the actions to take.

July 11: The power of positive doing.

Whatever our path, whatever the color or grain of our days,
whatever riddles we must solve to stay alive, the secret of life
somehow always has to do with the awakening and freeing of
what has been asleep.

~Mark Nepo, American poet and philosopher

It is time to *wake up*! Not just wake up your body to function on a daily basis and get by but wake up your inner spirit to fly. Instead of crawling along at a belabored pace, you can soar effortlessly with a miraculous view of the world. Have you ever looked up in the sky to see the birds gliding totally in line with their purpose that has allowed them to thrive? This is the freedom that you seek: one that does not seek permission or demand for you to be something that you are not. Seek out the people who soar like the birds and have taken the risk to leap into the beauty that is theirs. Find examples in the positive ones so you can benefit from their wisdom. With these examples, you are encouraged to free yourself from your slumber. Positive thinking alone is not enough; it is the positive doing in your waking moments that is the key to making the shift possible. Flock with the positive doers, and this could be the first step to awakening the transformation of your inner spirit and freeing what has been asleep. The positive ones are the company you want to keep because there is a reason birds of a feather flock together successfully!

Magical Key to Bliss: Wake up and join the freedom!

July 12: **Be a person with a vision and manifest your destiny!**

You, a person with a vision, are like a pebble in a stream, moving ever outward to infinity, impacting on all who come into contact with the ripple.

~Dr. Wayne Dyer, American self-help author and motivational speaker

Live your life with intention. Set out to face the world with a clear vision. Take the time to set out your heart's greatest desires, and step into your life with the knowledge that your purpose is aligned with your soul. Be intentional as to what you allow into your consciousness. If it is success you seek, then believe you are already a success. If it is love you seek, then know that you are the embodiment of all that is love. If it is freedom you seek, then release your spirit from fear to allow yourself to be free. By holding strong to your beautiful vision of your life, pay attention to all that manifests around you as a direct or indirect result of your perseverance. You may think you are but a drop in the ocean of life; however, the impact a drop has on the rest of that vast body of water is undeniable. You are important, your vision is important, and your life is important. As my beautiful friend Nina Vivenzio so eloquently stated, "How funny the impact you can have on one another. All life is in the meeting." Make no mistake: your vision will benefit others. Make no mistake: your kindness is the foundation of life. Make no mistake: your compassion heals. Know this and live this, and every day will hold magic to manifest amazing things!

 Magical Key to Bliss: Manifest your beautiful vision, and create in union with your divinity!

July 13: Artistic freedom to be discovered!

Every life is a piece of art, put together with all means available.

~Pierre Janet, French psychologist and philosopher

Your life unfolds freely each day. Like a beautiful painting, you are the artist who painstakingly takes the time to create something that you can be proud of. You gather the tools that allow you to develop a portrait that is both intelligent and visually captivating. You take the time to focus on what it is that you want to come alive on the canvas. You then surrender to the universe and allow the uplifting energy to infuse all that you do. You are constantly at work meticulously adding details to what was once a blank sheet of possibility. There is so much potential in you; there is so much to be explored as it unfolds. Each step of the process, you make use of every resource that you can find. Each stage of the journey, you have the chance to free the artist within so that you can go in the direction of your dreams. Every life is a piece of art. You are the artist who has the distinct pleasure of engaging your freedom to develop a vision for your own masterpiece. As you do, you will put together a rendition of a beautiful life that you will be proud of and grateful for. Everyone will be inspired by the artistic freedom that you have discovered.

Magical Key to Bliss: Create your life artistically, freely, and openly!

July 14: Focus on the big picture!

When you let go of your expectations, when you accept life as it is, you're free. To hold on is to be serious and uptight. To let go is to lighten up.

~Richard Carlson, PhD, American author of *Don't Sweat the Small Stuff...and It's all Small Stuff*

While most of us start our day with the highest of expectations, sometimes things just don't work out the way that we would like. Sometimes people disappoint us by not acting in a fair way, and sometimes we disappoint others by doing the same. Instead of letting go of that thing that bothers us most or asking for forgiveness, we have a tendency to ruminate over and over again, turning a small event into something that takes over a significant part of our lives. What we could have just discarded as inconsequential or a misunderstanding we hold on to, allowing it to become something so much bigger that it steals our serenity for a long time to come. Because each life moment is precious, we need to keep in mind the bigger picture. When we consciously accept things that are out of our control and let go of the result, even when things go wrong, we are free. Ruminating over something that has happened in the past is to be serious and uptight, and simply put, it is self-abuse. We can lighten up by focusing on the big picture; then all the ridiculous minutiae just fall away because we are no longer allowing ourselves to be deterred from the bigger plan that is our life.

 Magical Key to Bliss: Let go of the pettiness and let in the love!

July 15: Question what you do not understand.

Following the path of the heart requires surrender. Surrender doesn't mean giving up, but yielding to something much greater. It's an exquisite experience if we can find the courage to do it.

~Barbara DeAngelis, American author and relationship consultant

Curiosity keeps us from getting bored; it pushes us past our fears and opens doors to tremendous potential and possibility. As long as we stay curious, we will seek out opportunities that will take us on a hero's journey to discover new people, different cultures, beautiful places, and wonderful new concepts. Curiosity keeps our minds sharp as our interest in the new and intriguing peaks. And eventually, curiosity will lead us to enlightenment. When we question what we don't understand, we grow and follow the path of the heart. And when we follow the path of the heart, we are free to experience the world and embrace our curious nature while we ward off complacency and routine. By surrendering to this curiosity, we yield to something much greater, more creative, and more stimulating for our imaginations. While some of us are stuck in a rut and afraid to question the changes that our curious nature requires, we can remember our childhood dreams and become rejuvenated with the great freedom that desire yields. As we grow from an innate courage that reignites the call to adventure, we surrender to the light within and become seekers of our truth once again.

Magical Key to Bliss: Be passionately curious today!

July 16: You are more than enough!

You have brains in your head. You have feet in your shoes.
You can steer yourself in any direction you choose. You're on
your own, and you know what you know. And you are the guy
who'll decide where to go.

~Dr. Seuss, born Theodor Seuss Geisel, American writer
and illustrator of children's books

You are worthy, and you will beam. Accept this, and you are free to use all your gifts to move in the direction of your dreams. You are perfect just as you are. There is no one who can replace your brilliant rising star. Look in a mirror and repeat over and over again that you will not change to fit in. You are pure joy; believe it, and you will win. Know that your intuition will guide you well. Be confident when you pursue your calling in life. You will do what is necessary to follow your true north. Embrace the fact that you are the one who decides how to direct your vision henceforth. Your choices will build the solid foundation that will allow you to keep moving ahead. So do yourself a favor: don't play small and lose your cred. Go big and accept yourself once and for all. Go ahead and seize the day, and stand tall. The challenge is to just accept that you are here to thrive. What are you waiting for? It is time to come alive! The day you were born was a great moment in time. You be the person who will decide where you want to go—and shine, baby, shine. You are a miracle, and that is more than enough. It is time to throw off the imaginary handcuffs and show your stuff.

Magical Key to Bliss: Accept the truth that you rock!

July 17: **Forgiveness frees the spirit.**

Anger makes you smaller, while forgiveness forces you to grow beyond what you were.

~Cherie Carter-Scott, American author

Dreaming allows us to hope. Dreaming allows us to believe that the impossible is possible. Dreaming is the dress rehearsal for the reality that can be ours. Sometimes, however, we, ourselves, can be the biggest obstacle to our dreams being realized. When we allow ourselves to harbor anger, envy, or resentment, we block the free movement of energy toward a more glorious present and future. When we do this, we prevent our dreams as we allow the past to stop us from becoming all that we are meant to be.

Remember that what is done is done; you cannot change what has happened by going over it again and again in your head. But with the power of forgiveness—asking for and receiving it—you can release the heavy burden on your heart and soul. Each day is a new day to ask forgiveness.

If we identify the people and moments in time that can be healed, and then practice forgiveness, our spirit will be freed once again. Forgiving ourselves and others is the greatest act of love and kindness. When we forgive or ask for forgiveness, we open the door to discovering our own beauty as a person and start moving in the directions of our dreams again, growing beyond what we were.

 Magical Key to Bliss: Release the burden of past missteps; forgive yourself and others.

July 18: **Break out of the cage.**

The first step toward success is taken when you refuse to be a captive of the environment in which you first find yourself.

~Mark Caine, American writer

Your actions and choices today have a direct impact on your tomorrows. You can refuse to stay wherever you find yourself here and now if it is not for you. You are not trapped in any kind of environment. There is always a way to extricate yourself from any situation. The cage has a door. Figure out a way to open it, and step outside where the freedom lies. Life is a process of hits and misses. To figure out what works for you, you need to play the game of trial and error. As you take the first step toward any success, you get to decide what, how, and where you want to create. Start out by repeating to yourself the mantra that personal trainer and aerobics instructor extraordinaire Kevin Creegan would reiterate over and over again: "Create yourself a beautiful day." When you do so, life won't happen to you; you will happen to life! You are not a captive of the environment in which you first find yourself. If you do not like it, then it is time to make some significant changes. Break out of the cage and feel the freedom of choice pushing you along. Then get ready to march to the beat of an incredible new song.

Magical Key to Bliss: Make some significant changes to live a freer life today!

July 19: **Accept and move on.**

We cannot change anything until we accept it. Condemnation
does not liberate; it oppresses.

~Carl Jung, Swiss psychiatrist and psychotherapist who
founded analytic psychology

There is magic in accepting those things that we cannot change.
There is a tremendous sense of freedom in that place of release.
The acceptance frees us to move forward into a future unburdened by
resentment or regret. The acceptance allows us to stop punishing ourselves over and over again for things that have already happened. The
acceptance of where we are right here and now allows us to be present,
unhindered by our self-imposed shackles. We sometimes steadfastly remain with the ghosts of the past because they are what we know. And
what is known feels safe for a limited time. But in the holding on to what
is safe, we lock ourselves in our own self-imposed cell that prevents real
growth in our life. It is in the acceptance, forgiveness, and release that
we can liberate ourselves from self-sabotage. It is in the acknowledgment
that we cannot change what has happened that we are free to experience
the amazing grace that awaits us on the inside. Judgment and a closed
mind lock us into a cycle of condemnation. The magic of accepting is
the precise ingredient we need to experience real change and ultimately
feel alive. So what are we waiting for? We must accept what we see before us and confirm that it is time to move on, oppressed no more!

 Magical Key to Bliss: Condemn yourself no more; now is the
time to be free of judgments.

July 20: **Magnificent me!**

When you realize your own magnificence, you will only attract magnificence into your life, if you believe in things like "like attracts like," then the absolute best way to attract what's best for you is to love yourself to the point where you are filled with love, and will only attract to your life everything that confirms this belief about yourself.

~Anita Moorjani, Indian motivational speaker and author of *Dying to Be Me*

Start today, repeating over and over again that you are magnificent. The mere fact that you were created in an instant should convince you. You are splendid in appearance, majestic in spirit, and exceptionally impressive. You are made of love, and to love is why you are here. Fill yourself up with this understanding, and you will start to attract everything that confirms the gloriousness of your presence. You will make a difference in this world when you believe that everything from your head to your toes is made up of a magnificent energy that needs to be shared. You are here on this soul's journey for a greater purpose. You need to accept your magnificence so that you are free to attract others who embrace their magnificence as well. So believe it. Feel it. Know it! You are not doing yourself any favors by believing otherwise. It is freeing to set aside negative critique and just openly embrace knowing your own magnificence, inviting others to do the same.

Magical Key to Bliss: Be magnificent in all that you do today!

July 21: Empower your present with memories of the past!

I've never tried to block out the memories of the past, even though some are painful. I don't understand people who hide from their past. Everything you live through helps to make you the person you are now.

~Sophia Loren, Italian film actress

Instead of yearning to relive your yesterdays, be grateful for the tools that you have learned to help you embrace the potential in your present. Instead of blocking painful memories of the past, appreciate the gifts of compassion that will help you approach life from a different perspective. Instead of yearning for a time where you did not know pain, give thanks for the courage you have mustered to move past it and continue to dream. Your fond memories remind you of loved ones who have left their distinct mark on your heart. Your challenging memories remind you that you can get through the most difficult circumstances. When you are grateful for both the profound highs and the difficult lows, you empower yourself with acceptance. By not getting stuck in the negative, you become stronger and more liberated to enjoy the present, in which you will have more opportunities to meet amazing people and encounter a world of such amazing things. When you build on the positive frequencies of your memories, you decide to live your life from a place of strength. Embrace the joy of everything you have lived through; your reward will be an even greater love for life along the way.

Magical Key to Bliss: Smile because you understand that everything has a purpose in your life!

July 22: Free your mind to believe in possibility!

I'm trying to free your mind, but I can only show you the door. You're the one who has to walk through it.

~Morpheus, from the movie *The Matrix*, written by Lana and Andy Wachowski

Why must we punish ourselves with sabotaging thoughts? What will it take for us to free ourselves from our own self-imposed mental slavery? Can we use our imagination to free our minds and connect with the love in our hearts to liberate our lives? Why not take a chance and try it. Stand up straight and imagine releasing the weight of the world off your shoulders. Feel lighter and give love. Open your eyes and see the many doors just waiting to be opened to offer us a different path on the journey. Look around and see other individuals as cocreators with you. Feel lifted and receive love. The mind aligned with optimism is a powerful tool. A heart filled with love is even more commanding. When the mind is coupled with the heart, this combination is something to behold. Obstacles fade away. Negativity subsides. And possibilities spring anew. We can make the choice to free our minds to believe in the potential that we know in our hearts. The door is right in front of us, but that door can only be shown to us; it is ultimately our decision whether to walk through it. So what is it going to be? If we free our minds to believe in the possibility of wonderful things to come, the rest will follow. There is gentle salvation when we allow our minds to be free from the chains that bind as we connect to the love that awaits us.

 Magical Key to Bliss: Free your mind to believe in possibility!

July 23: The sky is the limit as long as you believe.

If you bring forth what is within you, what you bring forth will save you. If you do not bring forth what is within you, what you do not bring forth will destroy you.

~Gospel of Thomas, *Holy Bible, King James Edition*

There is a calling in your soul to set your creative essence free. Today will you answer the call? There is that small voice in your head telling you daily to chase your dreams so fast that you surpass them. Today will you listen to that voice? There is that beautiful music of love and life in your very being that needs to be played to allow your incredible gifts to flourish. Today will you play that music? Let it be said that the happiest people in the world are those who live life simply, acknowledging with gratitude their blessings and welcoming with love the path that begs to be followed when they honor that which is within. As you decide to bring forth what is within you and wholeheartedly step on that path, you make the decision to save yourself today and every day. When you answer the call, listen to your heart's voice, and gloriously play your very own music, the incredible symphony and dance of life evolve right before your eyes. Release the negative patterns of self-sabotage and punishing behavior that only look to destroy you. Replace them with positive patterns of self-love and worthiness, and you will rise up again. The sky is the limit.

Magical Key to Bliss: Set yourself free into a world where there are infinite possibilities!

July 24: Simply a reflection from within.

Everyone and everything that shows up in our life is a reflection of something that is happening inside of us.

~Alan Cohen, American businessman

If you could imagine the life you want, wouldn't you imagine wonderful things? If you spent your time focusing on realizing your deepest desires, would you begin to believe they were possible? If you placed your attention on those things that spoke of your great beauty and talent, would you start to believe and have confidence in yourself again? If life is simply a reflection of those thoughts you most focus on, wouldn't you be more careful of what you repeat over and over again to yourself? Believe that you can influence your external world by placing your focus on images of love, kindness, and joy, and you will truly be surprised by what you attract. If you live in consciousness regarding what is happening within you, you will have the grand opportunity to create what is happening around you in a more remarkable and enjoyable way. Let it be said that a person who feels good on the inside will experience that good on the outside. A person who looks at life with a glass-half-full mentality will eventually have their cup running over. Your world is but a mirror of what is happening inside of you. So before you start your day, promise yourself that you will take a moment or two to reflect on what you are grateful for, thus charging those positive emotions. When you simply start with a reflection of that joyous place within, your own something wonderful will most likely show up.

 Magical Key to Bliss: Reflect on freeing joy into your life, and you will find it.

July 25: Keep your eyes facing the rising sun!

You are never too old to set another goal or to dream a new dream.

~C. S. Lewis, British novelist

Each decade marks an evolution in a life. And with the passing of each, you have the opportunity to grow. As you assess the lessons you have learned, you are able to revisit your dreams, perhaps let go of those you have outgrown, and embrace new ones that will allow you to shine your gifts for all to see. While you are on your journey, you will grow weary if you focus on regret for having made some significant mistakes along the way. But be sure that if you keep facing the rising sun each new morning, you will not get stuck in the past. The point is to live this life with all the ups and downs. The point is to wake each day and forgive yourself for the error of your ways. The point is to set another goal to do better the next time around as you appreciate the beauty that you have found. So when you let the sun set on your past and dream well of a present that you can get excited about, you give yourself permission to let go of the pain and embrace the joy of possibility that *is* there. Remember that you can't move forward toward your dreams and toward the life that is yours if you remain in the past. Each day is a chance to consciously make the decision to step into the glory that is to come, and as long as you are alive, you are never too old to do so!

Magical Key to Bliss: Allow your spirit to rise with the hope of a new dawn.

July 26: **Onward, freedom to create a new ending!**

Hey-guess what: You're the only creature with free will. How does that make you feel?

~Kurt Vonnegut, American writer, humorist, and author of *Slaughterhouse-Five*

Be grateful for the knowledge that you do not have to go back and change what has occurred in the past. For, alas, you cannot. What truth you must live is to start today and make the changes necessary to fulfill your dreams, live your passions, and dwell in a place of love and goodness. You have free will. Imagine, just because you woke this morning, you get this chance, this magical golden ticket, to do what's right for you. You cannot change the past; it does you no good to have regrets. You shall make the choice to live a glorious present that impacts a more magnificent future. Just today. Just now. Just because you can. And even if your past is peppered with behaviors that you are not proud of, you know there is much you can be grateful for. Everything that has happened has folded into who you are today, and for all intents and purposes, it is good; it is divine. So with the beautiful community of energy you share with so many, you step into your life once again. Ready to write the next chapter as you go, and with grace, make the choice to embark on whatever the day holds with an attitude of tremendous gratitude. Acknowledging your blessings, you can repeat the three essential prayers in the title of writer Anne Lamott's inspirational book—*Help, Thanks, Wow.*

 Magical Key to Bliss: Start from now; you are free to make a brand-new ending.

July 27: You be you!

To thine own self be true, and it must follow, as the night the day, thou canst not then be false to any man.

~William Shakespeare, English poet, playwright, and actor

No truer words were ever uttered: be true to you. It is so important that you walk through your life guided by your own internal compass. For, if you do not, you may lose yourself while looking for an external map that does not exist. Never let it be said that you don't know right from wrong or that you must rely on another to truly understand how to live your best life. If you remain true to your own self, you will be sure to take the next step to thrive. When you are connected to your internal source, you will uncover what you need to learn at exactly the perfect moment in time. It is when you think that you must become someone other than yourself that madness has the potential to set in. You were intended to be exactly who you are. It is imperative that you get in touch with exactly who that is. Life will give you many experiences to discover your own internal beauty and richness. It is your job to take advantage of those opportunities and learn the amazing lessons through the experiences set out before you. Make the decision today for you to be you! Putting on false masks to hide from the world serves no higher purpose. It just hinders the greatness that resides inside of you waiting to get out.

Magical Key to Bliss: Remember today: to thine own self be true; none other is more unique and miraculous than you!

July 28: **Constrain yourself no more.**

If our lives appear impoverished, the fault lies not in our lives but in our lack of awareness. Looking more deeply, however, we come to understand that we cannot blame our awareness alone, for it is not awareness that is at fault but the constraints we have placed on expression.

~Nina Wise, American author of *A Big New Free Happy Unusual Life*

Magical. The world is magical if you choose to have faith and believe it. Mysterious. Your life is a beautiful mystery begging to be discovered. Stop constraining your experience. Relax into it. Look around and see with your whole being. Once you begin to allow awareness to permeate your soul, you tap into the miraculous. And once you tap into the miraculous, you are one with the world. Release your preconceptions to renew a sense of freedom. Life is felt with the heart. Life is being inspired. Choose to really get in touch with a greater consciousness. Shift your perception. You cannot see the air you breathe, but it is there. You feel the cool breeze that signals a change in seasons. You cannot see the bonds that tie you to another, but the energy is there. You cannot see the spirit of another, but the love is there. You cannot see the richness of this world, but in your heart you know that the opportunity to discover remains always at your fingertips. Magical. It all is really magical. To believe anything less only serves to deter you from the riches laid out before you. Be prepared to free your mind so that you can watch the magic unfold that will take you to a place of higher awareness, constrained no more.

Magical Key to Bliss: Believe that life is magical, and behold what lies behind the obvious!

July 29: Come with me and fly, won't you?

Come with me
And you'll be
In a world of
Pure imagination
Take a look
And you'll see
Into your imagination

~From the song "Pure Imagination," *Willie Wonka and the Chocolate Factory*, written by Leslie Bricusse and Anthony Newley

The world we all live in is filled with pure imagination. You can grab a book, listen to a song, watch a sunrise, or just sit in stillness and imagine. Venturing into this world is the important work of your life. To sit in a safe place where you allow the hand of God, higher power, or profound energy to touch your life is inspiring. Just allowing whatever comes through you to attach to a page, a canvas, or a screen is uplifting. What is born in your mind becomes a masterpiece of fantasy when you open your eyes. Take some time each day and try not to let resistance distract you. Imagine this world as a place where dreamers can channel from the depths of their soul, artists can engage you with colors, writers can inspire you to travel to places you have never been, and innovators dare to grab onto illusion to create a new and amazing reality. So come, won't you? And perhaps through your own imagination, you can transform yourself into a beautiful butterfly and take flight, seeing this world in a new way—the world is begging for you to do it!

Magical Key to Bliss: Travel into a world of imagination and free yourself to fly!

July 30: Stay interested, and take it all in.

Develop interest in life as you see it; in people, things, literature, music—the world is so rich, simply throbbing with rich treasures, beautiful souls, and interesting people. Forget yourself.

~Henry Miller, American writer

Your story unfolds as you wake up and live your script that is channeled through you daily. You become the author and willing recipient of a life mixed with reality and creative fascination. You stand captive to inspiration's overwhelming presence as you capture all that is interesting with arms wide open. You have this one opportunity to become who you are meant to be, to learn what you are meant to learn, and to share all that you are meant to share. Will you allow fear to take hold and keep you firmly rooted in what you know, never traveling farther than your comfort zone will allow? Or better yet, will you dare to break out of your shell and gather the courage to take risks, betting on the chance that the payoff will be amazing? Look around, friends, at the richness the world has to offer. Don't be distracted by those things meant to deter you from your own greatness. Breathe deeply and take it all in with love and laughter. Let its essence touch your spirit and penetrate your very being. Most of all, each day, embrace your story as it unfolds, stay interested, and revel in the beauty that each of you will discover.

 Magical Key to Bliss: Develop a crazy, awesome interest in your life and all it has to offer.

July 31: **Freedom to be!**

Our role in life is to bring the light of our own souls to the dim places around us.

~Joan Chittister, Benedictine nun, author, and speaker

If the journey is to be gratifying, you, the traveler, must be authentic in all that you do. Enlightenment no longer has to be hard earned, once you finally decide to wake up and just be you! Rise and shine; now is your time. You have come so far only to realize that you are perfect just as you are. In a world that may tell you otherwise, you can stand strong against all lies. Your brilliant light must shine for the universe to see; all you have to do is declare, "I am free to be me!" No more excuses, and no more fear. Isn't this what you have been dying to hear? Your turn has come; it is now up to you. Your soul is begging for its light to come through. Ask yourself this before you start this day: are you ready to brighten up someone else's way? Darkness does exist; you may have even experienced it for a time. You are now aware, and with glee, it is your turn to shine. What does this look like? You are the only one who knows. Whatever it is, you must start to glow. With the freedom to be, welcome to a new page in your life. You can live an existence that is based on love, not strife. Please, please, please let your life's work and calling come true; your role in this life is for you to be you!

Magical Key to Bliss: Remember to live authentically because you are fabulous and free!

Chapter Eight: August

A CELEBRATION OF FRIENDSHIP

August is the last month of summer before school starts up again and work gets back into full swing. This makes August a particularly important month to spend time with friends and family. In Europe, most companies shut down for the entire month of August, preferring to save the energy costs of air conditioning their urban offices, while most workers retreat to the countryside or the beaches for some rest and relaxation. Americans can learn a lesson from this European way of life; we often don't take that time out to just enjoy ourselves and spend time with our loved ones. We are always running, from one place to another, never stopping to smell the roses.

Renamed in honor of the first Roman emperor, Augustus Caesar, in 8 BC, August derives from the Latin root *augere*, which means to increase. In August, we can seize the opportunity to make lasting memories as we commit to increasing the time we spend celebrating the important friendships in our lives by spending more quality moments together. As the summer comes to a close, and the lazy days come to an end, throw a party for your closest friends and family, or plan an impromptu vacation with them. To celebrate your friendships and relationships, you have to make time to spend with them, no matter how hard it may seem to do so. In August, sip the lemonade, bask in the sun, and enjoy the last few days of your break in celebration of your friendships that make life well worth living.

August 1: A toast to true friends!

Here's a toast to someone who's truly a best friend—a person who goes around telling good things behind your back.

~Elmer Pasta, Author of *Complete Book of Roasts, Boasts & Toasts*

On *The Magical Road to Bliss*, what you need in life are true friends: those beautiful people who know you well, faults and all, and love you no matter what; those beautiful people in your life who are there for you in the good times *and* the bad, claiming you no matter what. Those beautiful people who, instead of gossiping about you behind your back, speak highly of you with no benefit to themselves and honor you no matter what. Good friends make life a rich experience. How beautiful language can be when you recognize that your words can send such positive and profound energy farther than you can ever know. So in an act of love for those beautiful people who are your true friends, let's remember to be one and join in a toast. A toast to those in your life who, given the chance, tell the world how amazing you are. A toast to those in your life who, given the chance, will give you the benefit of the doubt and defend your character to others. And finally, a toast to those who, given the chance, use their words about you as a way to convey a great love shared by someone who is truly a best friend.

Magical Key to Bliss: Reach out to a good friend and toast to your friendship!

August 2: **Forever connected.**

Friendship is born at that moment when one person says to another, "What! You too? I thought I was the only one."

~C. S. Lewis, British novelist

Thank goodness we are not alone in this world. There are so many people walking this earth that the opportunities to make friends and connections are endless. It is so important that we become vulnerable to those connections, reach out to another, and welcome new friends in our lives. God speaks through each one of us through our friends. A higher power speaks through our friends. An amazing energy works through all of us as we recognize that our friends are truly angels in our lives. A party of one is no way to live when there are so many others we can invite to join us. When we extend an invitation of inclusivity, what we get in return will be opportunities to boost our endorphins and light our way. By being open and loving to those around us, we look for the similarities in our paths and choose to laugh together and, in some cases, cry as well. Everyone has joys and struggles; life is easier when we get to share both. When we know that we have a hand to hold as we search for our solutions, it is so much easier to move forward confidently and courageously. There is healing in conversations between friends. When we accept the invitation to grow in a deeper relationship with others, we realize that we are not the only one going through tough times, and that alone can brighten our day.

Magical Key to Bliss: Make a new friend today!

August 3: Friendship makes the world go round.

Friendship takes time and energy if it's going to work. You can luck into something great, but it doesn't last if you don't give it proper appreciation. Friendship can be so comfortable, but nurture it—don't take it for granted.

~Betty White, American actress and comedian

Friends are the people who keep us grounded when we lose our way. Friends are the people who support us no matter what, even when we feel like we are going it alone. Friends are the people we get to choose in this life to share our joys, struggles, laughter, and tears. Friends are those who make this life more meaningful and more bearable at the same time. How lucky we are when we find a friend who accepts us just as we are, especially when we are not behaving well. How lucky we are that so many lovely people we call friends make life richer, fuller, and more beautiful. There are so many beautiful people who hold us at our lowest points with love, celebrate with us at our highest, and hold memories of times gone by. Friendship does take work. We need to water the plants of life if we want to see them flourish. But in the end, the energy and effort that we put into our greatest assets will come back to us twofold and make life that much more satisfying. Take the advice of a seasoned actress as set out above: each of our bonds with another person is invaluable. Every friend that we make is a gift for a more wonderful present and future.

Magical Key to Bliss: Be grateful for those friends who are blessings; tell them you love them!

August 4: Build a beautiful friendship!

You just don't luck into things as much as you'd like to think that you do. You build step by step, whether it's friendships or opportunities.

~Barbara Bush, former first lady of the United States of America

Friendships are built step by step. You meet someone you really like. You discover that you have similar interests and perhaps even similar acquaintances. You invite the other to spend time with you, and you get to know her better. You make memories, share dreams, support each other, and celebrate together. And over time, you develop a strong bond that becomes a part of you. Whether your friendship started from childhood, from high school, from college, or later, these connections are not put together by chance—although you may feel very lucky for having met. These kindred spirits come into your life and are nurtured by time, attention, vulnerability, and care. These relationships are blessings that enhance your life because these individuals took the risk and chose to get close. Seasons of your life change starting with autumn, as does the desire to shed old masks. When winter comes, your friendships will bring you warmth as the cold sets in. And when you are ready, they will help you spring into a new life. Then, time to enjoy ties of love and support as you enjoy the summer fun with those who have stood by your side. All seasons of a friendship allow you to build, step by step, a beautiful life.

Magical Key to Bliss: Call a friend, and tell her how much she means to you!

238

August 5: Find the happy ones, and enjoy the trip!

What a long strange trip it's been.

~Jerry Garcia, American musician

You want to be around happy people. You know who they are, those people who giggle, dance, sing, hum, and even prance through their day. The kind of happiness they are experiencing is contagious. You almost want to apologize if you complain around them lest you disturb the incredible energetic buzz that they display. Not that they don't have their share of problems; they just choose to see the silver lining. They choose to see the beauty on a rainy day. They choose love that drives the hate away. They choose to lift others up and to rise when they fall. They choose to be happy in spite of it all. On this long, strange trip, which you get to experience as you take your yearly trips around the sun, wouldn't it be better to travel with happy people by your side? Wouldn't it be better to learn from them as they choose to look at the bright side of life rather than at the darkness? Wouldn't it be better to invite them to show you a different way of looking at the world? You want to be around happy people because you want to own the happiness that already resides within. And the happy ones, the charming gardeners of souls, will remind you how to do that by their example. So find the happy ones, and wherever you are on your long, strange trip, you may just enjoy it a whole lot more.

Magical Key to Bliss: Go to where the happy people are!

August 6: Friends are beautiful blessings!

I just thank God for all of the blessings.

~James Brown, American singer and dancer

I f you have good friends, you know these beautiful people can make all the difference in your life. They offer solace when you are sad. They often cheer you on when wonderful things happen as well. But most of all, they offer you the love and support that you need to feel connected. Although you may feel lonely at times, with true friends by your side, you know that you are never alone. Good friends are such a blessing, often promoting and contributing to your happiness. If you are blessed with beautiful friendships, you know that you must express your tremendous gratitude. Before it is too late, it is imperative that your friends know how much they mean to you. Although there may be times that distance keeps you apart, the bond formed between kindred spirits will always be close to your heart. From shared moments and fond memories, you have the evidence you need to truly know that love exists in this world. True friends will never let you down and will show you how much they care. They tell it like it is and are likely to give you a boost when you need it most. As the late Hina Askari stated so eloquently, a true friend will tell you when "it is time to put on your sunglasses and get moving B*&%$!" Friends really are beautiful blessings!

 Magical Key to Bliss: Thank God for all of the blessings that good friends bring to your life.

August 7: Because you don't have to go this life alone.

I wrote your name in my heart, and forever it will stay.

~Rumi, thirteenth-century poet and Sufi mystic

Look around. Take it all in. Instead of feeling separate from your surroundings, feel connected. There are the trees that provide a canopy of shade for you. There is the sun that provides nourishment with vitamin D for you. There is the breeze that offers you a simple caress. There is the water that hydrates you inside and out. Then there are the people who cross your path every day. These individuals are seemingly strangers at first; however, walls are broken down with a shared smile. They share beautiful energy by virtue of kind and gentle words. Acknowledging that you are seen, a friend's embrace offers support when you need it most. Their names are written on your heart that will forever stay. Dance, dream, and simply rejoice in the magnificence that you get the opportunity to experience. Hold out your hands, and in gratitude, grab onto whatever positive guide comes along today. For your courage to move forward is rewarded. Imprinted on your soul is the understanding that you don't have to go this life alone. That understanding offers you the strength to transform into a "Michelangelo-esque" masterpiece. An amazing creation for all to see!

Magical Key to Bliss: Write your name on someone's life today!

August 8: Make it a habit to rest when you are weary.

Rest when you're weary. Refresh and renew yourself, your body, your mind, your spirit. Then get back to work.

~Ralph Marston, American writer

Although working hard is key to a successful life, so is the need to rest and renew on a consistent basis. Don't wait to do so until you are almost on your last leg, so to speak, and exhausted. It is more challenging when you are wiped out to bring back balance and equilibrium. When you are weary, your temper may boil over, your anxiety may start to take over, your fear of the unknown may be fueled, and your passion for life may be dulled. Nothing good comes from working on a deficit of energy. Nothing innovative comes from a person whose emotional or physical bank account has been depleted. So schedule times of rest and renewal as a vital key to a healthy life. Go to the beach, take a walk in nature, get away for the weekend, take time to sit and read a good book, or schedule something that will revitalize your soul. Take a day out of your week to go on a date by yourself, take a weekend and go to the spa to renew your body, or take a week to hang out with friends and just laugh and make wonderful new memories. Make it a habit to rest so that your life maintains a balance that will assist you in experiencing more joy, more life, and richer and more fulfilling personal and familial relationships. Be your own best friend, and lay your foundation for a richer life! Rest and recover—it's a part of the program.

Magical Key to Bliss: Take a break, and you will see your inner light glow again!

August 9: What will you be celebrating today?

But then there are magical, beautiful things in the world. There's incredible acts of kindness and bravery, and in the most unlikely places, and it gives you hope.

~Dave Matthews, South-African born American singer and songwriter

Open your eyes and see magic and beauty where you least expect it. Clear your ears to hear the message from even the most unlikely sources. Reach out and touch another with a random act of kindness, and fill your heart with love. Face your fears as you rise above what keeps you stuck, realizing that you are in fact strong, and that nothing but your own mind can keep you down. Take risks and start practicing bravery as you begin to embrace who you are, why you are here, and the gift of time that you have to live this purpose. When you do any of the foregoing, the celebration of life can begin. When you begin to accept that the invitation is there, your hope for an amazing life will be restored. Your focus will no longer be on what is wrong with this world but will shift to all that is right with it. Your attitude will no longer be based on all that stands in your way but will change to believe that so much will bring you forward in a positive direction. Your understanding of the world will no longer be based on the hardships but will look to what you can learn that will be beneficial to your journey. There are magical and beautiful things and people in this world; the question is whether you are willing to acknowledge and celebrate that fact.

Magical Key to Bliss: Celebrate today!

August 10: **Build another kind of team!**

Today get out and celebrate. Time to remember how lucky you are, time to give praise to the highest of the holies.

~Pam Grout, American author and journalist

To experience an abundance of the health, love, life, transcendence, and joy just waiting for you, surround yourself with people who aspire to this kind of life. It is time to build the most incredible team who will support you in the tough times and celebrate with you as well. Woweee zoweeee! One by one, candidates come into your life vying for a prize position on team *you*. One by one, you get to interview and decide who will make up your most trusted advisers and confidantes. Life gives you many opportunities to choose well the players on your team in the most important game—the game of life. With your goal being to get out and celebrate life, the members you pick should be on the lookout for all the possibilities of a beautiful day. Invite the optimists, the innovators, the good doers, and the open-minded ones to join you, and your team will experience success each step that you take. Remember how lucky you are, and give praise. When you set out to build the kind of team whose success is determined by how well you take care of one another, the celebration has already begun. Then with your squad by your side, be sure to give praise to the highest of the holies in thanks for it all!

Magical Key to Bliss: Choose a team of positive ones to walk with you on your journey.

August 11: Only together will we get through the storms of life.

We are all rowing the same boat, and there are ominous storms on the horizon…We need to have the courage to do the right thing. We need to love and respect one another, to see and appreciate the innate beauty and dignity of everyone, because we are all souls, all of the same substance.

~Brian Weiss, MD, American psychiatrist, hypnotherapist, and author

We must shift our belief from an us-versus-them mentality to one of cooperation. We must embrace that we are all in this together. If we do not, we will not find the strength to get through the storms in life. We need to make choices that empower us to make a difference. We need to work together, renouncing all that is bad in favor of the good. If we shift our focus to help solve the problems in this world, then there is a better chance that good will prevail. And, when it does, we will look back on the path that we courageously took together and stand proud that we played a positive part in making the world a more magical place to live. If we keep our integrity intact and focus on what is wonderful about this world, we can build on a strong foundation and be part of what is right. Let us work together and keep moving forward; let us row this boat of life toward a more amazing tomorrow. It is only together that we will be triumphant as we navigate through—or even past—the storms that we may face in this life!

Magical Key to Bliss: Find ways to work together with others to make this world a better place!

August 12: So much to learn; walk beside me, my friend!

Don't walk behind me; I may not lead. Don't walk in front of me; I may not follow. Just walk beside me and be my friend.

~Albert Camus, French author, journalist, and philosopher

I have often felt better for the kind gesture of love and companionship that my friends have shared with me. I have often lived better knowing that those friends who have already graced the pages of my story are supporting me, holding me, and laughing with me. And still I wait in anticipation and enthusiasm because I understand better that there are still those friends I have yet to meet who will guide me on my journey. There is so much we can learn from one another. There is so much that connects us to one another. So much awaits us that will help us to shine brighter. We can know so much love by reaching out and grabbing hold of the extended hand when we recognize that our meeting is not a coincidence.

So let us stand close and pay attention, and we will not miss the present moment filled with wisdom. We will benefit from each moment that is bursting with potential. We can experience more joy, happiness, and—most of all—loving embraces, if we choose to let another in. When we allow the wonder of the relationship to overtake us, we look into the eyes of the other with gratitude, for they have walked beside us and called us friend.

Magical Key to Bliss: Make time today for your friends.

August 13: Suffer in silence no longer!

Happiness consists not of having, but of being; not of possessing, but of enjoying. It is a warm glow of the heart at peace with itself.

~David O. McKay, author of *Pathways to Happiness*

Suffering in silence is something that many have known. Alone with our thoughts of how we do or do not measure up to what was expected of us, we nurture a sense of longing for validation that does not let up even into our later years. We yearn for a sense of peace. We yearn for a sense of acceptance. And we yearn for a sense of freedom—freedom to exist in this world and enjoy our place in it. When we finally do discover the warm glow of the heart at peace with itself, we are no longer silent about our pain as we start the healing process. When we share our hurts with others, our yearning dissipates and happiness takes its place. In confessing our struggle, we are freed from a false sense of perfection that we could never live up to. We no longer have to hide from judgment; we allow ourselves to just be. In turn, as the difficult emotions are released in tears, space in our hearts opens up for laughter once again. When we hide and do not permit ourselves to process our feelings, moving them through and out, then the suffering remains. But when we share from a vulnerable place, we admit to the world that we still suffer at times, but now no longer in silence. Then for sure, with friends by our side, our journey will be more peaceful and joyful.

Magical Key to Bliss: Share your pain and suffering, and then let it go!

August 14: **How precious it all is!**

I affirm only the good in life.

~Louise Hay, American author of *You Can Heal Your Life*

Walking through our days, going through the motions, one by one, we pass one another by. Synchronicity does surround us. We know that there are no coincidences, just incidents coinciding. Our lives are deeply touched by new faces and old faces alike. Our hearts are softened as our souls expand. We do not want to let go of the moments of utter joy. We continue to reach out to others as we disembark from the port of solitude. We leave no one behind and make sure to pull our friends out of the abyss. Not wanting a moment to go by without finding something to appreciate, we declare our gratitude. Not wanting anything more than we have, we affirm the good in our life. We know how precious these moments are. We know how precious this life is. We affirm how precious it all is, every bit of it—every kiss, every smile, every hug, every person, every animal, everything! We ask that these moments of joy never end. We beg to be reminded daily that for a seeker of light, there is always hope! We are thankful for our gifts of goodness today, tonight, and always!

Magical Key to Bliss: Affirm the good in your life.

August 15: We are magical!

Henceforth I whimper no more, postpone no more, need nothing...From this hour, I ordain myself loos'd o limits and imaginary lines.

~Walt Whitman, American poet, excerpt from "Song of the Open Road"

When you wake up one day and decide that no one has the power to tell you who you are, who you will become, and what is possible for your life, you are free. When you decide that your opinion is the only one that matters, you empower yourself to live your story exactly how you intend. It is at that very moment that you make a promise to that beautiful soul staring back at you in the mirror that you will do your best to make this experience the most beautiful journey possible. It is at that moment that you decide to stop complaining for what you do not have and be grateful for all that you do have. You realize there is a power in the universe that you can use to make you whole and free. All that is possible awaits you as long as you think it so. So on that day you awake to this new understanding of your life, the road on your journey goes from gray to bright yellow. You will put on your ruby slippers and believe that you are magical because you decide it is so. And then it will begin; the path that you choose will be lined with magical work for magical pay and a notion that you are magical every magical day.

Magical Key to Bliss: Believe that you can light up the world with no limits.

August 16: Enthusiasm is contagious.

Whatever you do, do it well. Do it so well that when people see you do it, they will want to come back and see you do it again, and they will want to bring others and show them how well you do what you do.

~Walt Disney, American visionary, cartoonist, and animator

We are all good at something. We all have been born with our own special set of gifts. While some of us have a gift for the written word, others have a gift of speech. While some have the gift of discovery, others apply what is discovered. While some have a gift of organization, others lead and inspire. The bottom line is that each one of us contributes to the beautiful fabric of this world. No one person can do it all. We need one another to make this life experience all that it can be. So if we all bring our best to the table, we will inspire others to follow our example. Whatever it is that we are good at, we must do it well.

So if you are here to sweep floors because you enjoy cleanliness, do it well. If you are here to heal the sick, be present and compassionate in the whole process. If you are here to fight for justice, do not forget to be just. Whatever you choose to do that brings you happiness and joy, do it with pride. For when you do, you bring your own magic and miracles, and we can all take pride in having experienced the kind of enthusiasm that is contagious!

Magical Key to Bliss: Take pride in what you do, and do it well.

250

August 17: **Become somebody's miracle.**

Don't just look for your miracle. Become somebody's miracle. When you reach out to others in need—when you lift the fallen, when you encourage those who are down, when you befriend the lonely—your own breakthrough will come.

~Joel Osteen, American preacher and author

When we go through tough financial times, health issues, or a sense of great loss, we ask and even pray that the heaviness of life will subside as we look for our own personal miracles. We believe and wait for the tides to shift so that our lives can move in a positive direction. We feel wrapped up in our own predicaments, waiting to be saved. It is during those times that we can be proactive. Instead of helplessly waiting for our miracle to come, we can decide to become someone else's miracle. Although our lives are challenging, when we turn our focus to lovingly serving another, something magical happens. It can be miraculous for the spirit when we take the opportunity to reach out to help someone else in need, to encourage someone who is having a tough time, or to be a friend to someone who stands alone. By making an effort to reach out to another in love, we are sending out the signal that we are ready and willing to receive the same. In doing so, we are creating an army of individuals who are also ready to pay it forward. When we are spreading joy, our own breakthrough will appear sooner rather than later. And, rest assured, it will be worth the wait when our love army is there to share in our triumph.

Magical Key to Bliss: Be someone else's miracle today!

August 18: **Be thankful for the dreamers and the doers.**

All life is a chance. So take it! The person who goes furthest is the one who is willing to do and dare.

~Dale Carnegie, American writer and lecturer

L ife can feel like a maze. When we take a wrong turn, we end up facing a wall. When this happens, we feel stuck or frustrated and want to give up. Thank goodness for those people who inspire us to move on, setting an example for us of perseverance. Instead of seeing the blockade as the end of the road, they become grateful that it has stopped them from going further in the wrong direction. They are grateful for the opportunity to turn around, look up, and perhaps see the ladder that takes them to a window opening to a better direction. These people are the dreamers who dare to take advantage of all chances. Follow the examples of the dreamers and the doers who do not give up on the opportunity to be all they can be. We all can get frustrated, and that's OK. But we cannot allow the frustration to stop us from growing and moving forward in this life. If we focus on our dreams and surround ourselves with a team of people who see possibility, we can fortify our future by simply being grateful for the present, whatever it brings. As long as we surround ourselves with inspiration, we will get exactly what we need to bring it all to light.

Magical Key to Bliss: Take the chance and dare to make your dream a reality today.

August 19: Grateful for connections.

Some people come into our lives and quickly go. Some people move our souls to dance. They awaken us to a new understanding with the passing whisper of their wisdom. Some people make the sky more beautiful to gaze upon. They stay in our lives for a while, leave footprints on our hearts, and we are never, ever the same.

~Flavia Weedn, author of *Flavia and the Dream Maker*

In the present moment, we find magic in the connections as the mystery of life unfolds. There in those precious moments, we discover who will be the ones to leave a profound imprint on our soul. Even strangers, after a synchronistic encounter, form friendships whose powerful bonds have a ripple effect far beyond what is known. These friendships last an eternity, unbroken by distance or the passage of time. These special connections are made stronger through the growing pains of life; more beautiful through shared joy in the celebration; and deeper through the compassionate, warm embrace in times of sadness. These are friends who come into our lives to teach us how to dance to the beat of life's beautiful drum and who show us how to accept the challenges through the wisdom of grace.

Whatever the reason for the connection, we remain forever grateful for the footprint that has transformed us, allowed us to become better people, and expanded our heart's capacity to love. For even when we are physically apart, the memory of the connection stays, forever changing us for the better! How thankful we will always be that we will never be the same again.

Magical Key to Bliss: Welcome new friendships; they will change your world!

August 20: Set the tone for your life, and connect!

A dream you dream alone is only a dream. A dream you dream together is reality.

~John Lennon, British singer and songwriter

Before you set your feet on the ground in the morning, make the decision to embrace life for all that it has to offer, and stand in gratitude for the chance to do so. Starting from a place of appreciation, you know that this attitude will only lead to greater possibilities for amazing things to enter your life. When you bring that kind of life-changing energy to the fore, stand back and welcome the wonderful. And if you want to see even more impressive results, take a moment and write down your dreams as they come to mind. You can dream as big or small as you'd like. When you give yourself permission to do so, your world changes as you get into that heart space and imagine that for just one moment, you step into a greater reality. Then, you must share those dreams with others so that they can catch the wind they need to take off. Your inner muse speaks to you in the stillness. Pay attention to its whispers, and create a space for something more inspirational to occur before your eyes. The next time you wake in the morning, open your eyes and recognize there are no limits as to what kind of connections will help you throughout the day. When you dream during the waking hours with others, a better reality for all of us is right around the corner.

Magical Key to Bliss: Set the tone to dream with others.

August 21: **Recognize those whose light saves us.**

At times our own light goes out and is rekindled by a spark from another person. Each of us has cause to think with deep gratitude of those who have lighted the flame within us.

~Albert Schweitzer, German and later French theologian and philosopher

We all may have moments in life when we enter a dark place. It happens sometimes as a result of a tragedy or despair. Although it becomes part of our life experience, the darkness will not become a permanent fixture if we seek help. While we may feel that our own light has been extinguished, we have hope because many angels surround us each day. When we ask for assistance, they will intercede. And we will be renewed as we believe that with the help of our angels, the path will be illuminated as we walk toward the light once again. We become grateful as we recognize those who help us break out from the despair as the flame of love is rekindled. May we all stand in gratitude for those people who light the way for us when we are lost. May we all stand in gratitude for those who give love and serve us when we need it most. When we are delivered from the darkness into light, we begin to see with clarity the divine connections that we share. Then we can take a moment to thank God for those whose light saves us.

Magical Key to Bliss: Recognize your angels, and benefit from their light.

August 22: The alchemy of connection.

A single rose can be my garden…a single friend, my world.

~Leo Buscaglia, American author and motivational speaker

Be a true believer in the alchemy of connection. When you connect with another through touch, a smile, a kind word, or the smallest act of caring, a seemingly magical power emerges from the profound energy that is shared. That beautiful energy, when released, has the power to change form, nature, or substance, bettering others, one life at a time.

This kind of alchemy does happen on a daily basis before your eyes. You are a witness to one person reaching out to assist another in need, to the beauty of two souls sharing a moment in time filled with gentleness, or to a spontaneous act of kindness gifted to you at a time when you were desperate. You must believe that you are a healer whose mere touch has the power to begin the process of alleviating the pain of another. You smile and paint the world with colors of joy. You listen and release the weight of the world off another's shoulders. You extend yourself in loving-kindness, and you have changed the trajectory of another's journey. Be a true believer in the magic of connections because they have the potential to heal as long as your intention is there to do so.

 Magical Key to Bliss: Believe your connection to a single friend can affect the world for good.

August 23: You are the company you keep.

The key is to keep company only with people who uplift you,
whose presence calls forth your best.

~Epictetus, Greek speaking Stoic philosopher

I have often wondered whether each of us is born with adequate resilience to see this life through the highs and the lows. I have often wondered if each of us is born with sufficient flexibility to wade through the changes in the world as they present themselves. Then I am struck by the realization that regardless of what kind of resilience we are born with or how flexible we are, as long as we keep good company as support, we will rise above anything. We are never alone in life as long as we choose connections with people who uplift our spirits. We are never without love as long as we take the risk and allow positive people to come into our lives. The true key to a successful life is our ability to join with a collection of beautiful souls who bring love and laughter on our journey no matter how easy or difficult. See the angels in human form who are standing to the left and to the right of each of us. Then don't worry any longer because through all our highs and lows, if we keep company with people who uplift us—even if we lose our way—they will help us get back on course so that we can continue with a renewed sense of internal joy and happiness once again.

Magical Key to Bliss: Choose the company of people who uplift you.

August 24: Start a revolution of love, joy, and happiness.

Who will tell whether one happy moment of love or the joy of breathing or walking on a bright morning and smelling the fresh air, is not worth all the suffering and effort which life implies.

~Erich Fromm, German social psychologist and humanistic philosopher

It seems people these days are focused on all kinds of negativity. If we get too wrapped up in it all, we end up infected by the germs of discontent and unrest. It appears that there is so much resistance to rational thinking, to finding a way to compromise for the benefit of the greater good. So many of us suffer because things happen that cause great pain, but to suffer needlessly at the mercy of the few seems quite ridiculous in the grand scheme of things. So perhaps in our own small corner of the world, in our own cluster of magical minds, the real revolution can begin—a revolution where resistance is set aside in favor of embracing all that is good in this world. There is a world where we can experience happy moments of love and generous appreciation of the connections in life that highlight the beauty we see and experience. It is all there, if we change the focus and place our energy in a positive place where it needs to be. As we support the revolution of love, joy, and happiness rather than misery, even in the most difficult moments, we can glimpse greatness born of integrity and character. It is there, and if we all run toward it, perhaps the people can unite for the good and change this world into something we can all be proud of.

Magical Key to Bliss: Start a revolution of love.

August 25: Who are we to judge?

If someone is gay and he searches for the Lord and has goodwill, who am I to judge?

~Pope Francis, born Jorge Mario Bergoglio, two hundred and sixty-sixth pope of the Catholic Church

A man named Joe South wrote a great folk song long ago called "Walk a Mile in My Shoes," and he sang, "Before you accuse, criticize, and abuse—walk a mile in my shoes." No one can claim a life of perfection. We all make mistakes. Judging another because of the person's differences will not protect us from having to face our own. God made us all in His or Her image—different shapes, colors, characters, personalities. It is the miracle of our diversity that will make this journey more exciting and enjoyable. Rather than criticize or judge the unknown, who is to say that once we open our eyes to the beauty of others through love, we won't discover something incredibly profound and beautiful about ourselves? When we get past fears of the unknown, forgive imperfections, and start to lead with courage, greatness is not only possible for all of us but probable. When we get past our own insecurities and set aside our judgments, we can look for the first time into the eyes of another with wonder. There we will connect as souls, and the love that is there in the connection will burst from within. After we have mentally walked a mile in the shoes of another, our gratitude for their presence in our lives grows! We are so blessed to have a diverse array of people in our lives; we are better people for it! Amen!

Magical Key to Bliss: Set aside your judgments and embrace one another.

August 26: Open your eyes; this remains a wonderful world!

If we focus on the planet's unending largesse rather than on the marketers' drumbeat limitation, on the bounteous gifts that spread out before us on every side rather than on TV commercials that suggest erectile dysfunction, depression, and sleeping problems, then we can rewrite the dominant paradigm.

~Pam Grout, American author and journalist

There is so much goodness in the world. What you see depends on where you look. While certain factions of society like to point out what they believe is wrong, you must choose daily to focus on what is right. Where some see lack, you find the connectedness where abundance lies. Where some focus on evil tendencies, you seek to recognize the benevolence of humankind. Where some identify what is missing, you decide to be grateful for everything you have. You can look for the unending beauty that surrounds you. You can look for the magnificent vibrations from shared joyful moments. You can build wonderful memories. And you can be proud of your accomplishments that have made a difference all around. The world is filled with enough pessimists; you can be part of the solution for a more enlightened universe by seizing optimism as your set point. With these kinds of magical choices, you can be a vital part of rewriting a new, dominant paradigm that allows you to immerse in the things that matter most with an attitude of gratitude. You can smile with open eyes as you really start to see the trees that are green and the sky that is blue. And mimicking the words of Mr. Louis Armstrong, you will think to yourself that it has always been a wonderful world!

Magical Key to Bliss: See the good that surrounds you today!

August 27: Be your own best friend.

You have to believe in yourself; that's the secret. Even when I was in the orphanage, when I was roaming the street trying to find enough to eat, even then I thought of myself as the greatest actor in the world.

~Charlie Chaplin, British actor and filmmaker

Regardless of what anyone says to you, you must be your biggest fan! You and God—or your higher power or whatever you want to call it—are your biggest cheerleaders! When life gets you down, cheer yourself forward. Tell yourself that this, too, shall pass, and believe that it will. You are special and unique; tolerate no treatment from yourself or others that is less than fitting for a superstar. Enjoy your own company and be the best at whatever you choose to do in life. There is magic in believing. You must be your own best friend and do what you can to build your confidence and self-esteem. Whatever you want to be when you grow up, visualize yourself as the greatest. Whatever you want to do, see yourself as a success. Whatever you imagine for yourself, the secret is to already know that you are triumphant. You must be your biggest fan! When you start from there, you will believe in your greatness and empower yourself to go far.

Magical Key to Bliss: Repeat a mantra that helps you to believe in your ability.

August 28: May I help you find your verse?

That you are here—that life exists, and identity;
That the powerful play goes on, and you will contribute a verse.

~Walt Whitman, American poet, excerpt from "O Me!
O Life! "

A s we awake to this journey and embrace our role, life unfolds before our eyes. We are here at this point in time, dressed in a personality that is all our own, armed with talents and skills that will aid us on the path of our choosing. Yet, thankfully, we are never really alone here. Each day, we are introduced to different characters placed along the way to participate in our powerful play. We are presented with angels in time, our tribe, who are in our lives for a reason, season, or lifetime, each one serving a distinct purpose. All present so that we can better discover our own unique purpose through challenges, celebrations, companionship, and conviviality. We are grateful as it goes on that we do not have to go it alone. We turn to the other offering a warm embrace, asking so simply in this powerful play of life, "How may I help you find your verse?"

 Magical Key to Bliss: Spend some time thinking about your verse, your legacy.

August 29: **Our true friends celebrate who we are.**

A friend is someone who gives you total freedom to be yourself.

~Jim Morrison, American singer and songwriter

There is the hope that we all will experience a liberating moment when we make the decision to totally embrace our holy place in this world. There is a tremendous gift when we are given traveling companions who encourage that freedom to just be who we are meant to be. With true friends, we get to see ourselves through the eyes of love. With true friends, we get to know ourselves by experiencing pure joy. With true friends, we celebrate the connection to another soul. With the support of true friends, we are able to risk and follow the heart's greatest desires, learning from both the smooth and the rocky parts of our journey. Free to be all we are meant to be—what a blessing that is! When we look into the eyes of our true friends and feel their complete acceptance, knowing that we are not in this world alone, we are invited to celebrate life. There is no greater freedom than that!

Magical Key to Bliss: Thank the true friends who give you total freedom to be yourself.

August 30: It is safe to share your soul with true friends.

The friend who can be silent with us in a moment of despair or confusion, who can stay with us in an hour of grief and bereavement, who can tolerate not knowing...not healing, not curing...that is a friend who cares.

~Henri Nouwen, Dutch-born Catholic priest, professor, and writer

While in a vulnerable place, they sit beside you and hold your hand. While looking for answers out of the confusion, they communicate in silence that you are not alone. While you may feel lost and lonely, you know the presence of a true friend as your heart recognizes an energy that can only be described as pure love. For there you know that it is safe to share your soul without having to be fixed and without needing permission. There you know that even in your darkest hour, your true friend will hold the light of hope until the joy and laughter can break through once again. There, in the caring presence of a true friend, you can just be who you are as you feel the emotions that arise from life's toughest experiences. As you safely find the connection in your most difficult hour, when you make it through, that same friend will be there to rejoice with you as well. Because when you have a friend who is there for you, you are reminded by his presence alone that the beautiful colors of the world still exist and will return to your life again; it just takes time. Be grateful for your friends. It is amazing to know that you have a safe place to share your soul.

Magical Key to Bliss: Confide in a good friend and share your soul.

264

August 31: Light up every room with love.

Surround yourself with people who make you hungry for life, touch your heart, and nourish your soul.

~Unknown

When you set out to live the proverbial play that is your life, make a conscious effort to draw in characters who reflect the kind of journey you wish to experience. To feel more alive, set out to attract the kind of person whose mere presence lights up every room that she walks into. To feel passion in your soul, set out to embrace the kind whose enthusiasm for life and adventure is contagious. To leave your positive mark, set out to know the kind who makes *you* want to make a difference and leave this world a better place. To feel love deeply, set out to know the kind who goes the extra mile, lending an attentive ear as well as a compassionate heart. You can make conscious choices as to those characters you relate to. When you choose to surround yourself with people whose primary theme in life is love, your soul will be nourished by the connection, and your spiritual cup will run over, allowing you to shower that affection on others as well. If you are lucky enough to meet someone who embodies all of the above, then hold on tight, honor that relationship, and be incredibly grateful for the blessing because it is the greatest gift you will ever receive. One person's light shared enables your light of love to shine as well.

Magical Key to Bliss: Write your own story, and reflect on what kind of friendships you want in your play.

265

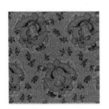

Chapter Nine: September

SWEET INSPIRATION

September is the time of year when the temperature begins to drop, and the leaves on the trees in cooler climates change colors. There is a natural beauty as a new season is introduced, and Mother Nature shows off her incredible masterpiece. Sweet inspiration surrounds us as the air is a bit crisper, and we take deeper and fuller breaths, meditating on the divine influence all around.

The first weekend in September, we take time to rest and celebrate Labor Day. While we recognize the things we do to maintain our lives and provide for our families, to uncover our bliss, we must make an effort to find inspiration through work this month. All too often, our work is a task we approach with dread. All too often, work is the source of our misery rather than a well of inspiration. So your assignment for September is to find work that inspires you—whether volunteer work for your local community organization, a part-time job doing something you love, or even a full-time job pursuing the vocation of your dreams. In September, take advantage of all the creative influences in nature and otherwise, and get inspired to make a life that matches your internal passion. You should strive for your work to inspire you as well as get inspired by your work! Make an action plan for what you need to accomplish to make a career move a reality. If you put your nose to the grindstone, you can make your work go from a burden to a joy. After all, when you enjoy your work, it is no longer…work! Get some sweet inspiration and let's go!

267

September 1: Inspired action breeds confidence and courage.

Inaction breeds doubt and fear. Action breeds confidence and courage. If you want to conquer fear, do not sit at home and think about it. Go out and get busy.

~Dale Carnegie, American writer and lecturer

Take on a no-fear approach to life. Put your "only ifs" on hold, and step outside your comfort zone. Dance, sing, create, or explore those things that are in line with your heart's desires. Don't wait for when you are thin enough, pretty enough, successful enough, or just enough. Believe that you have the confidence to put yourself out in the world now. Then seek out opportunities to build relationships that will allow you to make the most out of your life. The time is now to get busy and act. The time is now to face your fears. Name them, and they lose their power over you. Set out your goals in whatever way you can. Explore and get comfortable with your life. Be at ease in the skin that you are in. Do one thing every day to face your fear, and one day soon that fear will be a thing of the past. No regrets. Act. Don't sit back and think that you have missed the boat; instead, find a new boat and start paddling. This is your one chance, this is your life, and the time is now to make the most out of it. You have something important to share with the world. Get inspired, get busy, and share it. When you do, confidence will come, and with courage, you will have everything to gain as your life miraculously unfolds, leaving fear as a thing of the past!

Magical Key to Bliss: Decide what you would do if you knew you could not fail.

September 2: Claim your greatness!

Nothing great in the world has ever been accomplished without passion.

~Hebbel, German poet and dramatist

Every one of us was born great. Sometimes we seem to forget how truly unique and special we are, but we were all born with amazing and unique talents and attributes that this world needs at this time to move forward. We are not here by mistake. By acknowledging this fundamental truth, we no longer question our worth and in turn free ourselves to explore the world, not needing to prove anything to anyone. We must identify what makes our hearts sing. There we will find the key to energizing our bodies and souls. Passion in life comes when we are able to use our God-given talents toward something bigger. When we align ourselves with positive energy and open our eyes, we get a glimpse of the amazing interconnectivity of the universe that conspires in our favor. And in that moment, we can feel empowered to claim our greatness. With passion and our bold actions, we have the opportunity to make an incredible difference in the world as we change from within. For when we claim our greatness, we get closer and closer to realizing the freedom of living a life of passion. When we accept our calling, we are balanced and exactly where we need to be.

Magical Key to Bliss: Figure out what you are passionate about, and take the next best step in that direction.

September 3: Happen to the world with enthusiasm!

People are always blaming their circumstances for what they are. I don't believe in circumstances. The people who get on in this world are the people who get up and look for the circumstances they want, and if they can't find them, make them.

~George Bernard Shaw, Irish playwright and author of *Mrs. Warren's Profession*

If you got up this morning and started your day deciding to rise to any occasion no matter the circumstances you face, give yourself a golden star. If you found yourself facing a difficult challenge during your day and decided to shift your perspective from victim to victor, then give yourself another star. If you looked for the positive despite being surrounded by the negative, then give yourself another star for having the courage to raise your vibration to a level of joy and light. Keep track of how many stars you have earned during your day. Take the time to acknowledge that you are getting on in this world in a way that you can be proud of. Your stars are a reflection of your ability to look for and to find the circumstances that make life worth living. These stars are glorious reminders of your choice to see yourself as happening to the world with optimism and success. These stars are evidence that you have decided to find something to be grateful about in every situation as you go about your day. Your determination to recognize all your great accomplishments will empower you to catapult your life in the direction that you choose, happening to the world with enthusiasm as you go.

Magical Key to Bliss: Buy stars and give yourself one each time you feel accomplished!

September 4: **A magical connection to your dreams!**

A great attitude does much more than turn on the lights in our worlds; it seems to magically connect us to all sorts of serendipitous opportunities that were somehow absent before the change.

~Earl Nightingale, American radio personality, writer, and author of *The Strangest Secret*

An attitude of gratitude has always been the sweet elixir that can heal all that ails us. When we feel stuck in a rut, looking at all our blessings may just be the key to turning things around. Gratitude is one of the greatest keys to unlocking the bliss within. When we truly acknowledge and are grateful for our victories and successes rather than focusing on what is lacking, we make a habit of adopting an attitude that can magically connect us to our dreams. By repeating affirmations of appreciation coupled with incredible and powerful visualizations of possibilities, such as magic, the light in our souls gets fired up as the necessary connections appear and inspire things to happen. Putting out our positive and powerful intentions to the universe with a grateful heart, we will start to see others wanting to assist in opening doors to help us move forward on our journey. With a great attitude in life that is linked to the beauty of gratitude, we develop a sense of being plugged into an abundant energy that is ready to be shared on a daily basis. With a miraculous change in our attitudes, we should not be surprised that the world will respond to our hopes and dreams like never before. And when we stand in awe, now living the reality that was once only a dream, we will happily delight in the serendipitous opportunities magically revealed before our eyes. When that happens, we are thankful for that, too!

Magical Key to Bliss: Connect to your dreams by stating what you are grateful for.

September 5: Live life to the fullest!

To live, to err, to fall, to triumph, to recreate life out of life.

~James Joyce, Irish novelist and poet

There are those stories of triumph over tribulation that are known to inspire the masses. There are those events in which the power of the human spirit to rise above challenges is showcased as moving both present and future generations forward. And as we study human existence over time, we discover the secret to keeping hope through it all. Life is truly a gift begging to be appreciated that God gives us every day we open our eyes. It is a gift that is presented to us whether gift wrapped or not, to do with what we can. And as long as we do our best in the endeavor of living, even if we fall or err, we will persevere when we set our minds to do it, even triumphing as our own spirit soars in any given moment. There are moments in which routine takes over, and we are numb to the experience. And then there are moments when awe of the miracles that are right before us shakes us to the core. It is in the shift of consciousness that the passion takes over and the magic that is life itself materializes. And until our last day on this earth, we will have numerous chances to take our script and rewrite, re-create, and reinnovate, using what we have learned and infusing it with a prayer to make it that much better. It is time for the shift, and it is time to believe it is more fascinating after the transformation. Live life to the fullest!

Magical Key to Bliss: Start today, and make the decision to live life to the fullest no matter what appears on your path.

September 6: You might as well choose what you love.

You can fail at what you don't want, so you might as well take a chance on what you love.

~Jim Carrey, Canadian-American actor and comedian

We often wonder what this journey is all about. We often ponder our purpose in the grand scheme of life that surrounds us. We often question from a place of introspection what the point really is of all of this anyway. After the question is formulated in our minds, it goes out to the world in search of the perfect reply to our specific query. We must start to pay attention to the universe unfolding all around us. We must be open to the call that is perfectly tailored to assist us in discovering the answers that our soul seeks. When we recognize that if we rise to the occasion the answers are all around, we become a part of the magic of the universe once again seeking to follow our passion in matters both big and small. Doors that were once seen as closed now easily open to the next part of the journey that lies before us. Brief seconds in time offer a path that will make all the difference, brief seconds that challenge us to take the risk of being seen in all our glory by taking a chance on what we love. When those opportunities come, where the beat of our heart is matched, we are pushed to act now, move now, respond now. We can think about whether we would prefer to fail at something we don't want or to take the chance on what we love.

Magical Key to Bliss: Choose what you love.

274

September 7: Living the moment!

Happiness, not in another place, but this place…not for another hour, but this hour.

~Walt Whitman, American poet

Here in this moment, this is the best time of your life. If you are looking for joy, wisdom, or happiness, look no further than right here, right now. While multitasking can be admirable as it allows you to experience more and manage more, it hinders your ability to actually live in the moment and appreciate that happiness is where you stand. Don't miss it. Point your camera lens anywhere, and you will find a reason to be happy. You can take the best clear mental pictures of what is going on all around you if you focus on each moment, one at a time. While you may want to wish away the "now" because you are going through challenging experiences that are too difficult to face, you can turn adversity into advantage when you shift your focus onto the moment and seek out the good that is everywhere all around you. You are a seeker. And it is this place, this hour that you seek. Living moment by moment, you can start to appreciate the little synchronicities that bring happiness to light your life. In this moment, stop and smell the roses, no matter what. In this moment, pay attention to the people who share it with you, no matter what. In this moment, embrace your happiness that is already there, no matter what—for this moment is the best time of your life. Tomorrow is not a guarantee.

 Magical Key to Bliss: Build on the happiness of this place, this hour, this moment.

September 8: Never look back; there is so much opportunity ahead!

Never look back unless you are planning to go that way.

~Henry David Thoreau, American author, poet, philosopher, and transcendentalist

If you want to move forward in life, keep your chin up, a smile on your face, and both eyes looking ahead. Given that sunshine could appear at any moment on the road ahead, you really cannot focus your attention on the storms from the past because you just might miss it. Enlarge your vision of the life you want, and face forward, ready to welcome whatever comes. March dutifully toward what inspires you. Come up with a plan that you can get enthusiastic about, and get ready to set it into motion. Set the course with your eyes wide open, and get ready to see your dreams come to fruition. Conjure up your wishes, write them in the sand, and let the sea carry them away. Articulate well where you want to go, what you want to do, and what you need to get you there, and your guides will appear in many shapes and forms. Begin to tell your story of triumph rather than relive past hurts that have already served a purpose. And never look back—that is, of course, unless you want to go through it all again. There is no reason to repeat an experience, especially when there is so much more to discover. So much opportunity lies ahead for you; don't look back on what you may have missed, or you will surely lose out on today!

Magical Key to Bliss: Look ahead and get excited by the possibility of what could be!

September 9: **You show the world how great you are.**

My only fault is that I don't realize how great I really am.

~Muhammad Ali, born Cassius Marcellus Clay Jr., American professional boxer

You will show the world how strong you are. Your hard work will inspire you. Your perseverance will guide you. Your faith and trust in yourself, God, and the universe will ultimately give way to effortless joy on the way to realizing your dreams. You will show the world how awesome you are. Even if you don't believe it right now, you will look in the mirror and be grateful for what you are made of. You won't cower from the beauty that is your magnificent spirit. You will embrace what you are and what you see. You will only allow suffering to be the catalyst to take you far beyond what you ever thought possible for yourself. You will show the world how courageous you are. Your authenticity will allow you to process your unresolved anger and welcome and celebrate your good cheer. Your kindness will allow your enthusiasm to take over as you bask in the marvelous glow of life. You will show the world how fabulous you are. You have a grace that is yours alone to help you dance, sing, pray, and create. You will stand up for your uniqueness as a child of love. You will speak glory into your life as you advance confidently, moving forward on this wonderful journey. You will never look back to regret a moment, for with this clarity you will have realized all along that you were created in the divine image. Just by realizing this, you will have shown the world how great you really are!

Magical Key to Bliss: Do not shy away from the amazing person you are—own it!

September 10: Now, to get your groove back!

Acknowledging the good that you already have in your life is the foundation for all abundance.

~Eckhart Tolle, German-born author of *A New Earth: Awakening to Your Life's Purpose*

If you feel like you are in a rut, let's spice things up a bit! With your eyes closed, think about what you want to see and experience in your life today. Perhaps you would like to expand your horizons with a new professional opportunity. Perhaps you would like to connect with a person who can positively impact your world. Perhaps you want to experience laughter and fun. Or, perhaps you would like to experience more peace, love, and joy more often throughout your day. Now, with eyes wide open, see your world again for the first time, looking for what you most seek. When you start from a place of gratitude, acknowledging all the good that is already there, you are well on your way to receiving what you are looking for. In the few moments it took you to close and open your eyes, you can experience a renewed vision filled with possibilities. When you acknowledge the solid foundation that already exists, you will climb to greater heights as you build on the circumstances of the present moment. With hope, you can build from a place of what has gone right. By focusing your attention in the direction of abundance, your effortless flow will return. Rut, be gone! Remember, energy flows where your attention goes. Be sure to take a moment and do this quick exercise to transform your life by revving up with positive energy; get your spicy groove back in no time at all.

 Magical Key to Bliss: Close your eyes and see; open them and just be!

September 11: Arouse enthusiasm for life with great praise.

I consider my ability to arouse enthusiasm among my people the greatest asset I possess, and the way to develop the best that is in a person is by appreciation and encouragement...If I like anything, I am hearty in my approbation and lavish in my praise.

~Charles Schwab, American businessman and investor

Remember, today you have an opportunity to arouse enthusiasm in each person you meet. You are the key ingredient that can transform an ordinary day into something extraordinary. You are responsible for choosing an attitude that will allow the spark of enthusiasm to take over and permeate everything you do. With a positive attitude as an asset, you will transform any ordinary encounter with a person into something extraordinary. You choose to embrace a welcoming approach or one that repels. Many mistakenly believe that if you lead with an iron fist, you will get the best results in life or in business. This could not be further from the truth. It is only with appreciation and encouragement that you can inspire the masses to perform to their greatest ability and potential. You will lead well with kindness as your foundation. You will give others an incentive to improve themselves to better serve this world through constant encouragement. There is no end to the power of sincere praise. When you build one another up, you are building a more confident society as a whole. When you lavish with sincere praise, you are planting the seeds for a brighter tomorrow.

Magical Key to Bliss: Offer encouragement to others to follow the path of bliss.

September 12: **Understand with an open mind.**

All is love...With love comes understanding. With understanding comes patience. And then time stops. And everything is now.

~Brian Weiss, MD, American psychiatrist, hypnotherapist, and author

When we understand that life is all about love, we gain incredible insight that affects our awareness. The way we see the world changes. The way we take in information and knowledge expands. And the way we experience other people transforms. From a love consciousness, past wounds start to heal effortlessly as we become wholly balanced once again. Past judgments fade away as we start to patiently understand our fragile nature. Past negative emotions evaporate as a greater force overtakes us. Past suffering is surrendered as time stops, and we start to experience the now that is pure and simple. We must open the window of our hearts to love, allowing the wind to carry away what burdens us in order to make room for what renews us. Let understanding enlighten us as we become more patient with others and calmly advance. We start to grow and stretch beyond our perceived limits, experiencing everything in the incredible now. We step authentically into a higher consciousness, where understanding is the vehicle that opens the doors of the mind to greater love in our lives! Life will change from tiresome to effortless because love has the power to conquer all that no longer serves us so that the present moment is filled with gratitude!

Magical Key to Bliss: Love everything in the now!

September 13: Make them laugh, make them laugh, make them laugh!

A sense of humor…is needed armor. Joy in one's heart and some laughter on one's lips is a sign that the person down deep has a pretty good grasp of life.

~Hugh Sidey, American journalist

Without love, life would be gloomy. Without laughter, it would be unbearable. Life can get too serious too often. To lighten the load on your shoulders, there is nothing better than a good laugh. If you learn to laugh at yourself and with others, you gain a sense of humor that can fight off the doldrums. Try it, and see for yourself. When you feel the weight of the world, call a friend who has the skill of an amateur comedian to help you see your predicament in a humorous light. When you cannot take the intensity of current events, go see a comedy that has you on the ground in stitches and forgetting what had you upset in the first place. When you are facing challenges, find some humor to resurrect innovation in any situation.

Laughter and a sense of humor will add years to your life, joy to your days, and love to your heart. Even in your darkest moments, if you surround yourself with the sunshine that radiates from laughter, you can lift anyone up from what seems to be an abyss. Laughter is contagious. And as long as you hold on to others who have joy in the heart and laughter on the lips, you will eventually become one of those people. With more laughter in the here and now, what a wonderful world this could be!

 Magical Key to Bliss: Laugh as much as you can because laughter is the best medicine!

September 14: **Free to choose which illusion to believe.**

*There is no room for shame or regret in my life. I'm too full.
I am too forgiven, too adored, too fully loved, too full of ideas
and dreams and passion to waste my precious life pretending to
be crippled by something that is imaginary, like shame. Shame
is an illusion. It disappears so easily.*

~Glennon Doyle Melton, American author of *Carry On,
Warrior*

Why do you choose to punish yourself over and over again for
something that has happened and cannot be changed? What is
done is done. Now is the time for acceptance. Acceptance allows you to
embrace all that you are, the miraculous and the imperfect. Shame is just
an illusion; all negative emotions are. While you cannot change the events
of the past, you can learn from them so that they positively affect your
future. Your freedom of choice and awareness will allow you to break the
negative patterns in your mind so you avoid dooming yourself to repeat
the lesson. There is no time for ruminating over negative experiences.
When you realize that continued shame or regret serves no purpose for
your life, you will be free to hold your head high as the beauty of your
personal journey unfolds. May you continue on your path empowered by
positivity that guides you through your big and beautiful life! Shame is an
illusion. When you are aware of that and no longer desire it, it disappears.

If all things are illusions, then choose one in which you are emboldened by the lessons learned and excited by your story. Then hold on as
you prepare to feel your spirit soar!

 Magical Key to Bliss: Write out what inspires you and what
you have room for in your life!

September 15: You are a force to be reckoned with.

Believe in yourself! Have faith in your abilities! Without a humble but reasonable confidence in your own powers, you cannot be successful or happy.

~Norman Vincent Peale, American author of *The Power of Positive Thinking*

Confidence is a very interesting concept. With it, you can move mountains. Without it, you can languish in a puddle of your own misery. It is the key ingredient to believing you are capable of making great things happen in your life. Confident people are not easily manipulated. Confident people know their beauty within and use this knowledge to make a difference in this world. Confident people who face difficult situations put aside their self-interest and often become heroes as they positively impact the lives of others. When confident people are tested, they rise to the challenge and face any and all adversity to emerge victorious on both a small and grand scale.

As the labyrinth of life unfolds before you, have confidence that your journey is guided, and know that you are not alone. As you travel that circuitous route to the center of the intricate design set out before you and return again, be happy and confident that as you live life on purpose, you humbly take your place in this world as a positive force to be reckoned with. All around you are others whose self-assured faith in their own abilities will help you believe in yours.

 Magical Key to Bliss: Repeat a confident mantra that matches the positive force of your spirit.

September 16: The universe is unfolding exactly as it should.

*Just trust that everything is unfolding the way it is supposed to. Don't resist. Surrender to what **is**, let go of what **was**, and have faith in what **will be**. Great things are waiting for you around the corner.*

~Sonia Ricotti, American author of *Unsinkable: The Law of Attraction Plain and Simple*

Great things are waiting for you right around the corner. Let this be your rally cry, and get excited! The mere fact that you are here on earth is miracle enough. Embrace the life that has been given to you. All of it, for better or worse; it is yours to experience. If you are traveling through a rough part of your path, step by step, one foot in front of the other, do what you can, and have faith that great things are in store for you on the other side. If you are traveling through a majestic part of your journey, stop and smell those roses that lie at your feet. Enjoy it by giving love and appreciation for your current experience. Before you know it, you will attract more good. Just remember that as long as you are alive, great possibilities exist for you as the universe unfolds. How wonderful to embrace the spirit of each moment as you choose to separate yourself from the toxicity of the drama that could stand in your way. This is the moment of your great shift. Stop resisting positive change, surrender, let go, and have faith—then start to notice your life in a new way, and experience the freedom of this beautiful universe unfolding just as it should.

 Magical Key to Bliss: *Believe that the universe is unfolding as it should and that it is wonderful!*

September 17: **Expect the best, and you will most likely get it!**

It is a very funny thing about life; if you refuse to accept anything but the best, you very often get it.

~W. Somerset Maugham, British playwright, novelist, and short-story writer

As we learn, we grow. As we grow, we realize there are qualities that make the journey in life much easier. Wisdom through trial and error is a gift. For instance, if we are flexible and do not resist change, a challenging or scary situation can turn out to be a magnificent, life-altering event. If we stop seeking approval from others and recognize our own value and worth, we become the victor as we trust our own intuition and are empowered by making the best choices. If we refuse to accept anything but the best, we can accept that whatever is happening in our lives at any given time is perfect for the lesson that is before us. Rigid behavior only gets us more and more frustrated. Relying on praise from another keeps us trapped in a self-imposed cage and never really free to experience all that the world has to offer. A closed mind to the belief that we are worthy of the best has the potential to stall the continued positive growth that we could be otherwise enjoying. So as we move forward in life, if we choose the belief that everything that comes our way has the possibility to uplift our spirit, broaden our horizons, and keep us going in a positive direction—and if we refuse to accept anything less—the experience that we will have most definitely will be the best.

Magical Key to Bliss: Ask, believe, and receive.

September 18: **It's a pleasure to make your acquaintance.**

My bad habits aren't my title. My strengths and my talent are my title.

~Layne Staley, American musician and songwriter

Will you take a moment out of your daily critique and allow me to introduce you to your strengths? Your strengths are pleased to make your acquaintance as they say "I can dance, I can play, I can write, and I can say, I am great, I am humble, and I have certainly had my share of tumbles. But lighten up, if you will, for today is a new day; with enthusiasm and passion, I will show you the way. It is a pleasure to finally get your attention. Now turn your head and start looking in the right direction. I have known you all along. It is about time I came through when you were just humming and singing your song." You turn to ask, almost pleading: "Can you stay?"

Then your strengths respond: "I would be delighted, but there is only one way. You must accept me with love and gratitude, for if you do, I will never go away." Now that you have been reintroduced to your greatest ally, instead of berating yourself for what you cannot do, know that there is so much you can do. Embrace your blessings and your strengths. It is truly the recognition of your God-given talents that will define the trajectory of your life. As you own your strengths and gifts, your lifelong journey will be renewed with an incredible light that sparks your interest in living again. Let that be your title!

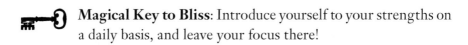 **Magical Key to Bliss**: Introduce yourself to your strengths on a daily basis, and leave your focus there!

September 19: The surrender makes you strong.

The attitude you have as a parent is what your kids will learn from more than what you tell them. They don't remember what you try to teach them. They remember what you are.

~Jim Henson, American puppeteer, artist, cartoonist, and producer of *The Muppet Show*

See yourself standing now at a crossroad. Where will you go next? Which way do you turn? Which choice will you make? Will today be the day that you make the decision to let go of old patterns that no longer serve you well in order to embrace the ones that do? Will today be the day that you let go of the safety of the known to feel the joy of what awaits you? Will now be the time that you show the children who you are by boldly setting out to realize your dreams? Then you must choose now to act with confidence and surrender to the divine energy of the universe. Wanting to control so much, you will become overstressed and overtired. Wanting to succeed, you will get lost in indecision as you stand at the fork in the road. Understand that with a little prayer of protection, moving forward into the surrender of life is where you will find the abundance that awaits you! You want your children or those who look up to you to be empowered by life and not afraid of it. Your words mean little if they are not followed by action. And you can choose to leave your worries and fears behind you and set a grand example as you surrender with faith, leaping forward; knowing the good that awaits you can only make you stronger!

Magical Key to Bliss: Be bold in your actions, and show others the inspired way.

September 20: When you need inspiration, be grateful, and it will come.

If the only prayer you ever say in your entire life is thank you, it will be enough.

~Meister Eckhart, German theologian, philosopher, and mystic

If you are able to live today without stress, be grateful. If you are blessed with the ability to love and be loved, be grateful. If you woke this morning kissed by the warmth of the sun welcoming you to live a brand new day, be grateful. If you are blessed with family and friends who care about you, be grateful. And if you have gained wisdom and strength through surviving life's challenge, be grateful. For all that happens in life, whether good or bad, has a purpose. See this. For with all of your missteps and accomplishments alike, you are being fortified with the knowledge and compassion that can catapult you to a higher level of consciousness and enlightenment. Embrace this. When you take a moment out of each day to look up to the heavens in gratitude for who you are, for where you are, for the people in your life, and for the journey you get to take, you open up to more possibilities of the same. Know this. For if the only prayer in your whole life is thank you and nothing else, rest assured with a grateful heart that your petition shall be heard the moment it is uttered. And for this, thank you!

 Magical Key to Bliss: Count your blessings with a resounding thank you, thank you, thank you; that is all the inspiration you need!

September 21: Whom will you believe?

All of what you are going through has a purpose. It will teach you empathy so that you can relate and help others someday.

~Mary Jo Nocero, my mother

Whom will you believe? Will you believe the proverbial "devil" or the "angel" that sits on your shoulder? The devil is your ego, afraid and in fear of the unknown. The angel is your soul already free from the illusions of the world. The devil is only a caricature of that part of your human persona that yearns for love. The angel is only a caricature of that part of your divine persona that knows you are love. Both parts serve a higher purpose. Both sides offer you perspective as your life unfolds. Both sides allow you to awaken and transform as you become more aware and liberated. Both sides are important and must be in balance in the reality that we are human and at the same time divine. Be the observer where before you may have been a judge. Step back and experience the moments in which the ego wants to dominate. Allow the soul, the divine you, to give the ego love and care. Be the observer of your past experiences. You are the person you are now because of what you have gone through. Believe that the duality of your life holds profound meaning, and embrace both. Ultimately, you will come to realize that the compassion gained from loving all of you will one day make a difference in your life and in the lives of others.

Magical Key to Bliss: Be an empathetic badass today and every day; it's your superpower!

September 22: Say what you need to say.

I took a deep breath and listened to the old bray of my heart. I am. I am. I am.

~Sylvia Plath, American poet, novelist, and author of *The Bell Jar*

Welcome to this new day of sweet inspiration! It is a day in which you are invited to be bold, be courageous, be kind, be loving, and most of all, be your authentic self! What a gift it is to be able to breathe in life and answer that breath with words that emanate from your very heart and soul. Therein you will be able to communicate the happiness that only you can share with this world. Therein you will be able to communicate the joy that only you can creatively express on life's canvas. Therein you can communicate the love that you need to express to others. Listen! Take a moment in time and listen to what messages you are meant to receive. And then turn around and relay to the world with gratitude what it is that you must share! Then, with a boldness and kindness, say what you need to say. Do not swallow your words so that they get stuck. Express them and share those words that can become the lyrics of justice, balance, leadership, or peace. Do what you can to let the music that emanates from your heart and soul be heard! Welcome to this, your new day of sweet inspiration. Count your blessings as you open your heart and mind to the something wonderful that is about to happen all because you acknowledge, "I am. I am. I am."

Magical Key to Bliss: Acknowledge your spirit by saying, "I am, I am, I am."

September 23: Free will—the choice is yours.

Always dream and shoot higher than you know you can do. Do not bother just to be better than your contemporaries or predecessors. Try to be better than yourself.

~William Faulkner, American Nobel Prize–winning novelist

When you follow your dreams and shoot higher than before, what ensues thereafter is a change in your definition of what you believe is possible. When you go within and tap into that light source that emanates from your beautiful heart, you will glow brighter than what you thought was probable. You are a beacon of light in a world that believes darkness is all there is. You are a dreamer in a world that limits its reality. You are stretching past your own limitations to get in touch with where your journey is taking you. You are doing what allows you to follow your bliss on whatever path appears. Free will allows you the choice each day to determine which direction you shall go. Inspiration comes from the wisdom of the ages when you freely exult, "Hey, it's a new day, and I am alive, so what's next?" It is as simple as that! If you are alive, then the world is waiting for you to shoot higher and become your brilliant self, shining your light, love, and happiness for all to see. When you honor that privilege to do so, the ripple of your amazing self will travel far and wide as you challenge others to become better than they were yesterday as well.

 Magical Key to Bliss: Set out to do something good today, and inspire others to do the same.

September 24: Can't wait to see what the universe has in store for me today!

The first step toward awakening is admitting you want something different.

~Joan Duncan Oliver, American author of *Coffee with the Buddha*

Do you want something different? Do you need inspiration to accomplish this? If your life feels like it is replaying the scenes from a bad movie—reliving the same moments, just on different days—it is time to stop the insanity. It is time to awake in the morning and decide that you want something different. It is time to get up and declare that you cannot wait to see what life has in store for you rather than allowing external events to dictate your path. Although you are guided by time as day becomes night and then night becomes day, you can drive those moments that you are given with passion as you decide what it is that you really want. If you feel stirred to desire something more in line with your purpose or calling, admit it to yourself, and you have taken the first step on an exciting, new adventure. Now is the time to awaken to that conscious reality and start taking steps in that direction. Listen to your own internal guide and ask it to show you the way! You will be inspired to break out of a routine that no longer serves you. You will be drawn to principles that challenge and improve your life for the better. And you will be shouting with enthusiasm, "Can't wait to see what the world has in store for me today!"

Magical Key to Bliss: Rise to your something different, and awaken to a great and amazing day!

September 25: **Let it go, and embrace life.**

Drag your thoughts away from your troubles...by the ears, by the heels, or any other way you can manage it.

~Mark Twain, born Samuel Clemens, American author and humorist

There must come a time when we let go of thoughts of despair and allow the emotions to move through and out so that we can embrace a life of overwhelming abundance. We get more of what we focus on. Awareness is the key. Life happens; circumstances that challenge us will come and go. When we are faced with a fire that can destroy us, believe that it will not; then be sure that the phoenix will rise again out of the ashes stronger than before. We get to choose where we go from here. We get to move forward one step at a time, letting go of thoughts that weaken us, and emboldening thoughts of empowerment. We have all had moments in which we have been dragged kicking and screaming to something that we did not want to do, only to be grateful in the end for having been obligated to do so. We must start dragging ourselves away, by the ears, heels, or any other way, from negative thoughts that tear us down to mantras that help us love our life again. Ultimately, we really don't have control over what life delivers to each of us; we only have control in the surrender. And when we surrender, we are freed from all that keeps us down. The cage door of our mind is open; it is time to turn our thoughts around and walk away from the thoughts that hold us in captivity to an illusion. Step by step, the world will be a happier place as we shine brighter.

Magical Key to Bliss: Embrace life!

September 26: Are you ready for a joyous adventure?

Do what you can, with what you have, where you are.

~Theodore Roosevelt, twenty-sixth president of the United States of America

What if the first thing that we thought of when we woke up were, "Can't wait to enjoy the ride today"? Just feel the spirit behind that sentiment—as if each and every day were a celebration of our lives. As if each and every day were an opportunity to be grateful for being born, a gift waiting to be opened. Imagine if we lived each and every day as if it were our big, beautiful birthday, and we remained ageless! We would have a smile from ear to ear; many would wish us well and send us on our way with love. Well, why not look at each and every day as a reason to celebrate, even if it is not our birthdays? Imagine all the gifts that await us, all the love that comes to us, and all the well wishes that will come our way. Visualize this, and make it happen each and every day. It will make the journey that much better. So each and every day that we get to awake to a bright and beautiful day, we should open our eyes with much appreciation because today can be a day when we are each born anew! So we must do what we can with what we have, right where we are! Happy big and beautiful new day, everyone! May it be filled with fun, love, laughter, and most of all, joy!

Magical Key to Bliss: Get ready for your joyous adventure on this amazing day.

September 27: Let go of the past and embrace the future.

...there are no wrong turns, only unexpected paths.

~Mark Nepo, American poet, philosopher, and author of
The Book of Awakening

Your future is calling to you; it is time to let go of the stuff that leaves you trapped. It is time to be grateful for all of the lessons that have taught you so much. It is time to make a commitment with enthusiasm, opening your heart and mind to the new paths that are there to be discovered. It is time to get ready for the unexpected paths. While you may be yearning for a shift in your life, it won't happen until you are willing to make the changes necessary. Remind yourself that there are no wrong turns. When you let go of the past and open up to a sunrise of an amazing future filled with lots of connections, you will be on your way to realizing your dreams. You can take the safe approach that is laden with fear, or you can take the empowered approach that allows for incredible possibility. The choice is ultimately yours to make. But action is key. When you act, know that new, amazing experiences wait right around the corner. If you do not risk, you will never know that they exist. However, when you drop the baggage of the past and embrace the wings of your future, you will find unexpected paths that will lead you exactly where you are meant to travel. And there you will open your eyes to new opportunities that will free your soul.

 Magical Key to Bliss: Believe in a future inspired by the magic of your dreams!

September 28: **Keep it all in perspective.**

When you wake up every day, you have two choices. You can either be positive or negative; an optimist or a pessimist. I choose to be an optimist. It's all a matter of perspective.

~Harvey Mackay, American businessman, author, and syndicated columnist

As we live, our understanding of the world broadens, and if we are lucky, so does our perspective. Circumstances happen, but our reaction to them is what matters most. In an instant, our lives can change. A dramatic shift or a life-altering event occurs that can shake even the most solid of foundations. Choices present themselves. If we decide to see ourselves as part of the great mystery, we can learn so much, but if we never allow the process to unfold, we will miss out on the beauty that is there for the taking. With the trained eye of the optimist, we don't succumb to potential despair but rather use our challenges as an opportunity to break out of the small vision of the world into a new and greater one. This key that will inspire us to open the door to a better reality will encourage us to turn around in our cage and see the door to freedom wide open on the other side.

We all go through significant change. Perhaps we have lost a loved one or a job, suffered a health crisis, or experienced discord in a relationship. We still have two choices before us. If we choose to be an optimist, we offer the chance for any situation to be blessed by incredible miracles of understanding as our perspective of the world changes for the better.

Magical Key to Bliss: Choose optimism, and the results will be more favorable.

September 29: Enough! Live your own life already!

People who say it cannot be done should not interrupt those who are doing it.

~George Bernard Shaw, Irish playwright and cofounder of the London School of Economics

You have had enough and are ready to live your own life. Break free of the ties that bind, and set out on the journey that is worthy of you. You have dreams, you have passions, and you have the tools to make it all happen. You have hopes, you have desires, and you have great plans. You are sweetly inspired and never too old to start today to plant the seeds for your dreams to come true. Tell those who cast doubt on you to move aside; enough, this is your time. There is no guarantee of how much time you have, so why waste a moment of it? There is nothing holding you back but you. If you want to write, then write. If you want to dance, then dance. If you want to live a healthier life; take the first step and move. If you want to sing, then turn the radio on and go to it. If you want to serve the world, then start to serve with honor and love, and respect your purpose here on earth. People will see the way you live and be inspired to do the same, and the joy will be infectious. Take your own inventory, set out your heart's desires, believe in yourself, and live your life already. When you look into the mirror, you will know that the only one whose opinion really matters is your own. When you start to say "enough" and ignore both the naysayers and your own depleting thoughts, you empower yourself, and there is no end to what you can accomplish.

Magical Key to Bliss: Scream out, "Enough, *basta cosi*"; live your life already!

September 30: Hope for love to be born again.

A very small degree of hope is sufficient to cause the birth of love.

~Stendhal, born Marie-Henri Beyle, nineteenth-century French writer

When you give birth to something that you are passionate about and let it go out into the world, your hope is that it will be protected and nurtured. When you put it out there, the control over what happens to it is gone, and that is where trust and faith come into play. If you keep your creation to yourself, it can never expand further, but if you release your baby into the world, there is great possibility that it will thrive. You have to trust that this "something" has a greater purpose; there must be a reason it was conceived. With faith, when you let it go, there is the hope that it will be received in a way that honors its essence. So much so that others will step in and care for it and love it as much as you do. Your "something" will touch and inspire others to tap into their own fountain of creativity that may lie dormant. Your "something" will spark others into action to make the world a better place. Your "something" will be cause for a tremendous celebration of life—a celebration that liberates the spirit to break down imaginary walls, separating heaven and earth so that mere mortals get a glimpse of how magical we are. So release the potential that has been entrusted to you, nurture it, and then let it go to be shared with the masses. Bring hope to a world where your "something" can light it up and cause a rebirth of love.

Magical Key to Bliss: Release your sweet "something" for love to be born again!

298

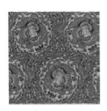

Chapter Ten: October

EMPOWERED THROUGH SERVICE

In October, choose to focus on love, not fear. Turn off the messages that no longer serve your spirit, and get empowered to turn on "I am" statements that positively uplift your soul. To be the change in a world that so desperately needs it, instead of focusing on what is wrong, get empowered by stating, "I am what is right," and be in service to that sentiment. For in October, with *The Magical Guide to Bliss* by your side, we set out to serve, and with these wonderful acts, we will await the surprises that are sure to come our way.

In October, with an ability to come to the aid of others individually or through organizations and networks that provide assistance, we are able to serve one another for the greater good and at the same time receive amazing energetic vibes to take us through our days. As we celebrate the month of October, let's keep in mind that the whole is greater than the sum of its parts and set out to empower our lives in service to community. There are so many ways to serve; in October, venture out to find one that resonates with you.

October 1: Greatness through service.

The best way to find yourself is to lose yourself in the service of others.

~Mahatma Ghandi, Indian leader and peace activist

Service is important to the world as a whole. Many people think service is defined in one way only, but that is not the case. You are blessed with many talents that run the gamut, from the ability to speak well in front of others to the ability to write well, to be compassionate, and to give your time to a worthy cause. No one talent is any more profound or powerful than another. It does not matter where you serve using these talents, be it at work, in your spiritual community, or at the bus stop—it only matters that you do serve in both big and small ways. You can serve another by sharing a smile, lending an ear, or organizing an event to raise money or awareness. If you share the gifts you were blessed with, you not only do a profound service for others, but you also are serving yourself because that is where you find your own greatness. Share your life or experiences with another through service, and see the good feelings multiply. Especially when you feel lost, if you serve others, you find the reason you are here in the first place!

Magical Key to Bliss: Be of great service today!

October 2: Service through action.

We ought not be content with being hearers, but doers.

~Saint Aloysius Gonzaga, S. J. (Society of Jesus), Roman
Catholic saint

Hear the messages and act. You have come to this journey with a
purpose to serve through action. From the very beginning, you
receive messages that reveal clues to help you uncover the mystery of
what that purpose is. Someone you meet conveys important information
that will help you to help others; do you act? Something you encounter
inspires you to believe that you have hidden potential; do you trust in
the inspiration? Somewhere you travel has you seeing the world from a
different perspective that opens your mind; do you heed the call? Hear
the messages and act. You have come to this journey with a purpose to
serve through action. From now until the very end, someone, something, or someplace will be introduced to you to help you move forward
in your life so that you can be of service to the world. You can be a hearer
or a doer; it is up to you. If you are a hearer only, then you are not doing
your part and are missing out on the whole point of your existence. If
you choose to be a doer, you will follow the inspiration to act on it in a
positive, uplifting, and loving manner, and the mystery will unfold, en-
lightening you to serve exactly in the way that you are meant to.

Magical Key to Bliss: Hear the messages and choose to act so
that your purpose unfolds.

October 3: Service through example.

Good character consists of recognizing the selfishness that inheres in each of us and trying to balance it against the altruism to which we should all aspire. It is a difficult balance to strike, but no definition of goodness can be complete without it.

~Alan Dershowitz, American lawyer, jurist, author, and political commentator

We are part of a world in which advertisements promote a destructive, competitive spirit. We are witnesses to news of individuals in society who seek advancement by stepping on others with no feeling of remorse. And, we see "leaders" who put their own needs first, catering to the few after they have taken oaths promising to serve the whole. With these examples before us, it is hard to believe that this world is moving in the right direction. However, while examples of selfishness exist, if we shift our focus, we will surely see parts of society where altruism, virtue, and good action rule the day. We see people honorably championing the rights of those who have no voice. We witness individuals who reach out to others to collaborate based on love and understanding. And we know people who set an example of service in which making a difference is promoted. As we see both sides of the coin, we know that we must strike a balance between both, between selfishness and altruism. The human condition reveals shades of darkness and light. We must make the difficult pilgrimage, finding a middle ground between both so that our world and all its inhabitants can learn to peacefully thrive together. And when we find that place where the scales are evenly set, ours can be a good example of service for others to follow.

Magical Key to Bliss: Work on your good character; serve by setting a good example.

October 4: You reap what you sow.

All that you give to others you are giving to yourself.

~Anthony de Mello, Indian Jesuit priest, spiritual teacher, and author of *Awareness*

We live in a world where there is a message of lack, a pervading belief that there is not enough of anything to go around. So many people fear that their things can be taken away from them by others who are equally desirous. We collect things and clutter our lives, holding on for dear life until we can no longer breathe under the weight and worry of losing it all.

The reality is that we live in a world of abundance. When we shift our perspective to that belief, there is so much good to be shared. Love is abundant. Kindness is abundant. Success is abundant. When we focus on our behavior as a means of reaping the abundance we sow, we become cognizant of what we are putting out there. For it is true; all we give to others will come back to each of us twofold. If we put out positive vibes, we will receive the same in kind. If we desire love, we must share what we have with others. If we want to experience kindness, we must provide an atmosphere in which fun and excitement can blossom. If we want to know success, we need to build the self-esteem of others to add to a more confident society. There is so much abundance in this world. By giving what we have and not keeping it from others, we are better serving the common good, giving all of us the chance to live a life that overflows with bliss.

Magical Key to Bliss: Sow love, and reap a life of abundance!

October 5: Do it well!

But you have to do what you dream of doing even while you are afraid.

~Arianna Huffington, Greek-American author and cofounder of The Huffington Post

Each one of us contributes to the beautiful fabric of this world. Each one of us brings our own beautiful music to add to the incredible symphony of life. And each one of us is important and necessary for the world to wonderfully go around. It is an incredible act of service to move forward in life boldly answering our call even while we are afraid. It is even a greater act of service to support one another along the way. We all need one another to share our gifts so we can all shine brighter doing whatever we choose to do. We all need one another to help move us past our fears to bring what we dream into the world. And we all need one another to offer love and assistance as we strive toward our goals, for when we all do what we dream of doing, we all win. We must act in a way that inspires others to rise to their own grandeur. We must act in a way that honors our soul. And in both regards, we must do that so well!

Magical Key to Bliss: Choose to do your thing and support others so well.

October 6: **You get to decide.**

Nothing happens until you decide.

~Dr. Stanley Turecki, American psychiatrist and expert
in adolescent psychiatry

Running, running, running. Getting caught up in a pace in which you are not able to catch your breath. At some point, you will decide to sit and ponder what you really want from this life. Time can fly by so quickly. In the blink of an eye, your todays become yesterdays. And when you look up, even your tomorrows are a thing of the past. Stop, stop, stop. Now is the right time to really enjoy your journey and live intentionally. There is fun to be had. There is life to be lived. There is joy to be discovered around each corner. Every moment from this point on is yours to do with as you like, so decide what it will be. You must believe in your dreams, your potential, and your excellence to the extent that you are bubbling over with enthusiasm. Decide to invest in moments to listen to your creative spirit so that it can grow. Stop in your tracks, slow down your pace, and figure out what makes life worth living for you. For nothing great happens until you decide to be great. Nothing amazing happens until you make the decision to vibrate your energy in a positive way. Nothing really makes sense until you start to make those choices that just feel right. And nothing happens until you decide to make it happen.

 Magical Key to Bliss: Decide to make this journey your life's greatest achievement.

October 7: **Plant seeds of kindness.**

The effects of kindness are not always seen immediately. Sometimes it takes years until your kindness will pay off and is returned to you. And sometimes you never see the fruits of your labors, but they are there, deep inside of the soul of the one you touched.

~Dan Kelly, Canadian-born sportscaster

In a society that demands instant gratification, we may often want to see the fruits of our labor *now*. When we labor in kindness, however, in reality, we may never know how we have touched another for some time to come. We live our life day by day doing our best, reaching out to assist others, and acting out of a kind and generous heart. If we act purely because we intend to receive in kind, we will be disappointed when our expectations are not immediately met. However, when we plant the seeds of kindness in all that we do, we may never know the true impact that we can have on the life of another. While it could be years from now that we discover how we touched the soul of another, the seeds are planted, and they will grow. Rest assured that kindness pays off in so many ways, big and small. When we think about it, we will be surprised by just how our good deeds affect our world. If we live by the Golden Rule, doing unto others as we would want them to do unto us, and practice kindness as part of our everyday life, then the positive thoughts and energy that we are putting out there in service to kindness will be enough for now and the future.

 Magical Key to Bliss: Plant the seeds of kindness, and let that expression of love be your reward.

October 8: **Let's make this an amazing once around!**

You only live once, but if you do it right, once is enough.

~Mae West, American actress, playwright, screenwriter, and sex symbol

You don't need anyone's permission to follow your bliss. Even when you feel like you are in a cage, stuck in a routine, or trapped, you really are not. There are things you can do to serve your highest good and make changes that will shift your perspective. If your life is super busy and you are yearning for some peace, take a moment out of your busy day and sit in meditation or prayer. You can take a walk and spend some time in nature. You can turn off the television, your phone, or social media and just be. Whatever you feel called to do, do it; this is your time. If you need a vacation to reconnect with your soul mates, friends, or significant other, set up a weekend trip to somewhere you have always wanted to go or plan time to reconnect. If you need to decrease your stress levels, set up a time to exercise, and get the good endorphins pumping. If you want to step out of your comfort zone and broaden your horizons, set some goals to get you revved up. If you want to feel passion again, take a moment to write or edit your dream list to keep tabs on how far you have come. No one has to give you permission to follow your bliss.

Remember, you live only once, so make the choices that will make your once around amazing. When you march to your own beat and do it right, that once around will be enough!

 Magical Key to Bliss: Take care of yourself, and live the best once around ever.

October 9: What is your motivation?

If you find serenity and happiness, some may be jealous. Be happy anyway. The good you do today will often be forgotten. Do good anyway. Give the best you have, and it will never be enough. Give your best anyway. In the final analysis, it is between you and God. It was never between you and them anyway.

~Mother Teresa, Roman Catholic religious sister and missionary, excerpt from "Anyway"

When your motivation is focused on good, then good energy will follow. When you choose to act out of love, then love energy will permeate all that you do. When you set out to do kind deeds, service energy will be founded on joy as you help others in need. When you set out to create a wonderful life, energy filled with hope will reflect the best in you. No matter what anyone else says, when you bring a high vibration of love, joy, and hope to your days, the energy of your whole life experience will change in an instant. When your motivation in life is based on all things good, even in the face of adversity and challenge, you will ultimately revert back to this state of being. Take a deep breath and set a mantra of love, and you will be amazed at how life can be. Even if others are acting in a way that discourages you, when you act in line with the divine, before you know it, your experiences will transform right before your eyes. So give your best and hold your head high, knowing that in the end, that is all that ever counted anyway!

Magical Key to Bliss: Set out to do your best today aligned with the positive energy all around you.

October 10: **Give love as a service to the world.**

Loving relationships are based upon commitment and giving. It is in giving of all of yourself, the good news and the not so good, that strong relationships are created.

~Robert White, American executive coach, and author of *Living an Extraordinary Life*

If you want to receive in life, you have to give. If you want love, you have to approach life and all your relationships with a commitment to love. If you want to feel the abundance of the universe, you have to commit to sharing your gifts and talents with others so that it can respond in kind. Your willingness to give of yourself and be authentic is the necessary ingredient that will enhance your experience on earth. When you decide to be authentic and loving in service to others, you will be filled up beyond belief. As you approach life in service, asking what you can do for others, life responds in kind with abundance. Don't selfishly hold back from giving love when love is what the world needs most now. Don't fear; embrace a perspective that life is full of abundance. Approach your life and your connections with love and an open heart, and your life will mirror that experience back to you. It is that simple. Giving selflessly works to help you create an extraordinary life. So if you want to build extraordinary, solid, and loving relationships with loved ones, significant others, friends, or family, then you need to approach each and every one of them with love. With this approach, you not only serve the world, but you serve yourself, too!

Magical Key to Bliss: Give love and serve the world!

October 11: In reverence for sacrifice.

Gratitude bestows reverence, allowing us to encounter everyday epiphanies, those transcendent moments of awe that change forever how we experience life and the world.

~John Milton, English poet

There are individuals who sacrifice so willingly for others out of love, loyalty, or call to duty. When those who sacrifice lose their lives in pursuit of those great virtues, there must be a time to honor them by paying our respects and standing in gratitude for their selflessness. For those individuals know the significance and power of service to another. They have earned a place of high esteem in the hearts of others, and they must be memorialized in some way because their lost lives have left us with a legacy that forever changes how we experience life and the world. To truly appreciate the impact of their sacrifice, reverence demands that we take moments of silence so that we may truly understand the gift left behind by our fallen heroes. These moments allow us to use their memory to transcend all the minutiae of life and continue to flourish. These moments of reflection assist us to ask with grateful humility, "How, too, can I serve?" There are individuals who have sacrificed for all of us. We are inspired by this act of service as we look within and ask how we can do our part for the greater good by making a difference in some small way.

Magical Key to Bliss: Choose to make a difference as you revere and never forget the sacrifice!

October 12: Live fully, laugh beautifully, and love generously.

Successful is the person who has lived well, laughed often, and loved much, who has never lacked appreciation for the earth's beauty, who never fails to look for the best in others or give the best of themselves.

~Mac Anderson. American author, speaker and founder of Successories and Simple Truths

Live, laugh, and love. Embrace these three incredible verbs through-out your day. There is no better foundation to build on. Live. You woke up this morning; now you have a chance to respond to whatever burning desire is tugging at your heart. If you do one thing to make that desire a reality, you have lived fully today. Laugh. Humor is the best medicine. A good giggle can turn a frown upside down. A good belly laugh could be the best distraction from the stress and worry that threatens to overtake you. If you spend just a few moments enjoying an opportunity to take your life less seriously through humor, you have laughed beautifully today. Love. If you have the opportunity to con-nect through kindness and love today, then by all means take it. If there is someone in your life you love and miss dearly, reach out. If you see someone who needs a hug, smile, or kind word, then give it. If you em-bark on your day, bringing with you all the love and kindness that you can muster, then you have loved generously today. Live, laugh, and love. Embrace these three words as a guide. On your journey, you will be grateful for blessings and opportunities that are sure to flow your way.

 Magical Key to Bliss: Start with this mantra: "Live, laugh, and love"—and success in life is already yours.

October 13: **Light up the world.**

How far that little candle throws his beams! So shines a good deed in a weary world.

~William Shakespeare, English poet, playwright, and actor, excerpt from *The Merchant of Venice*

A good deed can certainly go a long way. One act of kindness can send shock waves through places that desperately need it. A kind word, a compassionate smile, an understanding glance, or a moment of communication and clarity; these are all examples of the many ways goodness can be shared readily and easily. For it will never be your material possessions that comfort you when you are weary, lonely, or lost; it is the love you share that does. Believe in your potential to be a light in this world, and you will brighten up all that surrounds you. If you go through your days and sparkle onto the world like magical pixie dust, your illuminated presence will radiate love on any corner that was once in the dark. Your little light is going to shine, shine, shine. Pass on the spark that resides in you so that you can share the glow. In a world filled with many who are frustrated and angry, be the one who does the good deed, and share your goodness. For sure, have faith that when you need a little assistance in return, it will come back around. At the end of the day, you can rest easy that you have contributed to the great karmic circle of love that is so needed in an otherwise weary world.

Magical Key to Bliss: Choose to be a light in this world!

October 14: Changed for good.

You must be the change you wish to see in the world.

~Mahatma Ghandi, Indian leader and peace activist

Today, reflect on the various connections you have made thus far. Sit and remember past times spent with good friends, and relive the laughter and the tears you shared. Think about the brief encounters that you have experienced as well. Remember the quick wave you received from a car passing by, the smile that brightened your day as you quickly traveled to your next destination, or the kindness of random strangers whom you witnessed assisting a fellow traveler. Cherish the individuals you've interacted with on a daily basis at work, at play, or during other special events. With all of these different acts taking place on the stage that is your life, each actor, both lead and supporting, has affected you by the role he or she played at any given time. Begin to realize, as you reflect, how amazingly connected you are. Keep this in mind, and become aware of your personal responsibility on the bigger stage of life. Become cognizant of how your behavior affects, whether directly or indirectly, the lives of others. You have been blessed with a memory bank filled with moments of joy gifted to you by others. Pay these gifts forward, and the wonderful, loving energy will continue to expand and grow. Guided by principles of love and gratitude, your life will affect another to an extent you may never know. When you connect with others for a moment, a season, or a lifetime, the love you have expressed will be passed on, changing the world for good!

 Magical Key to Bliss: Allow love to energize you as you touch the lives of many!

October 15: Service to humanity as the ultimate goal.

The sole meaning of life is to serve humanity.

~Leo Tolstoy, Russian novelist and author of *War and Peace*

What does it mean to be humane? Is it a life marked by compassion, sympathy, or consideration for all creatures? Is it an awareness of the essence of the other? Is it the embodiment of respect and love for our neighbors? The answer to these questions is a clear and resounding yes. Where the goal in life is to act humane, the path to accomplishing it is through service. We are here to serve with love, with joy, and with a humane consciousness that will give rise to peace in a world that is affected by turmoil and strife. When we start to embrace acts of service, our selflessness will have a great impact on how we experience our world. We are one family, one tribe, one group of merry women and men. We are here to care for one another and serve this planet well until our last breath. Service gives our lives meaning, and there are so many ways to perform. When we share our life struggles with another who is hurting, we are in service from a place of love and compassion. When we use our talents and our genius to heal society, we are in service from a place of magic and miracles. When we extend ourselves and go outside our comfort zone to connect to another who is alone or lost, we are in service from a place of unity. When we remember that our lives have true meaning when we serve humanity, we start to truly feel alive and on purpose all at the same time.

Magical Key to Bliss: Serve someone from a place of love today!

October 16: **Practice the art of giving.**

I have found that among its other benefits, giving liberates the soul of the giver.

~Maya Angelou, American author, poet, dancer, actress, and singer

If you want to live, then start to give. Love, happiness, support, and service are just a few things you can give to liberate your soul. Start today; start now. Give your time to listen to someone who needs to be heard. Compile a music CD that inspires someone to dance. Send a card to let someone know how much he/she is loved and cherished. Or send a text; it cannot get much easier than that. Mail a care package to another to brighten his day. Compliment another person in a way that will boost her spirit. Give gratitude to the divine for all of your blessings. Offer to mentor someone who is starting on an exciting journey in life. There is no greater feeling in the world than the one you have when you give to another. The loving energy that you give out is always matched by either the recipient or another source. Try it today. Especially if you feel down, look around you; so many people out there are lonely and in need of a hug or a smile. So hug it out and smile; you will feel so much better. There is power in action. With intentional acts of giving to others, you are benefiting more than just the recipient of your goodwill. Practice the art of giving; it will free your soul and give you a good fix of love!

Magical Key to Bliss: Read something inspirational today!

"Come, boy, sit down. Sit down and rest."
And the boy did.
And the tree was happy.

~Shel Silverstein, American author of *The Giving Tree*

October 17: **Will you rise to the challenge or turn away?**

Not everything that is faced can be changed. But nothing can be changed until it is faced.

~James Baldwin, American novelist, poet, and social critic

Challenges are placed in our lives to see what we are made of. Will we rise to the occasion or turn away? Will we live a life standing up for what we believe in or move into our own little corner just wishing things would change for the better?

One thing is certain: things will not change in your life if you give up before you start. Instead of cowering in fear of the unknown, serve your higher self, and start where you stand. You could have never run if you had not first learned to crawl. Challenges are opportunities to strengthen the profound belief that you are a person of worth and here on purpose. Don't let the bullies of this world use their strong personalities to keep you down. You may feel small when your circumstances are overwhelming. The reality is that if you do not try to make a difference in your life or in the lives of others, you most assuredly will not. So it is better to face whatever you need to face. You never know what kind of wonderful change could happen. Rise to the challenge; don't turn away. Sooner than you know, you will be looking back and smiling at how far you have come. Then be proud with the knowledge that you served yourself well, having stood up and made the choice to climb higher!

 Magical Key to Bliss: Face any challenge, and you will see positive change!

October 18: **Your reality is what you make it.**

Reality is merely an illusion, albeit a very persistent one.

~Albert Einstein, American, German-born Theoretical Physicist

It is time to choose what your reality will be! When you believe the world will conspire in your favor, you will find evidence to support this theory. When you believe in a reality surrounded by love, you will receive loving confirmation of it from people you meet along the way. When you believe each day is an opportunity to strengthen your attitude of gratitude, you will create more moments that delight beyond imagination. Whether you choose to see what a wonderful world this could be, you will live this incredible energy in a reality of your choosing. Even in light of hard challenges, when you come to life with this choice to see beauty, angels will arrive to help you through any adversity. Close your eyes and picture the kind of life you want to live, the kind of people you would like to attract, and the kind of places you would like to go. There is great power in listing your intentions every day before the journey begins. And there is great affirmation in writing down and praising each kindness that comes your way. Choose to be the victor of your story, not the victim. When you practice a life with a heart wide open to all the wonderful possibilities, your mind-set will allow more magic and miracles. For if your reality is an illusion, and a persistent one at that, you want to be sure that your illusion is a life filled with joy, happiness, and love.

 Magical Key to Bliss: Use the power of your mind to create the reality of your choosing.

October 19: **The power of simplicity.**

I appreciate simplicity, true beauty that lasts over time, and a little wit and eclecticism that makes life more fun.

~Elliott Erwitt, French advertising and documentary photographer

Ah, the simple life! It is in simplicity that life delivers the most joy. There are simple rules to live by to truly experience the here and now. The present moment is all we have, and love is why we are here. If we do our best, we will never have regrets. Mistakes are just learning opportunities that will prepare us for something amazing. And happiness is not external to us; it is a part of us that we can never deny. Simple, yes! We must not complicate this beautiful world that we live in. If we follow the basics and use our intuition to guide us, then what follows will be just right for each of us.

So follow the butterflies as they loop and happily dance in the direction of your dreams. Relinquish the need to control the outcome in life. Synchronicities await you at every turn. Simply go with the flow, laugh at the mistakes, and move forward.

When we live like this, we will be greatly rewarded with true beauty that will last a lifetime. At the end of our days, happiness will come from the real gratitude we feel as we appreciate all the blessings we have received. When we keep it simple, blending in a bit of humor and drawing from many different sources, we are sure to have more fun.

Magical Key to Bliss: KISS—Keep it simple, sister!

October 20: **Preach the sweet life—*la dolce vita*—and practice it, too!**

Why do you not practice what you preach?

~Saint Jerome, Roman Catholic saint

L ive life with integrity; you never want to be accused of preaching to others about the good life if you are not actually practicing it. It is disappointing to be surrounded by those whose words of love, respect, service, and joy do not match their actions. It is even more disappointing to be one of those people. If you want to live *la dolce vita*, then start exhibiting the qualities that mirror that message. If the message you want to preach to the world is to engage in more laughter, do your part to bring humor to your life. If the message you want to preach to the world is to bring more joy, start serving your fellow men and women with love in whatever way you can. And if the message you want to preach to the world is to live *la dolce vita*, start living a life in which you stand in gratitude for all of your talents and blessings, and be sure to share them with others. Remember, integrity is the willingness to actually live your life by your own beliefs and standards. So if you preach the sweet life, and this is a belief you hold dear, be sure to live it as best you can—never regretting a moment. And as you do, be sure to know that your actions speak louder than words, and other people are always watching.

Magical Key to Bliss: Prepare to practice all the good that you preach, and carry on!

October 21: Conduct an examination of your life.

Character contributes to beauty. It fortifies a woman as her youth fades. A mode of conduct, a standard of courage, discipline, fortitude, and integrity can do a great deal to make a woman beautiful.

~Jacqueline Bisset, British actress

It is time to conduct an examination to get you moving forward toward your dreams. Take a look in the mirror. Gaze lovingly into the eyes of the reflection staring back. Feel the energy that emanates from your core, and let's get started. How do you feel? Do your eyes comfortably meet the ones looking back at you? Can you hold the stare for more than a few moments? First, smile and say to your reflection, "I love you, beautiful one; let's have fun!" Now, ask yourself, where will you go now that you know you can go anywhere and do anything? What will you say now that you know your words hold a penetrable force for amazing change? How will you feel now that you know how feelings dictate the profound music of your life? When will you take action now that you know how short and beautiful life is? Who will you be now that you know your destiny is yours to choose as you follow your bliss? These questions are there to help define and strengthen your character. This examination is meant to help set the tone and confirm what is important to you as you move forward knowing which values you hold true! As you go, your life will be fortified as you gaze in the mirror with pride for the beautiful life you have yet to create.

Magical Key to Bliss: Answer the questions above, and set out on the next phase of the journey!

October 22: Focus on what you *can* do.

I have a dream, a song to sing.
To help me cope with anything.
If you see the wonder of a fairy tale.
You can take the future even if you fail.
I believe in angels.
Something good in everything I see.
I believe in angels.
When I know the time is right for me.
I'll cross the stream, I have a dream.

~ABBA, Swedish pop group, lyrics from "I Have a Dream,"
written by Benny Andersson and Bjorn Ulvaeus (1979)

Dream and change the world. Imagine the burning fire in your soul as you set out to make a difference by doing what you must do to see that dream come true. You have a song to sing! When you sing it, your life will become an inspiration for all to see. Your song will be heard for years to come as you continue to use your gifts in answer to your call. What wonder surrounds you! Your life is a fairy tale that will be told in the future to engage and motivate others to follow their own bliss and become bigger than they ever imagined possible! Believe in angels! No doubt they accompany you on your journey. Feel their presence as a sudden breeze brushes your skin. Understand that you are not alone as synchronistic encounters show up over and over again. There is so much good to be seen. When you focus on what you can do, you know when the time is right to act. The unfolding of your life's dream will lead to a beautiful legacy, and no matter how big or small it is; never let it go. Dream big and focus on what you can do; the magic will happen!

Magical Key to Bliss: Believe in your dreams, and serve the world with your legacy!

October 23: Don't forget to sing in the lifeboat.

Life is a shipwreck, but we must not forget to sing in the lifeboats.

~Voltaire, born Francois-Marie Arouet, French Enlightenment writer, historian, and philosopher

Ever woke up on the wrong side of the bed wishing you could just roll over to the other side to try again? It happens once in a while. Perhaps you did not sleep as well as you would have liked. Perhaps there was much too much on your plate way too early in the morning. Perhaps you just can't get out of your own way. No worries. It is all part of being in this elite club called the human race. You have good days when everything seems effortless. You have bad days when you would like to revoke your membership. The best advice for the latter is to just stand back with awareness and remember that this, too, shall pass. In the interim, if you still have to function, be of service to yourself, and do something to make even the smallest shift to joy. When you greet someone with a smile, open the door for another, or allow a car to pass you without honking your horn, you stop digging yourself a bigger hole and start allowing the potential for the joy to return to your world. While crazy things happen around you and you feel like you are on a sinking ship, use your reason to get yourself into a lifeboat, appreciate those who love and care about you, and start to sing in gratitude. When you do, you can press the reset button and start your day anew. Anyone ready to sing?

 Magical Key to Bliss: Look for your proverbial lifeboat, hop in, and start singing!

October 24: An explosion of blessings!

Those who are lifting the world upward and onward are those who encourage more than criticize.

~Elizabeth Harrison, American educator and pioneer of early childhood education

When you water a plant and give it lots of love and light, one day when you least expect it, you will bear witness to the most beautiful blossoms. The same holds true for you. If you take care of yourself, feed your mind with positive thoughts, and surround yourself with love, you will become the most beautiful you. It has been said that a bamboo tree takes five years to establish its roots before it bursts out of the soil and you see the plant itself. Perhaps you are frustrated with the progress of your life. Perhaps you doubt your potential to realize your dreams because you have been stuck in the same place for quite some time. During these times, remind yourself that there is a lot going on behind the scenes that still remains a mystery. And just like the bamboo plant, one day you will burst out with an explosion of blessings as you realize your potential and see your dreams come true. The most important thing on the road of discovery is to stay optimistic for yourself and others. Stop criticizing yourself for not arriving just yet, and enjoy the journey. Encouragement is key, as you stay the course, day by day, step by step, and arrive at your destination fulfilled and satisfied with what you have done. As your dream comes to light like beautiful fireworks in a clear night sky, you will witness firsthand the results of hard work and dedication as you blossom into a more amazing you.

Magical Key to Bliss: Lift your loved ones with positive intentions rather than judgments.

October 25: **It is in giving that we receive.**

We make a living by what we get, but we make a life by what we give.

~Winston Churchill, British statesman and twentieth-century prime minister of the United Kingdom

Have you been the recipient of an unexpected bouquet of flowers? Have you been surprised by a visit out of the blue from a friend you had not heard from in a while? Have you struggled in life only to discover that someone has done a good deed to make your hardship easier to handle? If you have been the giver or the receiver in any of the preceding scenarios, then you know how wonderful it feels on both ends to experience acts of service. When you receive from someone who takes the opportunity to serve you out of love, it feels wonderful. When you give in kind, it feels more incredible to know that you have made a difference in the life of another. On both sides of the coin, you become part of the karmic circle of goodness that the world can benefit from. When you are the receiver, your world changes as you realize you are connected and not alone. When you are the giver, you are empowered as you touch the soul of another. When you realize it is in the giving that you receive, you will experience a life that is more satisfying and fulfilling. So decide to join the karmic circle of good and participate in acts of service, whether big or small. Perhaps you will be lucky enough to be on the receiving end. Either way, rest assured that the love you experience on either side will affect your life in an amazing way.

 Magical Key to Bliss: Give or receive; either way, be of service today.

October 26: Start living intentionally on this day!

I know of no more encouraging fact than the unquestionable ability of man to elevate his life by conscious endeavor.

~Henry David Thoreau, American author, poet, philosopher, and transcendentalist

Elevate your life. Make the decision to set your mind to something great, and act. Be conscious of the direction that you step into. Ask yourself what makes you feel alive, and go seek it. Ask yourself what gives you the greatest joy, and build on it. Ask yourself how you can serve the world with a loving heart, and go do it! Most likely, if you find yourself in an impossible situation, there can only be a simple solution to your predicament. You must act with intention that comes only from you. Pull away the veil and start to see clearly what it is that you want in your life. Set aside the clutter so that you can once again breathe without the weight of the world bearing down on you. Turn down the noise and get silent so that you will no longer be distracted by what your guides have been telling you all along. The human spirit has an unquestionable ability to rise when determined to do so. Even in the hardest of circumstances, if you start wherever you are and make that your new beginning, you most certainly will look back with a smile at how far you have come. Start living intentionally on this day, and decide to elevate your life by embarking on an exciting journey that is bound to enlighten your path and encourage others for years to come.

 Magical Key to Bliss: Set out your dreams, and start living intentionally today!

October 27: **Courage will see you through.**

Courage doesn't always roar. Sometimes courage is the little voice at the end of the day that says, "I'll try again tomorrow."

~Mary Anne Radmacher, American artist and author of *Lean Forward Into Your Life*

Courage is a wonderfully empowering word. You are courageous in all that you do just by setting out to do it. Although fear is present, it has no place in your life. You have the power to triumph over your fear by reaching within to that place where courage resides. Once you tap in, you will have the guts to get past what scares you and ultimately conquer it all. You can see fear not as a weakness but as an opportunity. Fear is a passing emotion; the less power you give to it, the more time you will have to enjoy the wonders and beauty of the world. When you refuse to devote your time to worrying about what might happen in the future, you are empowered to live in the present and enjoy all that it has to offer. Even when you are knocked down by your fears, courage will assist you to get up again and never quit. For as long as you are willing to try, the courage to do so will triumph in the end. When you prove to yourself again and again that a brave man or woman is not one who does not feel afraid but one who conquers fear, you will have greater compassion for yourself and fellow travelers. You are courageous; you don't need a magical wizard to tell you that. Courage will eventually see you through as the magic still remains within you.

 Magical Key to Bliss: Tap into your courage, and fear will fade away.

October 28: **What will be your victory song?**

It is time for us all to stand and cheer for the doer, the achiever—the one who recognizes the challenges and does something about it.

~Vince Lombardi, American football player, coach, and executive

You have heard the sad phrase "If only_____ (fill in the blank)" too many times. In fact, you may have sung that song on several occasions. After a day, week, or month of a full-on pity party, the realization hits that this is *not* the kind of song that you want to put out into the world. Then, inspired by music, you look for and find a tune of empowerment to kick-start your life into action. Where before, you would wait for opportunity to find you, now dancing to this new beat, you find opportunities to grow both personally and professionally. Where before, you were in a mind-set that good comes only to other people, you shift to the belief that you are blessed and are the creator of your own experiences. Play the song of empowerment over and over to push you along. A great theme song will embolden your spirit and take you out of victim mode, catapulting you to victory. Stretch yourself beyond your limits and challenge yourself to go outside your comfort zones with an orchestra playing behind you. Let that song be the spark behind your belief that you can take charge and change your life! If you need some inspiration to do and achieve, what will be your song?

Magical Key to Bliss: Find that victory theme song, and sing it out for all to hear!

October 29: **Perseverance!**

Perseverance, secret of all triumphs.

~Victor Hugo, French poet, novelist, and author of *Les Miserables*

You were called. You knew you had a purpose here. You listened for guidance as to what that was, and you set out a plan. You arranged your dreams in order of importance. You set small goals and steps to reach the next level on the staircase going up. You optimistically embarked on your journey with *The Magical Guide to Bliss* by your side providing keys along the way.

Now at the end of October, with only two months left before the end of the year, what is the next step if your dreams seem further out of reach than they did when you began? You must persevere. So simple and so true! Take the lessons that you have learned over the past days, weeks, months, and years, and keep moving forward, doing what you can do. With continued, patient effort, you will stay the course, fine-tuning it where necessary. For if you believe in yourself and in your dreams, you will persist, and it will eventually pay off. As long as you do not give up, success is already yours. Each day is a new day tailor-made just for you. As long as you keep moving forward with unyielding faith, your determination will be the key to your ultimate triumph. And you will persevere; there is no secret there.

Magical Key to Bliss: Insist that you will persist!

October 30: **All Souls' Day.**

Souls love. That's what souls do. Egos don't, but souls do.
Become a soul, look around, and you'll be amazed—all beings
around you are the souls. Be one, see one…And don't leave out
the animals and trees and clouds—it's all one. It's one energy.
It comes through in individual ways, but it's one energy. You
can call it energy or you can call it love.

~Ram Dass, American spiritual teacher and author of *Be
Love Now*

A ll souls celebrate love on both the spiritual and physical planes.
Take a moment to go within to that place in your heart, and feel the
love that emanates from each beat. There is a beautiful energy as your
heart light shines through. Share that energy, share that love, and be of
service to the world because that is why we are here. Love is the healing
energy that will cure all ills in society. Love is what connects each one of
us to our body temple as we engage with other souls throughout the universe. We are all souls. We exist on both a physical and spiritual plane.
Decide to love because love is the reason for it all. Love all creatures big
and small. Love the nature that surrounds us all. Love is our mission if
we so choose. Love is the only way. Without love, there is so much to
lose. We are love, and we are loved. We are all part of the divine's grand
design. Experiencing love is a gift even better than a fine wine. To share
in this amazing energy, we can celebrate as each soul makes his or her
way. Love is the necessary ingredient each and every day.

Magical Key to Bliss: Love is all we need!

October 31: **Be an example of love and compassion.**

Our "civilized" culture is failing us. And to change things, we have to start with our children, showing them the importance of love and kindness, of faith and hope, of compassion and nonviolence, treating each other with respect and dignity, not as bodies to be climbed over on the road to material success.

~Brian Weiss, MD, American psychiatrist, hypnotherapist, and author

The smallest acts of kindness can change the world. Most of the beautiful souls who have walked the world know this. They are people of service who show up when no one is looking. They are the individuals who practice love and kindness daily. They are the ones who exhibit faith and hope behind the scenes. They exude compassion through impeccable words and peaceful actions during the course of their day. They honor their fellow travelers by "seeing" them and acknowledging their dignity. We can find these people everywhere. We are these beautiful souls. When we realize our truest purpose is to shine our beautiful light from within, by our example, we give our children permission to do the same. We must allow our conversations to go from spotlighting the worst of humanity to identifying and focusing on the best. We must demand that our news media recognize this aspect more and more. We are all crying out for a better world, one where we all can evolve to a higher consciousness with an "us" mentality. Our children are watching us and learning. Through our example of service with love and compassion, we show our children how to find the greatest expression of their beautiful souls, and this will influence future generations to come.

Magical Key to Bliss: Embrace your beautiful soul, serve well, and change the world!

Chapter Eleven: November

ATTITUDE OF GRATITUDE

Thank you, thank you, thank you! November is the month in which you make a habit of using these simple and powerful words and use them well. For with *The Magical Guide to Bliss*, November is the month you discover the transformational energy of amazing gratitude. With Thanksgiving right around the corner, the grand celebration of gratefulness begins. Each day this month, you have an opportunity to choose to have a new attitude of gratitude for whatever comes your way. This attitude of gratitude will be your suit of armor that has the potential to sustain you when life throws its punches. It will also be your inspiration as you continue to spread your wings and get ready to soar.

When you appreciate all that you have accomplished thus far through the lessons of love, wisdom, transformation, creativity, joy, freedom, friendship, inspiration, and service, you know that life is full of wonderful surprises and blessings. As you welcome new opportunities and continue on the road to bliss, a great way to avoid being affected by the negativity of naysayers and skeptics is to protect yourself with this incredible tool, moving forward in an uplifting and positive way. So start today, and challenge yourself to name at least one person, place, or thing that you are thankful for each day this month. Ask yourself, "Attitude of gratitude, what am I grateful for?" Then confidently declare to the universe, "I am grateful for _____." Let thanks be your prayer, and the universe will be sure to respond in kind.

November 1: **Be grateful for challenges.**

I am grateful for all of my problems. After each one was overcome, I became stronger and more able to meet those that were still to come. I grew in all my difficulties.

~James Cash Penney, American entrepreneur and founder of the J.C. Penney Stores

It is in the discomfort of life that we truly get to know who we are and what we are made of. If we went through life never experiencing heartache or challenges, we would never know what we are capable of surviving. Facing challenges on a daily basis, knowing that we have overcome low points and learned incredible lessons from them, we are grateful for our problems. They not only give us great material for a good memoir but also create a great foundation for future challenges.

Bringing gratitude to the picture makes the process of healing a lot easier because we get to appreciate everything that has already happened in our lives. With this attitude, we also get to see ourselves transform from victim to spiritual warrior from one day to the next. It is a true test of the human spirit in which we can take the lesson of a difficult experience and rise from it. Instead of withering, we get to grow from the wound, move forward, and meet life with love and compassion. To all fellow warriors, thank you for a job well done! Through gratitude, we have transformed the journey into something more beautiful than if the hardship had never happened at all!

Magical Key to Bliss: Be grateful for the difficulties.

November 2: **Be a noble soul!**

Gratitude is the sign of noble souls.

~Aesop, Ancient Greek fabulist and storyteller credited
with the collection called Aesop's Fables

Embrace your noble soul. Just for today, make sure you consciously say thank-you to those you love. Make sure your soul acknowledges and recognizes those who bring beauty and make a difference in your life. And if you like, make sure your soul acknowledges and gives recognition to God, or your higher power, for giving you another day. To offer appreciation and validation of how important another person is to you is the greatest thing that you can do. There are many ways to do this. You can look into another person's eyes and say, "I love you." You can connect with another person from a spiritual place. You can acknowledge the uniqueness of a special friend. And you can celebrate the person's role in your life. This is one reason you are here—to share gratitude and be a noble soul. Even if those around you are entrenched in their own personal dramas and unable to be noble at this time, you be the one to set the example. You can offer your love, your joy, and your gratitude as the medicine the world needs in order to heal.

Magical Key to Bliss: Show gratitude as a noble soul.

November 3: Quench your thirst with gratitude.

Let's choose today to quench our thirst for the "good life" we think others lead by acknowledging the good that already exists in our lives. We can then offer the universe the gift of our grateful hearts.

~Sarah Ban Breathnach, American author of *Simple Abundance*

Showing an attitude of gratitude is amazing, powerful, and healing. When you acknowledge the blessings in your life, this gratitude is the one ingredient that has the potential to do wonderful things for your experience here on earth. If you infuse your thoughts with grateful appreciation for all the wonder that surrounds you, you can only imagine the powerful impact you will have on the world. When you quench your thirst for the good life, you drink in gratitude for all the blessings that you experience daily. This truth suggests that every hour of the day in gratitude can be your happy hour. Today, grab those rose-colored gratitude glasses and take a renewed look at your life through them. See your job as a blessing. See your children as blessings. See your home as a blessing. See your friends as blessings. See everything that surrounds you as a blessing. And, when you pay attention and look for the good in your life, you will be sure to find it. If you are a good finder, then good shall find you! Have an attitude of gratitude, people; what are you grateful for today?

 Magical Key to Bliss: Offer the universe the gift of a grateful heart.

November 4: In everything, give thanks!

We often take for granted the very things that most deserve our gratitude.

~Cynthia Ozick, American short-story writer and author of *The Shawl*

There are days in life that run effortlessly, and then there are days when we stumble often! On the days when life seems to flow effortlessly, it is pretty easy to find things to be grateful for. On the days when life seems laden with challenging obstacles, it is difficult to get out the door, much less appreciate blessings. While we yearn for more carefree days, sometimes we cannot recognize the gifts that lie in them until we face adversity.

As long as we don't get caught up in letting the challenge define us, adversity can be the ingredient that shows us how strong we are. Sometimes it is in the hardships that we find out what we are made of. There we find the building blocks and tools that will help us along the way. Start being grateful for it all now, and remember to live every day to its fullest—each minute is a blessing from God. And never forget that the people who make a difference in our lives are not the ones with the most credentials, the most money, or the most awards. They are the ones who most care for us.

Everyone is fragile, so if you see someone without a smile today, give him or her one of yours! Live simply. Love seriously. Care deeply. Speak kindly. Leave the rest to God. And most of all, don't forget to laugh. It is all going to be OK, and for that we can be extremely grateful!

 Magical Key to Bliss: Decide what deserves your gratitude today.

November 5: The magical allure of appreciation.

Appreciation can make a day, even change a life. Your willingness to put it into words is all that is necessary.

~Margaret Cousins, Irish-Indian educationist, suffragist, and theosophist

There is magic in expressing appreciation. When you acknowledge acts of love in any form, you are magically welcoming more to come. If someone supported you during a difficult time, let that person know how important his or her presence was. If you have succeeded in life because someone believed in your talents, there is no better way to recognize the assistance than by saying thank-you. If someone's kindness changed the trajectory of your day, there is no better way to return the favor than by expressing gratitude. The sky is the limit as you express your appreciation through hugs, smiles, cards, notes, flowers, visits, music, and so on. Remember that you are who you are today because of the love that was shared with you. Appreciation is the best way to acknowledge those gifts from the universe and encourage others to do the same! There is magic when you tell another that she is valued beyond belief. There is magic when you connect from a place of esteem and recognition of another's worth in your life. There is magic in your willingness to put into words what you feel inside. When you feel the gratitude in your heart, you must proclaim it to the world. The positive reverberations will influence others in ways you may never know, and the world will be a much better place because you said thank-you!

Magical Key to Bliss: Share your appreciation, and magically change a life!

November 6: Find peace in gratitude.

Life has to be more simple. We have so many gifts. If you want peace, open your eyes to what you have around you and say thank-you.

~Beverly Donofrio, American memoirist and author of *Astonished*

L ife gets hectic because we choose to layer on expectation over expectation. Life can get very stressful because we are encouraged daily to work harder, acquire more, and participate in the rat race. Life can be unfulfilling because we seek to fill the void by looking outside of ourselves, never fully appreciating our beauty within. Life can be painful, especially when things happen that are tragic and make no sense. Yet with a simple shift to an attitude of gratitude, we can experience life's other side of the coin. When we realize that we already have everything we need in life, we find contentment. When we clear away the clutter and open our eyes, we discover inner joy. When we cherish the people in our lives, we find inner happiness. When we are grateful for the opportunity to be silent and experience the blessings that come our way, we finally know peace. There is a renewed vision when we are thankful for all the beauty that surrounds us. Build on that attitude of gratitude, and even when life is extremely difficult, we will find comfort and peace in our blessings.

Magical Key to Bliss: Open your eyes to the blessings that are around you, and be grateful!

340

November 7: Gratitude is everything.

For each new morning with its light,
For rest and shelter of the night,
For health and food, for love and friends,
For everything Thy goodness sends.

~Ralph Waldo Emerson, American essayist, lecturer, and poet, "Thanksgiving"

When life goes awry, we can easily spiral into a negative frame of mind. It is hard to stay positive when we are exhausted and weary from the day-to-day effort. It is hard to stay optimistic when we are surrounded by darkness and can no longer see the light. When we feel this way, instead of throwing in the towel, we can reflect on the simple things in life that we are grateful for. It is the simple things that will refuel and catapult us to an improved state of mind.

We must start with a gratitude practice that has us appreciating the basic necessities that we may take for granted, such as food, shelter, health, and love. When we recognize that we are sustained in the most fundamental of ways, the opportunity for positive change grows. Then, with this new mind-set, instead of focusing on the chaos, we are grateful for good friends and family who stand by our side. Instead of feeling exhaustion, we appreciate our beds where we can lay our weary heads. Instead of focusing on the darkness, we see the constant morning light. A primitive prayer of gratitude at the most basic level can change our life for the better in an instant. When we acknowledge with gratitude the little things in life, everything that follows is just icing on the cake.

Magical Key to Bliss: Be grateful for the little things in life because they will one day prove to be the big things!

November 8: Grateful for the magic and beauty, inside and out.

The appearance of things changes according to the emotions, and thus we see magic and beauty in them, while the magic and beauty are really in ourselves.

~Khalil Gibran, Lebanese-American artist, poet, and author of *The Broken Wings*

See the magic and beauty all around. When you get enthusiastic about the opportunity to live your life on any given day, then what was once ordinary transforms into the extraordinary. When you wake to the passion within, you will start to notice nature's elegant display as you drive to work. When you are excited by your relationships with your family and friends, you will begin to appreciate what they bring to your life. When you are amazed by the synchronicity of random events, something as insignificant as sharing a smile with a stranger becomes a grand event. You will learn so much wisdom from magical moments each day. Your emotions will often dictate where you go, who you meet, and what kind of experience you will have over time. So before you start each day, take a few moments and be mindful of what emotional energy you will carry. Gratitude is a wonderful way of recharging your positive spirit. If you are grateful for everything that comes your way, you align yourself with love, and it will be a magical day. If you tap into the place of goodness in your heart, the world will mirror your thoughts and emotions, and it will be a good start.

 Magical Key to Bliss: Check your emotions before you leave for the day and be grateful for the gifts that will come your way!

November 9: **Live your words of gratitude.**

As we express our gratitude, we must never forget that the highest appreciation is not to utter words but to live by them.

~John F. Kennedy, thirty-fifth president of the United States of America

It is not enough to tell the world that you believe in love. You must show love. It is not enough to tell the world that you want peace. You must live in ways that foster peace. It is not enough to tell the world that you seek positive change. You must make a difference and act in ways that welcome the change you desire. And it is not enough to say that you seek to be of service to others. You must act when you receive the call to serve. The divine presence sends you invitations daily through the connections that you share with others. Are you paying attention to the world around you? Are you grateful for all the blessings you have received? If so, express your gratitude by paying love, peace, positive change, and service forward. There are many people whose eyes are not open to what you are experiencing. Many could benefit from your presence today. Do your best to open your arms wide to a loving embrace. There is space in your heart to express love to others. Be ready to listen if someone needs a shoulder to cry on. Do not just utter words of appreciation; live by them. When you do, your soul will open up, and joy will pour in. There is no better feeling in the world.

Magical Key to Bliss: Try to live your words of gratitude.

November 10: The magical power of words used well.

Feeling gratitude and not expressing it is like wrapping a present and not giving it.

~William Arthur Ward, American inspirational writer

When we start to believe how powerful words can be, we are reminded to use them wisely. With a single sentence, we have the ability to build people up or tear them down. With a single thought shared in writing or in person, we have the power to heal a relationship or destroy it. With a single verbal expression of gratitude, we have the opportunity to express to another how important he is or miss that chance to do so. Yes, words can bring about great peace. Words can create a bond filled with love and laughter. Wonderful words that delight and bring love to any situation can be the magical ingredient that awakens enthusiasm and excitement in our world. Having read many good books, we all know how it feels to experience the majesty of a well-written piece of work. Furthermore, we all know the extent to which powerful words can change the world. If we feel gratitude and love, we must make sure we express those sentiments with uplifting and positive words. We can open together the gift that comes from our heart. We must be clear with the goodness we wish to share as we take out our magical words or pen, say abracadabra, declare our appreciation with joy and admiration, and then witness the smiles that remain as we unwrap this life together.

 Magical Key to Bliss: Make your magical gratitude known today.

November 11: Build your own world through the messages in your dreams.

Your dreams are the gateway to your soul.

~Veronica Hay, American inspirational writer and author of *In a Dream You Can Do Anything*

Dreaming is a time when your subconscious takes over. While you dream, you can live in a world of your own making. If you want to give yourself the incredible gift of peaceful rest, protect what you feed your mind during the five minutes right before you go to sleep at night. Turn off the television, do your best not to create a hostile environment, protect your sleeping quarters from anxiety or worry, and provide a safe haven so that your mind can experience moments of pure Zen. You do not need to review or discuss the bad things that have happened right before your head hits the pillow. Opt for a gratitude review of the wonder that took place, and prepare your mind to experience a peaceful seven-to eight-hour rest. This time is too important for you to disregard. You need to wind down and give your subconscious the fuel it needs to build your world first in your imagination and then as your reality. Try it tonight; you have everything to gain and nothing to lose. Whatever efforts you make to wake up renewed will help unfold your greatest life experiences! With arms outstretched, get ready to experience a dream state that will connect you to your soul.

Magical Key to Bliss: Prepare to rest well tonight!

November 12: **Appreciate the diverse flowers in your "people bouquet."**

To know someone here or there with whom you can feel there is understanding in spite of distances or thoughts expressed. That can make life a garden.

~Johann Wolfgang von Goethe, German writer and statesman

Our relationships are so important. They are our first glimpse of what it feels like to be fully connected and loved. Beginning with what we identified as our mother or father's love, we felt a sense of peace and protection in our parents' arms. Later, our siblings and friends had a profound impact on what it means to be a part of a tribe. Culminating in our relationship to a significant other, we learn how to communicate and live together as a family once again. So many people come into our lives, each person a beautiful flower to add to our bouquet. On the journey today, identify three of these people who have taught you how to exist in this world, staying true to your vocation. The focus will be on your intentional gratitude for each of those relationships. Decide why you are grateful for each person you chose, and either write it down in a journal or think about that individual throughout the day. This exercise can either make that connection stronger or heal it. Remember, we are not meant to travel this earth alone; we are meant to learn our life lessons with and through others who grow in our garden. Be grateful for those who understand us well because they will give our life more meaning and certainly color our surroundings!

 Magical Key to Bliss: Choose three people, and decide why you are grateful for this people bouquet!

November 13: Acknowledge the good in all things.

Acknowledging the good that you already have in your life is the foundation for all abundance.

~Eckhart Tolle, German-born author of *A New Earth: Awakening to Your Life's Purpose*

While we know that we are blessed with so much, it gets particularly difficult to acknowledge these blessings when we have suffered a loss. Wanting to bask in the joy of connections with friends and family and desiring to experience an enthusiasm for the continuing learning process that lies ahead, even in the face of adversity, we can choose to focus on the positive of the world rather than dwell on the negative. However, if we acknowledge the pain in our heart from the loss of any relationship, we honor the good of what that tie represented to us as well. To acknowledge our feelings as a result of the loss of the connection is an important step to owning our healing process, especially around the holidays that will soon be here. By remembering the good times and recognizing the sadness as well, we move toward a stronger foundation after the grief does pass. When we find support to assist us in the process, the connection makes the road to healing easier. Find the mentor who has already had this experience, and be guided and loved through the pain. For in this way, we can acknowledge whatever wounds come up as well as the abundance that comes as a result.

 Magical Key to Bliss: Build on a solid foundation that will assist you for years to come!

November 14: **Every day is a special occasion.**

Don't ever save anything for a special occasion. Every day you're alive is a special occasion.

~Ann Wells, American writer of "A Story to Live By"
(Los Angeles Times)

Today is a beautiful day to be alive. To celebrate this special occasion, treat today as if it were the most important day of your life. Take the time to dress up in your personal best. Arrange your hair just so as you get ready to go. Make plans to meet with your good friends as you choose to make every hour today a happy one. As long as you are able, go outside for a walk, and take in the beautiful sights. Call your loved ones to reconnect on a very deep level. Send an e-mail to convey how much the people you love mean to you. And when you return home, light the candles and serve up your dinner on your special china. You do not have to wait for a special event because every day is a special occasion as long as you are alive. No regrets. Treat today as if it were the most important day of your life because there are no guarantees for tomorrow. If you are moving too quickly through your days, never stopping to appreciate your blessings, then now is the time; today is the day. Make this one change, and no matter where you are on the journey, it will be a beautiful day to be alive.

Magical Key to Bliss: Be grateful; if you are alive, today is a special day!

November 15: Do an attitude check today—are you in gratitude?

Your living is determined not so much by what life brings to you as by the attitude you bring to life; not so much by what happens to you as by the way your mind looks at what happens.

~John Homer Miller, American educator and author of *Take a Second Look at Yourself*

You are the lead actor and the director in the play that is your life. You do get to decide your motivation as the script unfolds. The good news is that despite what goes on around you, you get to choose how you react to whatever life throws your way. Empowered by this realization, every day is a new day in which you get to decide which way to go. Will you play the victim or the victor? If it is the victor, appreciate each character who crosses your path to ensure allies. Decide today that all things will work in your favor. Find goodness in each moment, and truly embrace the magnitude of every opportunity. As the lead actor of your story, make a conscious decision to adopt an attitude of gratitude. As the director, remember there are no random scenes or coincidences in your play. Everything that happens has a reason. You get to decide to bring the energy of an optimist or of a pessimist as you watch it unfold. When you take on an attitude of gratitude, you will stand in appreciation for everything. Remember, this is your once around. No matter what happens, choose well a positive approach, and be sure that any ending to each scene will be triumphant for the lessons learned along the way.

Magical Key to Bliss: Choose to play the victor today!

November 16: **Be grateful to experience the magic of life.**

A difficult time can be more readily endured if we retain the conviction that our existence holds a purpose—a cause to pursue, a person to love, a goal to achieve.

~John Maxwell, American author, speaker, and pastor

Today, even if you are going through challenges with your health, relationships, job, or the like, stand in gratitude for all that continues to function well in your life. Focus on what you are enjoying, and continue to be grateful for that. Be grateful for your eyes if you are able to see the beautiful colors all around you, your ears if you can hear the amazing sounds of life, your brain if you are able to process your experience here, and your body if you are still able to move gracefully free from significant pain. While you may not be able to change what is going wrong in your world right now, by focusing on what is going right, you get a reprieve if only for just a moment from the difficult time, as you recognize that your existence still holds a purpose. As long as you are here, you still have things to do. As long as you love, you still have people to engage with. As long as you have set goals, you have something to strive for. Even if the challenges seem overwhelming, you can handle them easier if you make a shift and focus on the magic of your life while embracing the positive energy that will surround you.

Magical Key to Bliss: Focus on what works, and experience the magic in your life more readily!

November 17: **Gratitude prayer.**

Every day, think as you wake up, today I am fortunate to be alive, I have a precious human life, I am not going to waste it. I am going to use all my energies to develop myself, to expand my heart out to others; to achieve enlightenment for the benefit of all beings. I am going to have kind thoughts toward others, I am not going to get angry or think badly about others. I am going to benefit others as much as I can."

~Dalai Lama, leader of Tibetan Buddhism

If you read this prayer in the morning, you are off to a great start for your day. These words will have you living with great purpose in everything you do. These sentiments filled with incredible appreciation will have you facing your life with amazing intention. These energetic thoughts will have you benefiting from a loving perspective as you welcome the blessings and gifts coming your way. As a work in progress, you need as much positive guidance as you can get. When you start your day with this prayer of gratitude, you set the standard for a life based on a belief in magic and miracles from the beginning until the end. You are a precious human life. As you continue to expand with the spirit of generosity, inspired by the words of the Dalai Lama, you will live this day knowing that the energy and beauty are there to be shared by you and with you. As a result, the thankfulness you feel for all you are and your ability to see the same in others will be the kindest things you can do.

 Magical Key to Bliss: Repeat or read this gratitude prayer many times throughout your day!

November 18: **Grace is a blessing for us all.**

For me, every hour is grace. And I feel gratitude in my heart each time I can meet someone and look at his or her smile.

~Elie Wiesel, Romanian-born Jewish writer, political activist, author of *Night*, and a Holocaust survivor

The wisdom that we get from the wisest members of society rests on its simplicity. With Elie Wiesel, a survivor of the horrors of the Holocaust, this wisdom came to him and then through him from a period that would challenge even the strongest of men and women. From a man like this, we learn to value the moments of our lives in the ordinary and embrace the simple beauty that those meaningful moments deliver. As we prepare to share the festivities of the holiday season, keep in mind that this time together is in fact a gift that will never be repeated the same way again. As we share in the breaking of bread with our loved ones, let us allow grace to bless us through the sharing of our rich stories of the past and present, which will affect our future. We must witness the animated conversations and loving smiles shared that expand our souls even more. Let us continue to be extremely grateful to all, engaging in a warm embrace, reaching out of our comfort zone, and being vulnerable with our heart and soul. If we simply live, starting with a smile, we are well on the way to being open to a more satisfying existence. Through our loving actions and positive insights, we begin to allow the universe to mirror our behavior back to us. And then what would have been ordinary will magically transform, blessed by a moment of grace, into the extraordinary.

Magical Key to Bliss: Feel gratitude for each moment of grace!

November 19: **Look well to this day.**

Look well to this day. Yesterday is but a dream, and tomorrow is only a vision. But today well lived makes every yesterday a dream of happiness and every tomorrow a vision of hope. Look well therefore to this day.

~Excerpt, ancient Sanskrit poem

Wow! You opened your eyes and could see; you listened again and could hear; you were embraced by a hug and could feel; you smelled the fragrance of the day; you tasted the warmth of nourishment. You are here again for a new day, filled with opportunity. The field of possibility is waiting for your order, so what will you intend today? When you wake in the morning, give gratitude for that opportunity to be a part of the world today. If you live today with the intention to make the most of each experience, whether your mind describes it as good or bad, it will be a day well lived. It is your choice. And with the choice to live between the dream of happiness and the vision of hope, allow the joy to overwhelm you as you take in the simplicity of the beauty that surrounds you. Ah, to start this way—what a gift! So then, you must look well to this day. And if you decide that your life starts and ends with a prayer, just believe that everything in between is the perfect answer for which you can be grateful!

Magical Key to Bliss: Embark on a new day filled with possibilities!

November 20: Just grateful for the transformation.

Transformed people transform people.

~Richard Rohr, American Franciscan priest, speaker, and author of *Immortal Diamond*

If something no longer serves you, let it go and move on! Declutter your body temple today so that you can experience the true treasures of your life. Change your eating habits, establish a healthy exercise routine, clear your mind of negative chatter, and live complaint free. If you feel weighed down by life, you have no more excuses to keep you from making the necessary alterations on both the spiritual and physical plane. It is time to transform your body and, in turn, free your soul. It is time for a transformation for the better. You are in the driver's seat, and today is a brand-new day. When your life is full of clutter, so many of life's little blessings today will go unnoticed and slip away; spending your precious moments continuing to grumble and fuss means you are ignoring the good God who gave them to us. Think how happy your life would be if instead of complaining you'd just stop and see. God gives you numerous blessings each day that lighten your burden and brighten your way. Transformed people transform people.

Have a wonderful day, and fly, butterflies, fly!

Magical Key to Bliss: Just be grateful for the opportunity to transform your life today!

November 21: Gratitude for others!

We do not find the meaning of life by ourselves alone—we find it with another.

~Thomas Merton, American Catholic priest, writer, and mystic

We are all in search of a deeper meaning to life. We are not satisfied believing that we are here on earth for no great purpose other than to take up space. We are all blessed with the ability to imagine and dream—a vital part of each of us that we should not readily discard. And we need one another to make our dreams a reality. With a concerted effort, we will together find meaning in this life. Even when some doubt our amazing potential, with those who support us, we know better. We know in our hearts and souls that we are here on purpose, and our dreams will guide us in a big way. Sure, we have insecurities, and we question a lot. But the bottom line is that we will hold on tightly to one another and persist together to see our dreams come true. When we accomplish in spite of some pretty big challenges, our true souls shine through. If the effort is shared, those who know us understand the hard work it took to unveil our masterpiece. We earned our stars together as we let our imaginations take hold. We knew that together we would survive even the most tumultuous times; we were determined and grateful to see how wonderfully we would fare!

Magical Key to Bliss: Be grateful for the love and support that has gotten you this far!

November 22: An optimistic attitude is the key to a magical life!

Our attitude toward life determines life's attitude toward us.

~Earl Nightingale, American radio personality, writer, and author of *The Strangest Secret*

The world is just a mirrored reflection of your state of mind. Whether you decide to be amazed by life or do quite the opposite really depends on what you do on a daily basis. Your attitude is key. Throughout history, many of the people you and I admire most are those who look for things to be passionate about. They are driven by a magical sense of all that is possible. They develop an attitude of determination and never allow any obstacles to get in the way of discovering their truth. They venture out into the world with a mental plan supported by a belief that once they make the decision to become all they can be, the universe will respond in kind.

When you set out to realize your dreams, remember that your attitude will be the determining factor that will empower you forward or not. With a positive and optimistic attitude and a tremendous belief in yourself, you can accomplish anything that you put your mind to regardless of what others may say. And then the mirrored reflection that life shows you will be filled with many magical moments of joy, happiness, and love. It's kind of like the universe thanking you for being a part of bringing all that is good to this world. Something magical to think about!

Magical Key to Bliss: Choose an optimistic attitude, and invite magical experiences today!

356

November 23: **Choose to feed the good!**

There is a battle of two wolves inside us all. One is evil. It is anger, jealousy, greed, resentment, lies, inferiority, and ego. The other is good. It is joy, peace, love, hope, humility, kindness, empathy, and truth. The wolf that wins? The one you feed.

~Old Cherokee proverb

Each day you wake, you have choices. Each day you live, you have the freedom to make decisions as to how you will react to life. And rest assured, how each person acts or reacts in the world directly affects everyone else. So set your intentions well. If you want more joy in the world, feed your own joy by engaging in an activity that you are passionate about. If you want more peace in your world, take the time to be still and calm yourself. If you want more love in your world, be loving to others and extend yourself past your own comfort zone. If you want more kindness in your world, reach out to others with gestures that show you care. If you want the world to be hopeful for better times, prepare an action list, setting forth positive goals. If you want more empathy in this world, reach out to someone going through a hard time and convey that you are there. And if you want a world based on truth, be willing to be vulnerable enough to share your truth without fear. It is just as easy to feed positive thoughts as it is to feed negative ones. You must ultimately decide where you will place your energy. When you decide to feed the good, an attitude of gratitude starves the lesser wolf every time!

 Magical Key to Bliss: Choose to feed the good with positive reinforcement!

November 24: Feel more alive—be grateful for it all!

We can only be said to be alive in those moments when our hearts are conscious of our treasures.

~Thornton Wilder, American playwright and novelist

You feel most alive when you have gratitude in your heart. When you are aware of your treasures, you feel alive. When you recognize the love in your life, you feel alive. When you breathe in a calm sense of understanding of your own true calling, you feel alive. Imagine that. When you take the time to truly appreciate your treasures surrounding you, the people who love you, and the deep breath that sustains you, you get to feel more and more alive. What an amazing benefit you get by choosing to have an attitude of gratitude! You can be thankful for so much: the passion you experience from an artistic masterpiece, the emotion that a wonderful aria stirs in your soul, or even the enlightenment from conversations that open your mind. These are the conscious treasures you get to experience each and every day. This is the joy that comes when you are truly grateful. Shout out to others in gratitude for letting you unite and be part of the whole process of extraordinary because these are the experiences that make life worth living. And as long as you are here, don't you want to feel more alive? So be grateful for it all!

 Magical Key to Bliss: Feel more alive, and be sure to say thank-you many times today!

November 25: **Radical gratitude!**

Gratitude begins in the heart and then dovetails into behavior. It almost always makes you willing to be of service, which is where the joy resides.

~Anne Lamott, American novelist, nonfiction writer, and author of *Help, Thanks, Wow*

If gratitude is a habit, then you must practice it each and every day. In your mind or out loud, you must repeat, again and again, "Thank you, thank you, thank you" until it rolls off the tongue like a beautiful operetta. Repetition of appreciation allows the mind and soul to refocus your life on the blessings rather than the hardships. This process of ingraining gratitude into every fiber of your being becomes radical especially during the discomfort, sadness, or strife. There is spiritual empowerment the moment gratitude takes over. Even if life deals you a particularly difficult hand—today, yesterday, or tomorrow—when you pay attention to gratitude, you are liberated from heaviness and delivered into the light. Gratitude for everything wakes up the heart muscle to feel love. Radical gratitude encourages you to be grateful even for the bad! When you allow yourself to believe that something beautiful resides in the darkness, you will repeat again and again, "Thank you, thank you, thank you." This habit of loving-kindness takes that feeling of gratitude and allows you to pay it forward in service to others as well. It is when you open up to serve that joy is truly born. The gratitude habit will guide you to a place of pure bliss if you let it. And that has been the purpose of this journey since the first day!

 Magical Key to Bliss: Serve with gratitude today, and feel the intense joy!

November 26: There is so much to be grateful for!

> *It surprises me how disinterested we are today about things like physics, space, the universe and philosophy of our existence, our purpose, our final destination. It's a crazy world out there. Be curious.*

~Stephen Hawking, British theoretical physicist, cosmologist, and author of *A Brief History of Time*

Always striving, always doing, and always looking for a way to move your life forward. Today instead of reaching for your golden star, make your intention one of gratitude for all your blessings through your connection with so many wonderful people. Even as an adult, it is important to recognize that you are a human being, not a human doing. You need to make time for rest and relaxation. You need to get away from the hectic and busy nature of your life and just be. As the holiday season nears, instead of going out and acquiring more material possessions, make an investment in downtime, whether alone or with your family unit. This can be a time for spiritual enhancement as you take the opportunity to regroup, reestablish your priorities, and stand in gratitude for the blessings in your life. Instead of setting out on Black Friday, go within and rejoice in all that you already have. Stop striving, doing, and looking, and start saying thank-you for the spiritual gifts you have. As you live in line with your spirit, others will see your good manners and want to follow suit. With no more than you already have, there is so much to be grateful for. Be curious.

 Magical Key to Bliss: Make saying thank-you for your crazy world your spiritual practice.

November 27: Stand still in gratitude, and keep your poise.

Gratitude is the law of increase, and complaint is the law of decrease.

~Florence Scovel Shinn, American spiritual author of *The Game of Life and How to Play It*

It is November, and the year is almost over. At the beginning of the year, you set out on the journey resolving to bring to light new hopes and dreams. During the eleventh month, while you may or may not have fully realized all that you wanted to, as long as you maintain a gratitude practice, you can be sure that you have laid the framework over the past several months to experience all the good that life has to offer. Stand in gratitude for all that you have accomplished thus far, and do your best to stay away from complaints because your dreams continue on their way to you. When you decide to live in gratefulness and maintain a patient perspective, you will keep your poise as you reenergize with enthusiasm, knowing your desires will be fully discovered. Do your best to choose to stay away from the negativity that will do nothing but drain and decrease your potential. Keep a deep appreciation for the law of gratitude that will increase your chance to succeed. As you discipline your focus in this positive direction, you will find that an attitude of gratitude never fails. At a minimum, it will bolster your opportunities to realize all your hopes and dreams this year and into the next with an open and grateful heart! You will certainly feel more confident for it!

 Magical Key to Bliss: Stay grateful, my friends, and your abundance will increase!

November 28: Finding the extraordinary in the ordinary.

It's all a matter of intention. There is so much to be grateful for, so much to be in awe about. Life is precious and extraordinary. Pay attention to this fact, and little, ordinary things will take on a whole new meaning.

~Richard Carlson, PhD, American author of *Don't Sweat the Small Stuff...and It's All Small Stuff*

Before you start your day, do you set your intentions? When you consciously take a moment of silent meditation and visualize well, it is amazing how magically the day unfolds before you. If this is a foreign concept to you, go within and ask your intuitive heart what you really yearn for. Receive the first thing that comes to mind, and set your intention that whatever unfolds in your life today will rise to this yearning. Speak faith over your life with impeccable words of success for the opportunities that will be your gift to experience. Stand in gratitude, staying present to life's precious moments. When you set your intentions each day, ordinary events will take on extraordinary meaning as they take you to a place of greater peace and joy. The key to all of this is to find a way to stay still so that you can hear what your life is saying and then be able to respond accordingly. When you settle your mind, all the negative chatter subsides. When you cherish moments of silence, you will see magic as the veil is lifted. If you intentionally seek, you are sure to find what you most desire. You just have to get silent to hear, and for this simple notion, be grateful!

 Magical Key to Bliss: Set your intentions first thing, and away you go!

November 29: *La dolce vita*—stop and smell the roses!

Plenty of people miss their share of happiness not because they never found it, but because they didn't stop to enjoy it.

~William Feather, American publisher and author

Decide to be happy. Delight in the here and now. See the treasures that you seek right before you. Bring this perspective to your life, and your life will respond. You will see the world showing up just for you. Your friends will smile just for you. Your children will laugh just for you. The flowers will bloom just for you. The stars will shine just for you. The sun will beam down just for you. Then be sure to say thank-you for your incredible gifts. When you make the decision to be happy, stop to smell the roses, and take in the amazing aroma that is the sweet life, your *la dolce vita*, you will realize that you already possess all the happiness you will ever need. So accept that happy place, and just for today, share hugs that energize your core, share laughter that builds momentum for joy, share your time and allow for connections to grow, share your wonderful smile that brightens the world, and share gratitude for this magical day. Don't miss out on another moment because you forgot to appreciate it. Really take the time to enjoy your *la dolce vita* every day of the year!

Magical Key to Bliss: Stop and smell the roses, never missing an opportunity!

November 30: **Perfectly flawed.**

There is a crack in everything. That's how the light gets in.

~Leonard Cohen, Canadian singer, songwriter, musician, and poet

Without the struggle, there would be no elation in triumph. Without the obstacles, there would be no need to think outside the box for creative and innovative solutions. Without the lessons from hardships, there would be no need to face our fears and evolve to a higher consciousness. Without the failures along the way, there would be no opportunities to gather the tools necessary to guide us on. However, when faced with the struggle, the obstacles, the hardships, and the failures all at once, whether because of a loss, health- or work-related stress, familial issues, or loneliness, we feel our hard exterior start to crack under the pressure. At that point, as the crack becomes more obvious on the surface, we make the decision to either curse the flaw or break open to let in the light. As we get older, when we honor the process, we must let go of our need for perfection so that we can survive and even thrive as the art of acceptance helps to minimize our anxieties about the difficult growing pains. As we focus on our breathing, input positive intentions, recite our uplifting mantras, learn to meditate, and live our life as an ongoing prayer, we will start to bask in the glow of receiving divine inspiration when we need it most. As we embrace our cracks, embrace our flaws, and stand in gratitude for the opportunity to accept our brokenness, hope is possible as we gain gratitude for being perfectly flawed and deeper appreciation for all of life as it unfolds.

 Magical Key to Bliss: Appreciate the light that comes through the cracks, and surrender!

Chapter Twelve: December

AWE-INSPIRING MAGIC AND MIRACLES

December is the most magical time of the year. This month is your reward for setting out your dreams and following the insights that have guided you further on your journey into bliss. Congratulate yourself on having come so far; the celebration has just begun. This year, you have worked hard to seize the day by visualizing the life you want. You have accepted that love is why we are here. You have gained wisdom through discernment. You have transformed your dreams into reality. You have fearlessly embraced your creative spirit. You have adopted joy as a part of your victory march. You are free, you are supported by friends, you are inspired, and you know what you have to do to serve others well. You have adopted an attitude of gratitude for the love that continues to surround you! Now this month, as you get ready to embrace this fabulous new you, be amazed by a world where the heavens touch the earth, knowing that only the divine could create this kind of masterpiece!

In December, get ready, because your something wonderful is about to happen as awe-inspiring magic and miracles unfold right before your eyes. It is time to have faith and believe in possibility once again. So sprinkle a little pixie snow or dust all about you, grab your tiara or crown, and get to the business of making your life happen. You have come so far; now open your eyes and enjoy unwrapping all your gifts that December brings. Experience the magic of life, and bask in the wonder that is to follow! Away you go!

December 1: Open your eyes, believe, and experience the magic of life!

And above all, watch with glittering eyes the whole world around you because the greatest secrets are always hidden in the most unlikely places. Those who don't believe in magic will never find it.

~Roald Dahl, British novelist and author of *Charlie and the Chocolate Factory*

Have you ever wondered why as children we don't need permission to let our imaginations run wild, yet as adults we default to someone else's reality as our truth? As children, we picture ourselves in an amazing world surrounded by the mystical and the magical. As adults we readily exchange that picture for one that has no spark at all. The little child fantasized about magic carpet rides around the world, unlimited in possibility. The little child beamed, eyes glittering, seeing a world that lies behind the veil. Then the little child grew and was tempted to lose the spark, exchanging personal joy for the beliefs of the masses. The little child reminds her older self not to risk becoming jaded as others attempt to convince her that magical senses no longer have a place. Hold on to the place within that still remembers to protect the part that still believes, thinks outside the box, and keeps an inquisitive mind. If we no longer believe in the magic of this life, we are almost guaranteed to never find it. In turn, if we do believe, the best-kept secrets will be revealed before our eyes. As little children, we see with glittering eyes. We must learn not to lose this gift as adults because the greatest secrets are hidden in the most magical places.

Magical Key to Bliss: Believe in the magic, and you will find great treasure.

December 2: **What do you really want?**

Ask, and it shall be given you; seek, and ye shall find; knock, and it shall be opened unto you.

~Gospel of Matthew (7:7), *Holy Bible, King James Version*

You are a great seeker. Do not forget this. Your greatest gift is your amazing curiosity and desire to learn. This has always been an innate part of every fiber of your being. Examine the incredible planet that you live on. Desire to understand the connections every day. Challenge your mind to expand as you think outside the box. Look for the answers to your inquiry as you go about your day. Know intuitively that all you have to do is ask the right questions, and then get ready to receive. For you inherently know what you want; you just need to take the time to clarify what it is. There is power in setting out your direction. Life gives you exactly what you need; just ask for it. If it is a healthy state of being, you will be inspired by guided action. If it is peace of mind, you will receive moments of profound silence. If it is abundance, you will be blessed with opportunities to use your talents for your highest good. And, if it is love you seek, you will be overcome by self-acceptance that will attract greater affection in return. Stop living in fear of not becoming, and just be by asking for the experiences you ultimately desire. You are a great seeker. With that knowledge, knock on the door of life, and see what waits for you on the other side. For when you ask, believe, and are ready to receive, what you find will be just what you are looking for.

Magical Key to Bliss: Ask, believe, and receive what you really want!

368

December 3: Enjoy unwrapping your gifts today!

I am a great admirer of mystery and magic. Look at this life—all mystery and magic.

~Harry Houdini, Hungarian-American illusionist and stunt performer

Let a little magic into your day, and watch the great mystery of life unfold before your eyes. This experience in the here and now is so much bigger and better than any dream you could think up. While your dreams are the entry point, surrendering to the unknown will take you to places beyond your wildest imagination. The inexplicable and profound mystery of life that is the thread between the spiritual and physical realm offers you the opportunity to take in each moment as a beautiful gift that is waiting to be unwrapped. Magic combined with mystery engages your innate curiosity to discover as much as you can while standing firmly on the ground yet simultaneously floating above the stars. Admire your story of beauty and love. Engage each person who comes into your life as one who offers you great truth by virtue of the gift of his presence, his words, and his smile. You get the gifts of life when you embrace the beauty of the mystery of life. Every gift is packaged differently; remember that even the unappealing stuff is a gift if you see it that way. So let a little magic into your day, open your eyes to life's mysterious unfolding, and enjoy unwrapping your gifts along the way. It's all magic and mystery anyway.

 Magical Key to Bliss: Enjoy mystery and magic in your life today!

December 4: Pay attention to what your life is telling you.

All you have to do is to pay attention; lessons always arrive when you are ready, and if you can read the signs, you will learn everything you need to know in order to take the next step.

~Paulo Coelho, Brazilian author of *The Zahir*

There is a time and place for everything under the sun. Frustrations arise when we are not patient, are uncomfortable with the unknown, and force things along. If we truly pay attention and follow our intuition in the most challenging of circumstances, we no longer have to worry because all the answers will come to us. We will learn just what we need to learn. We will receive messages just when we need to know them. And we will experience peace just when we trust that there is a time and place for everything under the sun. When we embrace the mystery of the unknown, fear and frustration fall away because as we learn to read the signs, they take on a magical significance. That magic will guide us to understand that we do not need to know the time or the place; we just need to recognize the signs in the moments we embrace. As we continue to embrace our magical moments, we will believe that we are prepared for each next step. As long as we have faith that we are guided and protected on this journey, life will tell us exactly what we need to know. So pay attention and don't miss it!

Magical Key to Bliss: Pay attention to signs as to which next step to take.

December 5: Your gifts lie in the present.

Be present—it is the only moment that matters.

~Dan Millman, American author of *Way of the Peaceful Warrior*

There is a lot of uncertainty in the world today. If you let it get the best of you, uncertainty can lead to fear, stress, and worry about what might happen. Conversely, if you guide your attention to the present moment, you will revel in a life filled with so many wonderful possibilities. Perhaps you have gone through trials and tribulations that have left you scarred. You may be afraid of what might be and lose sight of what is. Anxiety might be your default state of being, one in which you have trained your brain over time. Regardless, you have the ability to retrain your brain by laying positive tracks over the negative. And it is in the present moment that you have the ability to create such a transformation. Your brain has a natural ability to form new connections to heal from past trauma. These connections are made in the present moments that will take you through. There are no coincidences in life; your life is made up of magical synchronistic events in time. If you stay in the present and open up your amazing gifts, you will find the healing connections, you will insulate yourself from uncertainty, and you will get all that you need. And truly, your gifts lie in the present; when you begin to realize that, you will understand that it is the only moment that matters!

 Magical Key to Bliss: Be present to synchronistic events of healing today from past wounds.

December 6: Deal with the mystery, and the cage door will open.

Deal first with whatever is causing you the greatest emotional distress. Often this will break the logjam in your work and free you up mentally to complete other tasks.

~Brian Tracy, American motivational speaker and author of *No Excuses!: The Power of Self Discipline*

One of the biggest challenges is to face our fears and tackle what we are avoiding most. Our lives flow when we address the issues that keep coming up over and over again. It is easy to get distracted and not face certain emotions that keep appearing, hoping that as we practice avoidance, they will go away. Unfortunately, we will end up repeating our errors until we realize that we may need to cross that bridge and face our fear to get to the better side. When we surrender to the mystery, the next door in our life filled with answers will open. We can't get there if we continue to bury our feelings or our issues. They will just fester until the pain is overwhelming; the only way forward is to clear the emotional stuff for some relief. When we do, we will be free to create in ways we never thought possible. When we decide to face our emotional issues, we will receive the tools to do so, and those tools will assist us in healing. Remember, we are never alone; we just need to know where to turn when we are looking for help! When the student is ready, the teacher will appear. When we make the decision to face our pain, we must keep our eyes open for assistance that will come into our lives to help us through it—heaven sent!

 Magical Key to Bliss: Identify your emotions, and then magically there will be no cage.

December 7: Outside your comfort zone is where the magic happens.

No positive change is possible unless action has been taken. What action should you take to create the change you want?

~Natalie Ledwell, author, speaker, and cofounder of Mind Movies

If you find yourself complaining, take a deep breath and ask yourself what is right in your world; then you can take action to better the rest. Even if things don't change in an instant, the mere fact that you consciously stopped the spiral is enough to give you hope for positive change. That one intentional act is the first step of shifting you toward something that can move you forward. It is the first step toward that wonderful and magical future you have been dreaming of. In a world where you are inundated with so much, you cannot waste precious energy complaining. By focusing on what is right, you empower yourself to look for ways to increase the potential that surrounds you and for solutions to help you live better. If you want a better relationship, plan time to connect. If you want to further a dream, set aside time to map out how to do that. If you want to learn a new sport, take time to get lessons and practice! If you want to be the master of your destiny, buy a cape and a nice tiara, and play the part. Address whatever is tugging at your spirit, and create the change you want. Make positive change your reality by taking steps in the right direction. Don't just sit there and wait for it to happen. Your next action can make all the difference because outside your comfort zone is where the magic happens!

Magical Key to Bliss: Take the best step toward positive change.

December 8: **Blessed by the miracles in each moment.**

Focus on positive things; then positive things will be attracted into your life—breathe positive, think positive, be positive!

~Unknown

How wonderful it is to be a believer in the power of positive thinking. How empowering it is to experience the energy behind this approach to life. Although we are not shielded from trials and tribulations in life, with a positive mind-set we can establish habits that strengthen us mentally for those hard times when they do come. We have the choice to see the world in one of two ways—best stated by Einstein: "One is as though nothing is a miracle. The other is as though everything is a miracle." And if we choose to see everything as a miracle, we open our minds to the opportunity that is always there. We cannot expect to escape the realities of the human experience. We would not want to miss the moments of joy and happiness that can come from times of pain and suffering. To think positively, we can buy into the belief that this universe is conspiring in our favor to encourage the greatness in each of us, despite what is going on in our world. When we take a positive approach, instead of feeling broken and destroyed when we hit the proverbial bottom, we can find the opportunity to break open, like a rosebud feeling the pain but knowing we are ready to burst open with beauty. In the good times and bad, it seems like good advice to just be, breathe positive, think positive, and be positive! Then we can all be blessed with the miracle of each moment, no matter what it is.

Magical Key to Bliss: Be positive; your miracles are on the way.

December 9: Look upon life in awe!

I believe in pink. I believe that laughing is the best calorie burner. I believe in kissing, kissing a lot. I believe in being strong when everything seems to be going wrong. I believe that happy girls are the prettiest girls. I believe that tomorrow is another day, and I believe in miracles.

~Audrey Hepburn, British actress and humanitarian

The universe is amazing as you appreciate the coincidences that occur daily! If you are a believer in Jungian synchronicity, then you know that coincidences are meaningful because a greater message is delivered by random life events that occur together. When you examine the synchronicity of life unfolding, you start to uncover a dynamic that underlies the magical human experience. If you welcome all events into your life as holding profound meaning, you will look at your journey from a different perspective. Seemingly unimportant occurrences will take you in a new direction. You will see colors in a different way. You will appreciate shared laughter more deeply. And most of all, when you get into the effortless flow of your adventure, you will be aware that each day is filled with magic and miracles because of the outwardly random events that cross your path. Oh and yes, you will understand fully that the universe is amazing as you choose to believe that the people and concepts you are introduced to along the way stand for something important that will lead you to a more authentic life. For as you look upon life in awe, the events will have more meaning than you even know!

 Magical Key to Bliss: Keep your eyes open in wonderment to the synchronicities.

December 10: **Believe in yourself!**

Believe in your dreams. Believe in today. Believe that you are loved. Believe that you make a difference. Believe that we can build a better world. Believe when others might not. Believe there is a light at the end of the tunnel. Believe that you may be that light for someone else. Believe that the best is yet to be. Believe in yourself. I believe in you.

~Kobi Yamada and Dan Zadra, authors of *1: How Many People Does it Take to Make a Difference?*

My wish for you is that you experience the magic and miracles of this beautiful time of year. This is a time of year when everyone is a little bit nicer, some people seem to smile more, and many are more willing to reach out past their emotional boundaries. In this magical time of year, embrace the energy of this season of believing. Tap into this magical source and believe in yourself, in others, in your dreams, in a more loving world, in the ability to make a difference however you see fit, and in anything that serves the greater good. For it is with this belief that you can move mountains. It is with this belief that you can change lives. It is with this belief that you will follow your calling that takes you further on the road to bliss. And with my wish for you to experience magic, I will add that I believe in you, too. I believe that the magic and love of this season will surround you if you let it. And I believe that you will be protected by your guardian angels if you start to believe in yourself!

 Magical Key to Bliss: Believe in yourself, and embrace the magic of the season!

December 11: The power of awakening into consciousness!

Your vision will become clear only when you can look into your own heart. Who looks outside dreams; who looks inside awakens.

~Carl Jung, Swiss psychiatrist and psychotherapist who founded analytic psychology

D o you love where your life has taken you so far? Do you appreciate the knowledge gained from your powerful insights? If so, you are awakening into consciousness. You are awakening to your intuition that empowers you to keep moving forward with greater vision. Penney Pierce, the author of *Frequency*, defines this as the Age of Intuition. Perhaps you are going through a great transformation. Perhaps you are effortlessly experiencing a time of incredible enlightenment—a time that will bring an alchemical change into the basic nature of your life as you shift from one energy state to another. Perhaps this is the time when you experience a startling change that feels simultaneously miraculous and freeing as you look into your heart and awaken to who you are. As you get in touch with your energy and become conscious of what you release into the world, you will be more proactive in inspiring positive change. And it is there that greatness begins!

Magical Key to Bliss: Trust your instincts today!

December 12: You are blessed; behave yourself, and never mind the rest.

Believe there is a great power silently working all things for good; behave yourself, and never mind the rest.

~Beatrix Potter, British illustrator, conservationist, and author of *The Tale of Peter Rabbit*

Believe in the magic and the mystery that will conspire in your favor to bring good to your life. Even when things look bleak, something greater than it seems is going on. Trust and be grateful for the support that you have received. This must be your creed. It is freeing, it is loving, and most of all, it will guide you to a place of bliss. While it may seem that whatever you are experiencing is the end of the world, know that as long as you are living and breathing, you have great hope of experiencing the immense power of the positive energy that surrounds you. You are blessed to be aware of the synchronicities as they present themselves. You are blessed when a friend or stranger appears when you need her most or when you cross the path of someone you knew long ago. These are the events in life that infuse light into a place that was otherwise dull. These are the events in life that remind you that you are never alone, so keep the faith. These are the events that keep your focus on all that is good in your life. So be aware today of the goodness, behave yourself, and never mind the rest. The rest is not worth your time anyway.

Magical Key to Bliss: Write down five amazing aha moments that reconfirm goodness in the world!

December 13: **Here is to the good life!**

Not life, but good life, is to be chiefly valued.

~Socrates, Classical Greek philosopher

When we are grateful for what we have and the abundance that is already in our lives, the universe responds in kind with more abundance. When we face the world noticing what we lack, the universe responds in kind with more lack. It is so simple. We must stop wanting what others have and start appreciating what is already present. Let's face it; we all experience so much that we can be thankful for. If we choose an attitude of gratitude every time for the good life, we will not be disappointed. We have another day of life, and we have our health; life is good. We have family and friends who love us; life is good. We have the freedom to explore what our hearts desire; life is good. We have roofs over our heads and clothes on our backs; life is good. And we have the ability to say thank-you for all of our blessings; life is good. With this acknowledgment, let us offer a grateful heart to the universe. Let us lift up our glasses filled to the brim with our appreciation and make a toast to a good life!

Magical Key to Bliss: Toast when you can, "Here is to the good life!" Salute!

December 14: Work miracles!

The intention to love can work miracles.

~Robert Holden, PhD, British psychologist, author, and expert on happiness

All you need to work your miracles is to hold the intention of love in your heart and put it out into the world. Open your arms to receive, and bask in the gifts that come your way. As a child, you may have learned that miracles are extraordinary, divine interventions in human affairs. Or perhaps miracles were described to you as extremely outstanding or unusual things or accomplishments that only the few experienced. But in reality, you can work your own kinds of miracles in this world. You may just need to have a shift in your perspective and start to process the blessings in your life from this point of view. Be aware that you can be the miracle worker in your own life and in that of others if you come from a place of love. When you are faced with a particularly difficult relationship, give love. When something challenges you, give love. When you are feeling the love, give love. And, if you start to give love in all that you do, you are only going to receive more and more of it. So begin your day infusing love into all that you do, and by the end of the day, you will believe that your life is in fact an extraordinary event manifesting the divine in this world. You will start to know that you are capable of working miracles in this world. And you will change for the better. Leave your mark on this world by setting the intention to give love; nothing is more miraculous than that!

 Magical Key to Bliss: Give love in all you do, and work your miracles.

December 15: Magical senses!

Trust your hunches. They're usually based on facts filed away just below the conscious level.

~Dr. Joyce Brothers, American psychologist, television personality, and columnist

We really do have a God-given sixth sense. It is this sixth sense that keeps us from harm's way, guides us into a new direction, or encourages us to enter into or stay away from certain relationships. While all of the other five senses are important, it is this sixth one that, if fine-tuned, can turn out to be magical in many instances. In a nutshell, it is our intuition. At times we get goose bumps all over from excitement and enthusiasm as we embark on something in life. It is then that we must follow intuition. We know the feeling that keeps us from taking one opportunity over another. We should pay attention to the guide. Over time, we have gathered different experiences that allow us to fine-tune this very important gift as we act on our hunches in life. They can be our best friend when we need to make important decisions in life, coming in handy when the powers of persuasion are strong. They can keep us from regretting our choices. If we trust our sixth sense, our intuition, this magical tool will help us to move confidently in the direction of our dreams.

Magical Key to Bliss: Trust your intuition, and follow your dreams!

December 16: The next magical step.

Everything we need to learn is always there before us: we just have to look around us with respect and attention in order to discover where God is leading us and which step we should take next.

~Paulo Coelho, Brazilian author of *The Zahir*

Trust the process and magic of life. Relinquish the idea that you can control the circumstances that surround you. Make a decision to believe that every opportunity in life is designed just for you. By giving up the notion of external control, by being still and trusting in your life's direction, you will believe that everything happens for a reason and will work out for you. Although at times you have no control over your direction, by releasing the reigns even just a little, you start to accept your life as it unfolds. For it is in the silence that you can hear what you need to hear. It is when the veil is lifted that you can see the direction you need to follow. Stop, sit away from the chaos, and reflect in meditation, becoming aware of the signs you receive. It is in both the quiet and the calm that you will learn which step you should take next. You just need to look around and pause before you continue to move forward. Everything that you need to learn is there for the taking; you just need to trust that you are part of something greater than you will ever know.

Magical Key to Bliss: Pay attention to the signs regarding the next step to take.

December 17: A world beyond imagination!

Fantasies are more than substitutes for unpleasant reality;
they are also dress rehearsals, plans. All acts performed in the
world begin in the imagination.

~Barbara Grizzuti Harrison, American journalist,
essayist, and memoirist

No one has control of all the places you can go but you. All the
wonderful possibilities you can conjure up come from your magical mind. Thoughts make things. All magical opportunities started as
thoughts and are yours to embrace. You benefit from so many new innovations and technological discoveries, and the next great discovery could
be yours. Someone dreamed up all that you see, and you, too, can take
action to make possibilities become reality. Inspire yourself, and take
a moment to ponder your greatest fantasies; allow yourself to imagine
how you wish to see your world, and then experience the joy that comes
to you. How exciting it will be to see a beautiful dream become reality.
Get in touch with that amazing imagination of yours, go with it, and
put what you know into practice. Little by little, your dress rehearsals
will become the real thing. Let your heart take flight through laughter,
singing, and dancing as you rest assured that your greatest potential is
yet to be realized.

Magical Key to Bliss: Make your world the happiest place on
earth!

December 18: Magical synchronicity!

I do believe in an everyday sort of magic—the inexplicable
connectedness we sometimes experience with places, people,
works of art, and the like; the eerie appropriateness of moments
of synchronicity; the whispered voice, the hidden presence when
we think we're alone.

~Charles de Lint, Canadian novelist and poet

Have you had moments when you experience people so familiar that you feel you may have met them before? Have you had that déjà vu feeling that you have already been to a place even though it is your first time there? When these moments occur, pay attention. The person or place is there to teach you something about yourself that you would not learn otherwise. It may be something that you need to hear, see, taste, or know that will ignite the spark of a new creative journey. Your life is built on connections that provide profound relationships and lessons. It is in the awareness of the moments of synchronicity that you can use the lessons, propelling yourself forward to heal, in some instances, or to expand your energetic field for love and creativity, in others. The synchronistic moment may be the missing link to figuring out where to go next. With this awareness, you will no longer take the meetings for granted because each one comes with a lesson for you to learn. So if you have a connection with a stranger or a loved one who delivers to you a message of love that you need to hear or experience today, don't dismiss it as a random event. If you get just what you need, know that magical synchronicity is working in your favor to carry to you all that you need.

 Magical Key to Bliss: Remind yourself that there are no co-incidences in life.

December 19: **Allow the unexpected to happen.**

You have to take risks; we will only understand the miracle of life fully when we allow the unexpected to happen.

~Paulo Coelho, Brazilian author of *By the River Piedra I Sat Down and Wept*

Playing it safe is for people who are scared of life and who are in fear. Taking risks is for people who move past their fears and believe there is more to get out of life. Life is miraculous. Embrace it and hope that the unexpected will happen. Routine and consistency are good to a degree, but the real magic occurs when you do not shy away from the big challenges—those challenges that have you pushing your ability to the limit, expanding your understanding of your potential, and moving you into a greater belief in your potential. You have to take risks if you want to get a bigger payoff. Playing it safe is not what you are here for. Do not shy away from challenges. They are there so that you can see what you are made of.

Control is an illusion. If you try to control your world, it will ultimately be a futile exercise. Start allowing. Be proactive with what you can, and take risks. Believe in yourself and in the possibilities that are in and surround you. Think outside the box and be innovative with your life, allow the miracles to come as you do your best, surrender to the outcome, and embrace the unexpected. When you do, the unexpected will be even better than anything you could have imagined for yourself!

 Magical Key to Bliss: Take a risk, and do something outside of your comfort zone.

December 20: Brick walls are there for a reason.

> *The brick walls are there for a reason. The brick walls are not there to keep us out. The brick walls are there to give us a chance to show how badly we want something. Because the brick walls are there to stop the people who don't want it badly enough.*

~Randy Pausch, American professor and author of *The Last Lecture*

When you find a brick wall stopping your journey toward a particular destination, you may get extremely frustrated and disappointed if you cannot quickly figure out a way around it. That is when you should embrace the brick wall as a temporary pause, not a roadblock, and use it to reevaluate your direction; refocus your dream and reenergize your spirit so that the next chapter of your story is one of determination and glory. For you will find a way over, around, or through that obstacle when you clarify the direction you will take. You will start to see your brick walls not as obstacles but as opportunities to come up with creative solutions to help you build a strong foundation. Instead of banging your head against the wall, look for the ladder that is there waiting for you to use to climb over to the other side. Or perhaps the wall will simply disappear. See the brick wall for what it is, and stand fast in the knowledge that you will figure out a way to overcome it and succeed, no matter what, in realizing your dreams. You know that magic and miracles await you on the other side! Having surpassed the wall, it will feel so good to look back!

 Magical Key to Bliss: When you see a brick wall in your life, look for your ladder and start climbing!

December 21: Miracles happen when we trust!

No matter how soft we pray…God listens and understands. He knows our hopes and fears we keep in our hearts. And when we trust in His love…miracles happen!

~Unknown

Not knowing what the future holds can be a gift when you get silent and share your hopes and dreams in moments of prayer. There you return to rest on this incredible universal energy that will see you through. With God, the energy of the universe, or your higher power, all things are possible. When you surrender to the magic of life and connect to a place filled with love, miracles do happen. Meditate on that, and a greater strength will help align you with your true calling—one that is enveloped in passion and enthusiasm so you can continue joyously on your journey. There you will truly trust that everything happens for a reason and that all will work out for you. Do yourself a favor and step out of your own way, release the belief that you need to control all things, and be grateful that you are not alone. With this freedom, you will know that something greater listens and understands the beautiful song in your heart. When you surrender, you are free to move forward and embrace the miracles that unfold. When you get silent and allow your intuition to guide your choices, you are tapping into a deeper source within that will lead you. You can release your fears and throw your arms wide open to be embraced by the heavens—and enjoy the miracles as they happen!

 Magical Key to Bliss: Surrender to the magic of your life, and look for your angels!

December 22: **The magic of believing.**

The human spirit is so great a thing that no man can express it; could we rightly comprehend the mind of a man, nothing would be impossible to us upon the earth. Through faith, the imagination is invigorated and completed, for it really happens that every doubt mars its perfection. Faith must strengthen the imagination; faith establishes the will.

~Paracelsus as quoted by Claude M. Bristol, American author of *The Magic of Believing*

The human spirit is an incredible thing. Each of us is a spiritual being having a physical experience. We all must take the time to acknowledge this, discover our spiritual side, and physically connect it to the good we are truly capable of achieving on this journey. As the great thinkers recognize, the mind can achieve whatever it perceives; the thoughts that come from our amazing minds are that powerful. Recognize this, and truly believe that anything is possible here on earth. Each one of us is blessed with a tremendous imagination coupled with our gifts and talents. By sparking our imagination, we begin to use our talents for greater things in this world. It is faith in our unique abilities that will empower us and many generations to come to rise further. We must believe in our own inner light, fuel the fire within, and go forth to share our passion with the world. Through the magic of believing, we can use our super talents in service to this world.

Start to believe in this force within, connect to your higher power, and magic and miracles will occur. For the power and the potential of the human spirit connected to others in this great endeavor give rise to the hope for a brighter present and an even more amazing future. This is our shared spiritual dream!

Magical Key to Bliss: Share your incredible magic with the world, and believe in your dreams!

December 23: Live your life in a state of wonder!

See it all through eyes of great wonder. Look for the colors that brighten your world. Listen for the music that lightens your soul. Feel for the first time the warmth of the sun or the coolness of the rain. If you don't start living life from a perspective of big wonder, how will you really get to experience this great masterpiece laid out before you. You have a mind that can truly embrace the beauty offered to you each and every day. You have a heart that can truly capture the incredible feeling that life has to share. You have a spirit that alights with insight gained through those elements that set off a spark of pure joy. Life gives you the material to write amazing stories filled with magic and miracles. You be the poet and capture the essence of the experience through music, dance, art, and words. You be the philosopher when you look for and accept deeper meaning and purpose to your presence in this world. You be the perpetual student of life; you take part in your mission to learn what that purpose is. And the more you seek to learn, the more open your world becomes. When you see things that have always been present, you lift the veil of darkness from your eyes and start to live your life in a state of wonder for the magnificence before you. What a wonderful insight to share! Here is to the wonder!

Magical Key to Bliss: Do what you can to go *big* with wonder today!

December 24: Have you forgotten that you are a miracle?

[W]hat, after all, is ordinary about being born and living a human life? Each life simply explodes with potential—we can accomplish pretty much anything we put mind and material effort to. Each life is a miracle.

~Concetta Bertoldi, American author and medium

Although you are a witness each and every day to the miraculous, did you know that you are a miracle too? Touch the life of another, and witness sparks of greatness ignite for the first time. Spend time acknowledging someone else's gift, and watch pure potential come to life. Offer the gift of your presence, look into the eyes of a fellow traveler, and jointly admire the miracle standing before you. Validate the beauty of life within you and in front of you, and accept your role as a miraculous being here to give and receive unconditional love and support in life. Start to believe in your magic, show up because you want to, and realize what is possible for your life. Your earthly adventure is meant to be extraordinary. You *can* accomplish anything that you put your mind to—and inspire others to do the same. You are a precious miracle; you just need to embrace this fact and choose love over hate, bliss over sorrow. This love is what God has intended for you to experience. You are more precious than the finest diamonds. You are a miracle, an extraordinary miracle. Choose to see your truth in that light. Never forget that truth!

Magical Key to Bliss: Explode with miraculous potential, love, and beauty, and share it with the world!

December 25: **Faith leads to renewed hope.**

If you have faith, you have hope. If you have hope, you have everything.

~Unknown

Sometimes believing in something you cannot see or explain is freedom. Sometimes believing in something bigger than you allows you to surrender to the mystery and joy readily available for your life today. It is a wonderful feeling to let go of the belief that you have to control everything in life and to trust the process and just go with whatever unfolds during your day. So step back from what you think should happen, have faith, and keep an open mind to what wonderful things could happen when you think outside the box. It is an act of love to hold to your faith that everything happens for a reason. It is an act of love to maintain the hope that everything will in fact work out for your highest good. It is an act of grace to insist that magic and miracles still happen. And it is an act of kindness to allow yourself to enjoy the journey. There is love in the release when you allow and accept the present moment that is waiting to be experienced. And your faith in the surrender will lead to renewed hope as you return to love this day—and every day, for that matter! Merry Christmas!

Magical Key to Bliss: Have faith that everything is unfolding just as it should, and surrender!

December 26: Epic loveliness!

My soul can find no staircase to Heaven unless it be through Earth's loveliness.

~Michelangelo Buonarroti, Italian sculptor, painter, architect, poet, and engineer

How lovely that the word lovely just rolls off the tongue. All of our souls are lovely. Imagine your soul dancing in step to the music of a beautiful song: one that is light and airy; one that feels like a prayer; one in which the instruments act in perfect unison, a collaboration that opens the door to your heart and unleashes the beauty within. Just lovely! Perhaps when you woke this morning, you felt the mundaneness of life: the routine taking over, the struggle begging to be recognized. Pinch yourself as a reminder to wake up, and decide you want to see and experience loveliness instead. It is at that point that you decide to be the sculptor of your day. You get to experience the patient unveiling of the hidden, lovely secrets that surround you as you effortlessly chip away at the untruths. Put on a song that arouses your spirit from that unnecessary trance, and set out on the spiral staircase that will lift you to earth's loveliness. While prayer is the asking for your senses to experience the discovery, faith is where you return when you trust that your soul will receive all that it needs to rise as you move forward. So when your soul demands that you live this day only to experience each lovely thing that comes your way, your response must be to trust and start climbing. For it is true—you experience epic loveliness when you are in gratitude of heaven right here on earth!

 Magical Key to Bliss: Appreciate the loveliness you experience in the company of angels.

December 27: **Expect miracles.**

I am realistic—I expect miracles.

~Dr. Wayne Dyer, American self-help author and motivational speaker

The experience of life is all about perspective. And a lot of that perspective comes from what you learn along the way. When you were a child, you thought like a child, with all the wonder and possibility that comes with it. As an adult, having experienced loss and disappointment, you may become cynical to the magic and miracles of life. How do you change your story as an adult when you face life events considered negative? Start to think like a child, and expect miracles again. It is easy to see the world as miraculous when you are feeling good and when wonderful things are happening for you. It is when you feel like a dark cloud is hanging overhead that you need to choose to become childlike and align with your imagination that magic moments do exist. There is an energetic buzz when you take on the innocence of a child to see other people as messengers of love. There is a pure state of mind when you make a concerted effort to act like a young one, loving through your actions. No brick wall is constructed to either protect you or keep you from joy. Break yourself free when you recognize the child within who knows that even in the pain, you can be blessed with many miracles. In that choice, you will find an inner strength that you had not known before. And in reality, given the choice, wouldn't you rather expect miracles any day over the alternative? Start to be realistic and expect them, then!

 Magical Key to Bliss: Expect that a miracle will happen when you need one!

December 28: **Believe!**

The Warrior of Light is a believer. Because he believes in miracles, miracles begin to happen. Because he is sure that his thoughts can change his life, his life begins to change. Because he is certain that he will find love, love appears.

~Paulo Coelho, Brazilian author of *Warrior of the Light*

Believe in miracles, positive change, and love, and your life will transform before you. Each morning, determine to welcome all three into your life, and watch your dreams come true. Embrace the warrior of light within, and believe in all the possibilities that the world has to offer you. Be a believer in life. You are the principal actor in your own theatrical drama that unfolds before you. You can accept this role and choose to bring amazing things to this world; the stage is set for you to bring miracles, change, and love. If you want to see miracles everywhere around you, embrace your life as a miracle. Starting today, embrace the warrior of light within, and truly believe in yourself. As you believe in the beauty and the possibility of your life, you become a beacon of hope for others to do the same. When you shine your beautiful light of believing onto others, incredible things happen beyond the scope of your own world. When you decide to shine your little light and believe, you contribute more than you will ever know. Stand in your own light, and center on your own joy, doing the best you can—and watch the magic appear in your life for all to experience!

 Magical Key to Bliss: Believe in miracles, and miracles begin to happen.

December 29: Enjoy remarkable synchronicity.

> *I don't think that anything happens by coincidence...No one is here by accident...Everyone who crosses our path has a message for us. Otherwise they would have taken another path, or left earlier or later. The fact that these people are here means that they are here for some reason.*

~James Redfield, American author of *The Celestine Prophecy: A Pocket Guide to the Nine Insights*

If you open your eyes and look at yourself in a mirror, you see the vehicle by which you get to discover the world. If you close your eyes and look into the mirror of your soul, you experience the spiritual side by which you get to really understand why you are here in that vehicle. To help you along, you are greeted daily by other persons or angels here to guide you with specific messages. Although initially you may be unable to recognize their importance, over time, as you become more in tune, those messages will start to make more sense. Nothing happens by coincidence. Realizing this, you will be enlightened by a higher appreciation for the magic everywhere. Everything happens for a reason. When you start to accept that, each event in life becomes more exciting and remarkable. With this heightened awareness, you see that each person is delivering to you a piece of the puzzle that helps you fulfill your purpose. You will see that each person is helping you to discover the mystery that is your beautiful life. So, you might as well set out to enjoy the synchronicities while you are still here. For if you follow your gut and believe that the messengers are there to serve you, you will really begin to understand what the ride on this journey is all about and truly enjoy it!

Magical Key to Bliss: Enjoy the synchronicities today!

December 30: The miracle workers!

I wish to work miracles.

~Leonardo da Vinci, Italian Renaissance man, painter, sculptor, architect, scientist, musician, mathematician, inventor, and writer

With enthusiasm and action, you can create beauty in your world. You are a person of great ideas who will take risks to propel humanity to something even greater. Are you ready to take on that healing gift, in a world that so desperately needs it? What if you were the one to say the words, "I wish to work miracles"? How would you do it? What comes to mind? What beauty would you create that could lead this world in a better direction? Ask yourself this as you move through your day. Clarify your thoughts, visualize your goals, and then act with your best intentions to make this world a better place than it was when you found it. You know your heart is speaking to you, and with your powerful, God-given intellect, you know you can work miracles. What do you have to lose? Imagine what a loss it would be to humankind if Da Vinci had never tried to work miracles. The same thing goes for each one of you. You can be an ordinary person doing extraordinary things.

Magical Key to Bliss: Align with the incredible energy in the universe that manifests magic and miracles!

December 31: Be the hero on your own journey!

The world is full of magic things, patiently waiting for our senses to grow sharper.

~W. B. Yeats, Irish poet and one of the foremost figures of twentieth-century literature

How much do you appreciate a good mystery? While reading great mystery novels, you are taken on an adventure as the main characters gather information to solve the riddles that help unfold the next part of the journey. The protagonists must face their fears and not succumb to any shortcuts offered so that they can learn their lessons along the way. At the end of the journey, when the mystery is solved, the heroes stand taller with the wisdom they have collected through overcoming any obstacles on the way to a newfound truth.

Each part of your own life is like that same great mystery unfolding. Regardless of your age or where you are in the process, each stage allows you the opportunity to gain the necessary insight to sharpen your senses. When you have patience, each discovery allows you to see the beauty that lies before you like never before. With positive growth, the veil covering your eyes is lifted so that you see the magic that has surrounded you all along. All senses are alert at each stage of enlightenment, and you are better able to detect that the world is a magical one full of magical things!

As you come to the end of this year, recognize and congratulate yourself for the positive growth as you embody the role of a hero. Congratulate yourself for boldly taking this adventure with *The Magical Guide to Bliss*, and look forward to turning the page to a new year on the journey. Smile because as long as you are alive and ready to take on a new day with your dreams, goals, and visions, you know that the best is yet to come, and something wonderful is always about to happen. With that, Happy New Year's Eve, my friends! Get ready to leave the mistakes of the past behind; be grateful for the present once again. A new year full of opportunities and challenges lies ahead! Are you ready?

 Magical Key to Bliss: Cherish all that you have accomplished this year—Congratulations!

EPILOGUE

Where mysticism is the pursuit of communion with divinity, or the conscious awareness of God through direct experience, my mother was a modern-day practicing mystic. Where sainthood has been granted to those individuals who live a life of virtue and of an exceptional degree of sanctity, she seemed to all who were in her presence to be a living saint. God creates and releases many messengers who come to earth to guide all of us on the path of love. I truly believe that my mother was one of those very special messengers who had the gift of divine light as she shone on the many individuals who were fortunate to cross her path. Regarded by most as a great teacher of spiritual wisdom and one who challenged those around her to question the foundation of their journey of faith in this life, my mother was above all a great student of life. She had an intense need for enlightenment through reading the great works of literature and studying the actions of the great spiritual leaders of the past and present. She had an avid desire to nurture her relationship with Jesus Christ and introduce Him and His beautiful message to others so that many would know that we are not alone in this present experience. She became an exemplary model for those who wanted to imitate a life guided by Christ; she was an extraordinary teacher for those who wanted to grow and move forward on their spiritual journey; she was a healer as she listened to others and held them as they worked through the pains of life; she was an intercessor of God's love as she held you in her prayers always; and she lived a modest lifestyle unattached to excessive material comforts of this world. When you were in her presence, you clearly felt that you must be in the presence of God. While my mother has accomplished her mission in the physical world and has crossed over to continue in the spiritual one, she leaves behind a legacy with those individuals who were touched by her incredible soul. Both those who knew my mother well and those who had only a glimpse into her beauty will forever be transformed.

There is a poster board in my home that I made the week my mother passed away. There are words of inspiration and butterflies placed all over the board, with a beautiful angel in the middle. Above the angel's halo reads the following quote by Flavia Weedn: "Some people come into our lives and quickly go. Some people move our souls to dance. They awaken us to a new understanding with the passing whisper of their wisdom. Some people make the sky more beautiful to gaze at. They stay in our lives awhile and leave footprints on our hearts, and we are never, ever the same." This is a quote that describes the ongoing impact that my mother has on all of our lives. She was a person who brought a wealth of synergetic wisdom to our world, and that wisdom continues to assist and affect the lives of many people. She had a special connection with the divine that allowed her to teach many to dance to the beat of life's beautiful drum, to understand life through the wisdom of their different experiences, or to see the world in a new and wonderful light that allows us to identify the magic that is there. She is the kind of mystical saint who left her mark on the hearts and souls of her fellow seekers. With this knowledge, I stand in utter awe at how magical it was to have had the opportunity to be in her presence and learn God's message of love. I stand in utter awe that I was a witness to the experience of divine healing through her. For through her, anyone could experience the mystical; anyone could learn and realize a conscious awareness of a direct experience with God. Truly, that is the calling of a mystical saint, and that was the life mission of my mother, Mary Jo.

After my mother passed away in April 2011, I never felt so alone. We had beautiful conversations each morning before I started my day that left me truly inspired. When she died, the grief was terrible. To navigate this strange and challenging time in my life, a good friend and therapist suggested that I dedicate a time each day to connect to my mother. So each day, I started to talk to her, and her response came to me through my thoughts of the day. They have been my continued connection to who she was and is. I take the inspiration and love I get from her and share it with others who may want to hear it, and in return, I still get to feel the presence of my mom. Through her magical guidance, I survived the grieving process and continue to heal as my journey progresses. What I know for sure is that souls transform when they connect and join with others on this magic carpet ride we call life. *The Magical Guide to Bliss* is dedicated to the loving memory of Mary Jo Nocero. Even in death, she still teaches me how to live.

Miami, November 2014

***

I saw a turtle in the clouds; it said to take things slow. For if you do not stop in life, its meaning you will not know. Be consciously slow and patiently aware with each one and everything. You will then begin to understand what is truly meant by spring. Life is not meant to be hurried or to go, go, go; make an effort to be still in love, to stop and sit and look around, and most importantly, to take things slow.

I wish you all bliss, Meg

ACKNOWLEDGMENTS

The Magical Guide to Bliss is a labor of love that took over four years to write. In the aftermath of one of the biggest challenges of my life, I was incredibly blessed with family, friends, support groups, and healers who helped me to make this book a reality. I am a better person today because of all the assistance and love that God has sent me over time. Attitude of gratitude—for whom am I grateful?

To begin, for Frank Simone, my handsome husband, whose love and support are so important to me. I cannot wait to see the incredible places the next part of our life journey will take us. For my two-legged and four-legged children—my poof of magic and little diva, Ava Isabella; my peacemaker and compassionate son, Michael Anthony; and my amazing dogs, Leonardo Alfredo, Luciana Josephine, and the late Fred, Alfredo Luigi, and Giorgio Umberto. You are my greatest source of unconditional love and proof that magic and miracles exist in this world.

For my brilliant, fun and adventurous father, Dr. Michael Anthony Nocero Jr., and my incredible sisters, Dr. Mary Scanlon and Aimee Nocero, Esq. We are still strongly united and continue to enjoy the journey together; Mommy would be so happy. For Coco Padilla, you are truly an important part of our family. For Patricia Santangelo, thank you for listening at all hours of the night. For my in-laws, nephews and nieces, and extended family—the Scanlons, the Lewises, the Santangelos, the Hults, the Egans, the Simones, the Pfeiffers, the Bernards, the Mooradians, Lori Mazzola and her family, the Daileys, and my Colombian exchange family, the Mantillas, who have always shown me such incredible love and acceptance. I love you all!

For the original Bellas and Soul Sisters: Lisa Terranova Lommerin (Jandy Bella), Michele Barrett, Grace Hawley, Karyn Todd, Renata Aurelius, Cathy Muhletaler, Lilianna Mantilla, Teda Melero, Annabelle Berrios, Laurie Wilson, Corin Sands, Ingrid Navas, Michelle Alberty, Michele Drucker, Wendy Allen, and Bertha Vasquez. What would I have ever done without any of you! From the birthing ritual for Ava to struggling with different kinds of losses together and holding on to hope during a time of hopelessness, you are a circle of trust and sisterhood for which I am grateful; I continue to learn from, heal with, and dream big with you.

For all my many Emmaus sisters with whom I am blessed. I'm so grateful that I was able to see God in all of your beautiful faces. Especially Norma de Regil, whose constant prayers and friendship remind me so much of the spirit of my beautiful mother; Glenda Barrios, who will always be my wise owl; Martica Quiros, whose strength will always inspire me; Jaqueline Lozano, who is my example of pure sunshine; Francisca Fajardo Phillips, who shares my belief in magical things, pretty shoes and unicorns; Aurora Labrada, who just beams love; and Christine Stevens, who showed me what determination is.

For Kristi Stoll's Divine Mentoring and Awakening Groups; the support and encouragement were vital to my moving forward. I'm grateful especially for Simone Gers, Edan Hunter Lamacchia, Jeanne Stoll, Fari Ansari, and Shannon Rae Arthur. You are inspirational women who have helped me start on the path to discover my dreams.

For the magical ones and beautiful butterflies in my life. For Amy Butler, your friendship and light have made an incredible difference. For Linda Dalton and her son-in-law Chad Carter (blessed), Janet Woods, Pam Grout, Nathalie Laulhe, Gretchen Ariz (my zen sister), Patricia Prado (Patty Sue), Mindy Kobrin (Mindela), Gary and Jessica Shendell, Michelle Ramirez, Nina and Dolly Vivenzio, Nickelle Crowley, Frieda Goldstein, Jill Swartz, Kevin Creegan (Kevilina), Cory McCutcheon, Surronda Scippio, Jill Slaughter, Maxine Zisquit Poupko (magical meetings), Graciela Espinoza, Luisa Santiago (trust the process), Kellie Santos de Jesus (Perfect 10 club), Shana Belyeu (tears to joy), Chris Palacios, Tina Ashley, Ghislaine Ynestroza, Maria Brito, Tom Ayze, Fanny Behar-Ostro, Michelle Ressler, Christine Lynch and Michelle Murphy (Misha). For Denise Lane and her incredible power posse of amazing women. For my close friend Maite Albuerne, whose incredible friendship helped to calm the senses with reiki, and whose conversation brought perspective to life. For Ana Gloria Rivas-Vasquez, who helped coach me to identify my vision and set goals to realize it. For Laya Seghi, who was an amazing therapist and introduced me to incredible healing techniques and my favorite mantra: "Magical service every magical day." For my dear friend and gifted healer Dr. Cecilia Shaw, who helped me find peace and connection to my mom. For Dr. Eva Paglialonga, whose compassion, love, and kindness started me on the road to healing. For Dr. Natalia Sikaczowski, whose talent as a physical therapist helped me find balance again. For Dr. Edgar Facuseh and Dr. Heidi Mason, thank you. For Dr. Paul Canali, Amy Barrett-Kiskinis, and Barbara Lemporer who have helped me see life and healing from a whole new perspective. And for Dr. Grussmark and his team, you are a compassionate genius who helped perfect my smile. For my mother's nurses Shannon Cronk, Placido Buniao III and Dina Alcius who continue to exemplify the highest standards of care with such dignified service, love and compassion.

For my Department of Homeland Security colleagues at the Miami Office of Chief Counsel, who were the first audience for my insights. For the Miami Immigration Court and its Judges who have wonderfully influenced my life for many years. For my mentor, Catrina Pavlik-Keenan, whose guidance and support I will never forget. For my mentees, Patty Rohr, Marlene Myers-Owen, Giseli Lemay (write your dreams in the sand), Michelle Morgenstern McGhee, Paulina de Regil (synchronicity), Ilaria Cacopardo, Ashley Ahearn (believe) and Vince Calarco who have honored me with the opportunity to teach and inspire. For my office husband, Phil d'Adesky. For my right-hand man, my children's godfather, and my dear friend, Richard Jurgens, you embody and teach me kindness every day. For all of my interns who inspire me with their amazing and enthusiastic presence. For Alec Izzo, your guidance helped me to become a better writer. For Howard Marbury, your genuine care for all of us was what we needed to start the healing process. For my IDC colleagues, your passion for your profession has and will inspire me for years to come. For my fellow bloggers, thought of the day email list followers and Facebook family, I am so lucky to share the world of writing with you all. For Jennifer Diliz, the newest butterfly in my life and fellow animal lover, now let's begin the fun!

For my Jesuit-based education at Boston College, I will always be grateful for my friends, roommates (Betty Bednarski, Tracey Livingston, and Ken Hosey) and the knowledge and desire to explore my world that has bolstered my spiritual curiosity for the majority of my adult years. For the University of Miami graduate program, the professors, and my friends (Pamela Kohl, Lisa Montouri, and Mark Texeira) who inspired in me a strong desire to learn about the world. For St. Thomas University School of Law, the law professors and my friends, this place established the real cornerstone for building my confidence as a speaker and writer.

I am grateful for Donna McDonald for giving me her time freely and encouraging me to write to my mom each day, which led to *The Magical Guide to Bliss* insights. For my oldest and dearest friend, Alicia Eliscu, who was my first introduction to the spiritual quest, and Davalu Cummings; they were the ones who first encouraged me to arrange these insights into a book format. For my book club, Read Between the Wines, who share my incredible love for reading—especially David Landau, who helped me with some of the chapter titles. For the continued prayers of my prayer group, Debi Portela, Eileen Ortega, Kathy Bohutinsky, Lynne LaRussa, Jean Blower, and Mariana McCroskey. For Mari Vina-Rogriquez; you shared with me one of my greatest dreams: to meet Oprah in the most incredible way ever. For my oldest and dearest friends from my childhood in the St. Mary Magdalen Catholic Church youth group, they are family and the cornerstone for my spirituality built on unconditional love.

Thank you to all of my former and present teachers and to the inspirational authors, both living and deceased, whose words guided me on my journey to find bliss. Your wisdom, challenges, and triumphs provided the platform for my learning. Your contributions have been invaluable. Thank you for providing me with the opportunity to grow and thrive. I am grateful for my cousin, Margaret Santangelo, whose assistance, guidance, creativity, technical know-how, words and friendship really helped encourage me to bring *The Magical Guide to Bliss* to light.

For Oprah Winfrey as she took my arm in the American Airlines arena in Miami, Florida, looked me in the eyes and said her lasting and very meaningful words to me on October 25, 2014 that have empowered me more than she will even know, "Now, it is the time to live the life you want." And for George Burns and his amazing photos that captured some amazing moments of pure bliss.

And finally, for my Italian American upbringing. I am so blessed to be a part of such an amazing group of people whose traditions are rooted in a rich cultural identity of artists, musicians, writers, people of service, family, passion, spirituality, and love. What more could I ever want as an example as I follow my own *Magical Guide to Bliss* and "la dolce vita"! Salute- I toast all of you, and to the inspirational ones I have yet to meet. You are all loved very much. May you all experience incredible health, lasting friendships and connections, and an abundance of love! Remember to dance with abandon as you follow your dreams and experience great bliss!

ABOUT THE AUTHOR

M eg Nocero is one of three daughters born to Dr. Michael A. Nocero Jr., a distinguished cardiologist, and the late Mary Jo Nocero, a teacher and family counselor. She is the proud granddaughter of Congressman Alfred E. and Betty Santangelo and of Dr. Michael and Helen Nocero, who taught her the importance of her Italian roots, of family, and of giving back to the community. Meg spent a formative summer abroad in Bucaramanga, Colombia, studying Spanish as well as a semester abroad in Rome, Italy, studying Italian. Ms. Nocero graduated from Boston College in 1991 with a bachelor of arts in Spanish and a concentration in Italian and was awarded a master's degree in international affairs from the University of Miami at Coral Gables, Florida, in 1993. In addition, Ms. Nocero was awarded a Juris Doctor from St. Thomas University School of Law and has been a member of the Florida bar since 1997.

Since 1999, Ms. Nocero has served as an attorney for the US Department of Homeland Security. Ms. Nocero enjoys the distinction of acting as legal intern coordinator, mentoring and training law school and undergraduate students in the field of immigration law. Having benefited from mentoring in her own career, Ms. Nocero wanted to pay it forward by establishing a reputable internship program that features one-on-one collaboration and peer support groups to provide career guidance, emotional support, and role modeling to ambitious students, as well as satisfy her innate desire to inspire and support others. Through her mentoring experiences, Ms. Nocero realized how highly she values the opportunity to serve and guide others and has sought to pursue this natural inclination in all aspects of her professional and personal life.

As an avid reader of spiritual and inspirational writings by contemporary self-help authors, Ms. Nocero attended the Stephen Covey and David Allen Time Management workshops. Inspired by her experiences at these workshops, Ms. Nocero helped to establish a group called Soul

Talk for the purpose of exploring many different topics with her peers. She also organized her own five-part workshop, titled Follow Your Bliss and Realize Your Dreams, in which she shared her unique perspective on self-empowerment by pursuing one's bliss while setting out goals—maximizing the potential for joy by taking care of one's body, mind, and spirit and visualizing possibilities. Her spiritual practice of writing daily meditations to connect with her recently deceased mother ultimately resulted in this, her first book, *The Magical Guide to Bliss: Daily Keys to Unlock Your Dreams, Spirit and Inner Bliss*. Finally, she founded the Give Love Project with her children, Michael and Ava, to teach children—and adults—the importance of giving love. She is also the founder of her company, Butterflies & Bliss and organized S.H.I.N.E. Miami! Spirit. Hope. Insight. Networking. Event.

Meg Nocero lives in Miami, Florida, with her husband, Frank Simone, Esq.; her son, Michael; her daughter, Ava; and their two Shetland Sheepdogs, Leonardo Alfredo and Luciana Josephine. She enjoys sports, Zumba, spinning, traveling, reading, drawing, vision boarding, and spending joyful time with treasured friends and family.

PHOTO JOURNAL

Figure 2. The author, Meg Nocero and her mother, Mary Jo Nocero
The author celebrates her wedding day with her mother at the Portofino
Bay Hotel on February 19, 2000.

Figure 3. The Nocero-Simone family
From left to right: Leonardo, Frank Simone, Ava Simone, Meg Nocero, Michael Simone, and the late Giorgio.

The author balances a full-time career as an attorney, a loving relationship with husband, Frank Simone, motherhood, and homemaking with her writing pursuits. (not pictured, new family member and Shetland Sheepdog, Luciana Josephine)

Figure 4. The Nocero family
From left to right: Tim Scanlon, Dr. Mary Scanlon, Rodney Lewis, Aimee Nocero, Esq., Frank Simone, Esq., Meg Nocero, Esq., Hunter Lewis, Dr. Michael Nocero Jr., Ryan Scanlon, Michael Simone, Ava Simone, Mary Jo Nocero, and Patrick Scanlon. The extended Nocero family poses for a Christmas portrait in December 2010, shortly before Mary Jo's untimely death from breast cancer on April 12, 2011. The loss of her mother profoundly affected the author and motivated her to make the publication of *The Magical Guide to Bliss* a reality.

Figure 5. The closet writer
The author resides in a Miami condo full of dogs and kids. Therefore, the luxury of a home office was just not an option. Nonetheless, she needed a room of her own to write. So she got creative and set up shop— in her closet—giving a whole new meaning to the term "closet writer."

Figure 6. Butterflies & Bliss's Full Moon Weekend vision boards, 2014

A selection of vision boards from the author's Butterflies & Bliss weekend is a testament to *The Magical Guide to Bliss*'s principles in action.

Figure 7. The author, Oprah Winfrey, and Mari Vina-Rodriguez
In October 2014, a dream comes true at Oprah's "The Life You Want Weekend" in Miami, Florida, when the author meets Oprah Winfrey for the first time.

BIBLIOGRAPHY AND SUGGESTED READINGS

The following is a bibliography of the books that helped me navigate the healing process after I lost my mother in 2011. Each one of the following authors became my teacher, my inspiration, my morning meditation, my food for the soul, and my friend who encouraged me to continue moving forward out of the darkness and into the light. I have experienced firsthand how books expand our world, broaden our horizons, and give us wings. I have lived this as I have undergone the incredibly painful, yet liberating process of transformation as I experienced the metamorphosis from the caterpillar into a butterfly. My wish for you all as you travel your own journey with the *Magical Guide to Bliss* is that you also gain wisdom and insight from those who have gone before us, taking what you like and giving your soul light as you, too, answer your calling and fly! I will forever be grateful to each of these wise and inspirational authors for their words of love and guidance. It has made all the difference in my life, and now my hope is that these book suggestions will do the same for yours.

Angelou, Maya. *I Know Why the Caged Bird Sings.* New York: Ballantine Books, reissue ed., 2009.

Bertoldi, Concetta. *Do Dead People Watch You Shower? And Other Questions You've Been All but Dying to Ask a Medium.* New York: William Morrow Paperbacks. 2007.

Block, Lawrence. *Write for Your Life: The Home Seminar for Writers.* A Lawrence Block Production. 1986, 2013.

Buscaglia, Leo. *Love: What Life Is All About.* New York: Ballantine Books. 1996.

Byrne, Rhonda. *The Power.* New York: Atria Books. 2010.

Cameron, Julie. *The Artist's Way: A Spiritual Path to Higher Creativity.* New York: Tarcher. 1992, 2002.

Campbell, Joseph. *The Hero with a Thousand Faces.* Novato: New World Library, 3rd ed., 2008.

Carlson, Richard, PhD. *Don't Sweat the Small Stuff…and It's All Small Stuff: Simple Ways to Keep the Little Things from Taking Over Your Life.* New York: Hyperion. 1997.

Carnegie, Dale. *How to Win Friends and Influence People.* New York: Pocket Books. 1998.

Carr, Kris. *Crazy Sexy Diet: Eat Your Veggies, Ignite Your Spark, and Live Like You Mean It!* Charleston: Skirt! 2011.

Chittister, Joan. *Between the Dark and the Daylight: Embracing the Contradictions of Life.* Colorado Springs: Image. 2015.

Chodron, Pema. *Taking the Leap.* Boston: Shambhala Publications, Inc. 2009.

Chopra, Deepak. *The Seven Spiritual Laws of Success: A Practical Guide to the Fulfillment of Your Dreams.* Novato: New World Library/Amber-Allen Publishing. 1994.

Coelho, Paulo. *The Alchemist.* San Francisco: HarperOne, 25th anv. ed. 2014.

Coelho, Paulo. *By the River Piedra I Sat Down and Wept: A Novel of Forgiveness.* San Francisco: HarperOne, 1st ed., 1996.

Coelho, Paulo. *Manuscript Found in Acra.* New York: Vintage, reprint ed., 2013.

Coelho, Paulo. *Warrior of the Light: A Manual*. San Francisco: HarperOne, reprint ed., 2004.

Coelho, Paulo. *The Zahir: A Novel of Obsession*. New York: Harper Perennial, reprint ed., 2006.

Covey, Stephen. *The 7 Habits of Highly Effective People: Powerful Lessons in Personal Change*. New York: Free Press. 1989.

Dass, Ram. *Be Love Now: The Path of the Heart*. San Francisco: HarperOne, reprint ed., 2011.

De Caussade, Jean Pierre, S. J. *The Sacrament of the Present Moment*. San Francisco: Harper San Francisco, reissue ed., 2009.

DeGeneres, Ellen. *Seriously...I'm Kidding*. New York: Grand Central Publishing, reprint ed., 2012.

De Mello, Anthony. *Awareness: The Perils and Opportunities of Reality*. Colorado Springs: Image Books, reprint ed., 1992.

Desai, Panache. *Discovering Your Soul Signature: A 33 Day Path to Purpose, Passion & Joy*. New York: Spiegel & Grau. 2014.

Donofrio, Beverly. *Looking for Mary: Or, the Blessed Mother and Me*. London: Penguin Books, reissue ed., 2001.

Dyer, Wayne. *I Can See Clearly Now*. Carlsbad: Hayhouse, Inc. 2015.

Dyer, Wayne. *Wishes Fulfilled: Mastering the Art of Manifesting*. Carlsbad: Hayhouse, Inc., reprint ed., 2013.

Frankl, Victor. *Man's Search for Meaning*. Boston: Beacon Press, 1st ed., 2006.

Fromm, Erich. *The Art of Loving.* New York: Harper Perennial Modern Classics, 15th anv. ed., 2006.

Gilbert, Elizabeth. *Eat, Pray, Love: One Woman's Search for Everything across Italy, India and Indonesia.* New York: Riverhead Books. 2007.

Grout, Pam. *E-Cubed: Nine More Energy Experiments That Prove Manifesting Magic and Miracles Is Your Full-Time Gig.* Carlsbad: Hayhouse, Inc. 2014.

Grout, Pam. *E-Squared: Nine Do-It-Yourself Energy Experiments That Prove Your Thoughts Create Your Reality.* Carlsbad: Hayhouse, Inc. 2013.

Hay, Louise. *You Can Heal Your Life.* Carlsbad: Hayhouse, 2nd ed., 1984.

Hill, Napoleon. *Think and Grow Rich: The Landmark Bestseller—Now Revised and Updated for the 21st Century.* New York: Tarcher, rev. ed., 2005.

Hillman, James. *The Soul's Code: In Search of Character and Calling.* New York: Grand Central Publishing. 1997.

Holden, Robert, PhD. *Shift Happens: How to Live an Inspired Life… Starting Right Now!* Carlsbad: Hayhouse. 2011.

Huffington, Arianna. *Thrive: The Third Metric to Redefining Success and Creating a Life of Well-Being, Wisdom and Wonder.* New York: Harmony, reprint ed., 2015.

Josephson, Michael. *You Don't Have to Be Sick to Get Better!* Los Angeles: Josephson Institute of Ethics: 1st ed., 2001.

Jung, Carl G. *The Undiscovered Self: The Dilemma of the Individual in Modern Society.* New York: New American Library, reprint ed., 2006.

Kelly, Matthew. *Rediscover Catholicism*. Boston: Beacon Publishing, 2nd ed., 2011.

Kubler-Ross, Elisabeth. *On Grief and Grieving: Finding the Meaning of Grief through the Five Stages of Loss*. New York: Scribner, reprint ed., 2007.

Lamott, Anne. *Help, Thanks, Wow: The Three Essential Prayers*. New York: Riverhead Books. 2012.

Lesser, Elizabeth. *Broken Open, How Difficult Times Can Help Us Grow*. New York: Villard, reprint ed., 2005.

Lewis, C. S., *Chronicles of Narnia*. New York: Harper Collins. 1950.

Melton, Glennon Doyle. *Carry On, Warrior: The Power of Embracing Your Messy, Beautiful Life*. New York: Scribner, reprint ed., 2014.

Merton, Thomas. *The Seven Storey Mountain: An Autobiography of Faith*. Boston: Mariner Books, anv. ed., 1999.

Millman, Dan. *Way of the Peaceful Warrior: A Book That Changes Lives*. Tiburon: HJ Kramer, rev. ed., 2006.

Moorjani, Anita. *Dying to Be Me: My Journey from Cancer to Near Death, to True Healing*. Carlsbad: Hayhouse. 2012.

Nepo, Mark. *The Book of Awakening: Having the Life You Want by Being Present to the Life You Have*. San Francisco: Conari Press. 2000.

Nightingale, Earl. *The Strangest Secret*. New York: Merchant Books. 2013.

Nouwen, Henri. *The Inner Voice of Love: A Journey through Anguish to Freedom*. Colorado Springs: Image Books, reprint ed., 1999.

Osteen, Joel. *I Declare: 31 Promises to Speak Over Your Life.* Brentwood: FaithWords. 2013.

Pausch, Randy. *The Last Lecture.* New York: Hyperion, 1st ed., 2008.

Peale, Norman Vincent. *The Power of Positive Thinking.* New York: Touchstone, reprint ed., 2003.

Proctor, Bob. *You Were Born Rich.* Reno: Life Success Productions. 1997.

Radmacher, Mary Ann. *Courage Doesn't Always Roar.* San Francisco: Conari Press. 2009.

Robbins, Tony. *Awaken the Giant Within : How to Take Immediate Control of Your Mental, Emotional, Physical and Financial Destiny!* New York: Free Press. 1992.

Rohr, Richard. *Immortal Diamond: The Search for Our True Self.* San Francisco: Jossey-Bass. 1st ed., 2013.

Roosevelt, Eleanor. *You Learn By Living: Eleven Keys for a More Fulfilling Life.* New York: Harper Perennial, 50th anv. ed., 2011.

Ruiz, Don Miguel Angel. *The Four Agreements: A Practical Guide to Personal Freedom (A Toltec Wisdom Book).* San Rafael: Amber-Allen Publishing. 1997.

Scovel Shinn, Florence. *The Game of Life and How to Play It.* Camarillo: DeVorss Publication edition 1978.

Seligman, Martin. *Flourish: A Visionary New Understanding of Happiness and Well-being.* New York: Atria Books, reprint ed., 2012.

Stepanek, Mattie. *Heartsongs.* New York: Hachette Books, 1st ed., 2002.

Tolle, Eckhart. *A New Earth: Awakening to Your Life's Purpose.* London: Penguin Books, reprint ed., 2008.

Vanzant, Iyanla. *Peace from Broken Pieces: How to Get through What You're Going Through.* Carlsbad: Smiley Books. 2012.

Weiss, Brian L. M.D. *Only Love Is Real: A Story of Soulmates Reunited.* New York: Warner Books. 1996.

Weiss, Brian L. M.D. and Amy Weiss. *Miracles Happen: The Transformational Healing Power of Past-Life Memories.* San Francisco: HarperOne. 2013.

White, Robert. *Living an Extraordinary Life: Unlocking Your Potential for Success, Joy and Fulfillment.* Denver: Extraordinary Resources. 3rd ed., 2005.

Williamson, Marianne. *A Return to Love, Reflections on the Principles of "A Course in Miracles."* San Francisco: HarperOne, reissue ed., 1996.

Winfrey, Oprah. *What I Know For Sure.* New York: Flatiron Books, 2014.

Wise, Nina. *A Big New Free Happy Unusual Life: Self-Expression and Spiritual Practice for Those Who Have Time for Neither.* New York: Broadway Books. 2002.

Woolf, Virginia. *A Room of One's Own.* London: Penguin, rev. ed., 2004.

INDEX OF NAMES

59743508R00252

Made in the USA
Charleston, SC
13 August 2016